RUSSIA

RUSSIA

THE STORY OF WAR

Gregory Carleton

The Belknap Press of Harvard University Press

Cambridge, Massachusetts
London, England

2017

First printing

Library of Congress Cataloging-in-Publication Data

Names: Carleton, Gregory, author.

Title: Russia : the story of war / Gregory Carleton.

Description: Cambridge, Massachusetts : The Belknap Press of Harvard

University Press, 2017. | Includes bibliographical references and index.

Identifiers: LCCN 2016046732 | ISBN 9780674972483 (alk. paper)

Subjects: LCSH: Nationalism—Russia (Federation) | War and society—

Russia (Federation) | Exceptionalism—Russia (Federation) |

National characteristics, Russian. | War—Mythology—Russia (Federation) |

Russia (Federation)—History—1991–

Classification: LCC DK18 .C37 2017 | DDC 303.6/60947—dc23

LC record available at https://lccn.loc.gov/2016046732

For Alessandro

Contents

A NOTE ON SPELLING

As is typical of most books on Russia, I use a mix of transliterations for names. Those that are more familiar, like Peter the Great or Alexander Nevsky, are rendered in their anglicized versions. Less familiar names duplicate Russian spelling, such as General Petr Bagration and Denis Davydov (instead of "Dennis"). Hard and soft signs are eliminated in the text proper but not the notes, and surnames ending in *-skii* are replaced with *-sky,* such as Dostoevsky. Place names are given in the traditional form found in works in English on Russian culture and history: for example, Kiev, Warsaw, Vilnius. Unless otherwise indicated, all translations are mine.

Selected battle sites referenced in the text; *places and dates not exclusive*

FINLAND

RUSSIA

Gulf of Bothnia

1941–1944

1240

Leningrad
St. Petersburg

Neva

Volga

1552

Kazan

ESTONIA

Lake Peipus

1471, 1611, 1941, 1944

Volga

1242

Novgorod

Pskov

BALTIC SEA

SWEDEN

1510, 1581–1582, 1941

LATVIA

1608–1610

Holy Trinity Monastery

1238, 1293

Vladimir

1238, 1293, 1368, 1382, 1439,
1571, 1612, 1618, 1941

1812, 1941

Borodino

Moscow

LITHUANIA

1514, 1609–
1611, 1632–1634,
1812, 1941, 1943

Smolensk

Kozelsk

Kulikovo Field

Riazan

1237, 1278, 1307

DENMARK

1758

Zorndorf
Sarbinowo

RUSSIA

BELARUS

1238, 1941

1380

1945

Berlin

1794, 1831, 1920

1941

Orel

1941, 1943

KAZAKHSTAN

Kunersdorf
Kunowice

Warsaw

Brest

1169, 1240,
1941, 1943

Kursk

1275, 1943

Don

1942–1943

59

POLAND

Kiev

1709

Donets

Stalingrad
Volgograd

Volga

CZECH REP.

1805

UKRAINE

Poltava

2014–

Austerlitz

SLOVAKIA

Dniestr

S. Bug

CASPIAN SEA

AUSTRIA

HUNGARY

MOLDOVA

Dniepr

SEA OF
AZOV

2000

SLOVENIA

CROATIA

ROMANIA

Crimea

annexed by
Russia 2014

2008

Height 776
Chechnya

BOSNIA AND
HERZEGOVINA

Danube

1854–1855,
1941–1942

Sevastopol

Abkhazia

South
Ossetia

GEORGIA

AZERBAIJAN

SERBIA

MONTENEGRO

BULGARIA

BLACK SEA

ARMENIA

ITALY

MACEDONIA

ALBANIA

GREECE

TURKEY

IRAN

ater of conflict

Prologue

Bully. Bear. Insatiable aggressor. To many the words are inseparable from Russia itself. Wherever one looks support can be found for such epithets. The annexation of Crimea and military intervention in eastern Ukraine; the earlier flash war with Georgia and flattening of Chechen dreams for independence; the inward turn to authoritarianism and open assault on civil liberties—all push Russia onto the stage of international villainy.

The images, to be sure, enjoy little favor at home. There the titles one hears come as if from a parallel world where all is turned on its head. Allusions to Russia the defender, the protector, and even the savior or liberator permeate state media, academic tomes, religious manifestos, and popular histories. In spite of how far apart the two worldviews are, sustenance for these alter egos can be drawn from the same events and actions. The distance between the two is as unbridgeable as the values that define them. They share, perhaps, only one feature. Neither is new.

Russia has long borne this Janus-faced reputation, no matter what flag it has flown or ideology it has embraced. Its image as villain stretches back virtually unbroken for centuries. Other nations have at times taken the limelight, but none in the modern age has been such a consistent member of the cast, as if history permanently and purposefully assigned Russia that role. Such longevity, however, also marks its double, presenting us with the paradox of reading the same history, just upside down. Is Russia a global power whose expansionist designs have made it, in the words of a Czech historian from the nineteenth century, "an infinite and inexpressible evil?"[1] Or is it a force for good, defeating titans such as Hitler and delivering the world from its darkest enemies?

War is where Russia's contested legacy has been forged. For a millennium its lands, along with those of Belarus and Ukraine, have been among the world's great battlefields. The scope, savagery, and frequency of conflicts that have ravaged this region are almost unprecedented. The largest armies, the biggest battles, the worst losses of life—all of these superlatives would rightfully, and tragically, point there. In the twentieth century, the celebrated philosopher Nikolai Berdyaev concluded that "the history of the Russian people is one of the most poignantly painful of histories."[2] Sometimes that pain has been self-inflicted: Berdyaev himself was expelled from Russia following the Bolshevik Revolution, whose aftermath took the lives of millions. Yet he also wrote these words just when World War II had devastated that area of the world like no other conflict in all of human history.

As a consequence, war saturates Russian culture. Many of its churches have been built to honor its military heritage—some directly on battlefields with icons of warrior-saints adorning the walls while they continue service as the country's heavenly guardians. Noted operas and ballets are devoted to war, while its dominance in cinema and television is unparalleled. The saturation runs so deep that Russia's most famous writers, many of whom wore a uniform, cannot avoid the subject, whether in novel, verse, story, or essay.

Yet war has had its deepest impact on how Russia sees itself in the world. Here the quantitative factor of saturation leads to a qualitative one, arming it with the impression that its experience of war is unique. Other nations fight, die, attack, and defend, but no other, runs this belief, has faced such a persistent wave of challenges and threats for century upon century. This perceived distinction is so great that it serves as the foundation for a Russian myth of exceptionalism.

As anyone familiar with Russia knows, iterations of a special destiny have long colored its political landscape. Yet the one that derives from war is, in and of itself, exceptional because it alone bridges the ideological turns Russia has taken in modern times, from the arch-conservatism of the Russian Empire in the nineteenth century to the revolutionary radicalism of the Soviet Union in the twentieth. And today, in the Russian Federation, it serves as the core of a neo-nationalist civic religion seeking to unite all citizens around a shared belief about their unique role in history and place in the world.

Not all who over time have embraced this legacy have done it for the same purposes or in precisely the same manner. However, when it is invoked, it issues from a common stock of assumptions, operates with a consistent vocabulary, and mobilizes along an interlocking emotional appeal. At its center lies a mythic view of Russia's history based on archetypal sets of causality, character types, scenarios, and outcomes around which remembrance of that past is structured. As this pattern repeats across genres and generations, it can downplay the profound differences that make each and every conflict sui generis and leave in their place perceived or imagined commonalities. In so doing, Russia's wars are pushed into a single frame of reference that, as held in collective memory, fosters a distinct national identity both born and bred in war.

The story that Russian myth produces is obviously a favorable one, and it shares key features with a generic "good war" paradigm: right versus wrong, just cause, noble sacrifice. At the same time, however, because of Russia's geographical location, its thousand-year legacy of conflict, and the unshakeable influence of Orthodox Christianity, it can take striking positions and make unsettling claims that, as it often appears to outsiders, veer off into irrational and even disconcerting directions.

Sometimes these are akin to the idiosyncrasies that mark any culture. Why should a soldier's death be the fitting—and often expected—end to a story? What role does the Holy Mother play in Russia's military heritage, and what is the fearsome weapon she wields? And how have

Russians earned the reputation, according to a papal envoy five centuries ago, of "defending their cities and fortresses like fanatics," oblivious to both "cold and hunger?"[3]

Others bear far more weight, especially when projected outward. What is Russia's response when others paint it as a predator? When does an attack or occupation become a defensive maneuver? On what grounds might a president insist that Russia has saved civilization not once, but several times? And what, ultimately, are the stakes of employing war as a cornerstone of national identity?

The answers to these and other questions take us deep into Russian history and back to the present day, yet through a mythic lens that omits nuance, recalibrates events, and generally steers us along a path of national greatness in the face of an often hostile, unforgiving world. This does not mean, however, that the narratives we find are mythological in the sense of being fantastical or made-up. They can operate within (relatively) realistic parameters by grounding themselves in actual occurrences. In this way, they express concerns, anxieties, and desires that have discernible and sometimes legitimate roots. Just as one could say about the myths favored by any nation, the history is there as much as it is not.

This conundrum demonstrates the power and attraction of myth. It allows for a degree of creative liberty that is not necessarily untrue or implausible in order to make sense of complex realities. This is how nations can always place themselves on the side of the good and come out on top even in the direst of circumstances. To this degree, the myth that gives voice to Russia's past is no different than those heard elsewhere. What distinguishes it, however, is that it centers on war—in other words, when the stakes are greatest in the game of storytelling.

This is why myth can be so consequential, no matter its sometimes tenuous relationship to the historical record. It provides a road map to understand what is remembered, what is championed, and what is challenged or denied in a nation's collective sense of self. It reveals the ways in which products of a given culture, from a poster to a presidential speech, gain intelligibility and acceptance at home while often producing offense or confusion for others. Through myth one can anticipate what historical connections might be drawn to shape an argument for domestic consumption, and while it does not necessarily offer the tools to foresee what actions a country might take, it does allow one to predict, with certain accuracy, how a conflict is likely to be framed—and that ability, in some circumstances, can be half the battle.

Most often we associate mythic history with official circles of power, yet it would be a mistake to see its production only and always as a propaganda ploy dictated from above. Scores of thinkers, writers, and filmmakers have also contributed to Russia's sense of military exceptionalism. It is a way of thinking about the nation and people that has enjoyed solid currency across society for over two centuries. The discursive repetition and cross-fertilization of an idea that can transcend ideological differences—even those that have torn the country apart—have made it, in effect, the default way for understanding Russia at war. Challenges have come to it, but none so far has toppled it. Indeed, as one of the clearest signs of its fortitude, flexibility, and appeal, there is essentially no place or period in modern Russian politics and culture where one cannot hear some variant of its expression. For many, it is the lifeblood of their nation's history.

What follows is a journey through Russia's civic religion that is anchored deep in this sense of exceptionalism. The national narrative it favors and that fuels *Russia: The Story of War,* it should be underscored, is decidedly lopsided—akin to an American version of itself that tucks slavery and the treatment of Native Americans away in a corner, or a British imperialism heralded as the beneficent march of Western civilization across the globe. Points of emphasis, given thematically, include how this self-image operates as a shield against accusations of belligerence, assuages anxieties and fears, accentuates the country's prestige, and, when needed, promotes national insularity as a virtuous destiny. The heart of its creed lies in a past modeled to match the present that shines in perpetual triumph yet bristles with sharp lessons delivered by history's punishing hand.

This book, conceived and nine-tenths composed before fighting erupted in eastern Ukraine in 2014, offers itself as both an invitation and an introduction to see Russia through the lens so many Russians have themselves internalized. It is neither an apology nor a justification for the country's policies or actions, but issues from the conviction that we cannot fully understand Russia without recognizing its experience of war and the resulting stories it tells of itself. We need not condone them, but to ignore them or, as is commonplace in the West, to dismiss them as ludicrous, as the product of delusional fantasy, handicaps our ability to understand how they have profoundly shaped Russia's self-image and worldview.

In short, if war is often inseparable from our impression of Russia, the same holds true there as well. It's just different. Quite different. After all, who else has a patron saint for nuclear bombers?

1

Pedigree

On the ninth of May, the sun always shines in Moscow. The Kremlin has made it so, dispersing the clouds to ensure that nothing can spoil the parade rumbling through Red Square. It shines on an array of tanks and rocket launchers, on soldiers in contemporary and period uniform marching alongside, and on an ever-shrinking group of elderly veterans, chests bristling with medals. It banks off the wings of jets soaring overhead as they release trails of white, blue, and red smoke. And then it shines on the Russian president as he informs the nation and the world that they are there because on that day in 1945 a darkness lifted with the surrender of Nazi Germany.

May Ninth is Russia's greatest secular holiday, commemorating a war that itself is crowned with superlatives. In the deadliest conflict ever, Russia led the Soviet Union in crushing the largest army the world had yet seen and thereby saved humanity from the worst evil it has ever known. In so doing, no country has paid a higher price in human lives. The official number of dead in the war now stands at nearly twenty-seven million, or approximately one out of every seven Soviet citizens—man, woman, and child.

Victory Day, as the holiday is formally known, marks when Russians of all ages show unbounded pride in that generation's triumphant sacrifice. They are encouraged to take to the streets bearing photographs of family members who served—and often perished—in the epic struggle against Hitler's forces. Through the blood of the fallen, it is claimed, they share a "sacred kinship" that transcends politics and class, bringing Russians together across eleven time zones as one family united by the war. No other nation remembers World War II in such an elaborate, annual ritual, and no other has made it the centerpiece of a civic religion, a subject of veneration so strong that Russia's role in that victory is often evoked as fulfilling providential destiny.

However it might be expressed on that day, this conviction also rests on the belief—often operating as an undeniable truth—that this chapter of Russian history is, in fact, not unique. World War II was not the first time Russia has been called to play a salvational role; not the first time its people and land have been sacrificed to protect others, indeed whole civilizations, from destruction. Instead, collective martyrdom, particularly for the sake of Europe, is a recurring chapter and, more importantly, is one embedded in the very saga of how Russia arose as a nation. Shared across the centers of authority— political, religious, military, academic—the narrative behind this conviction takes us back seven centuries before the Nazi invasion and reads roughly as follows.

A Nation Born of War

In the thirteenth century, Russia as we understand it now didn't exist. The lands from Kiev to Moscow and then continuing northeast to where the Volga originates were dominated by East Slavs (in whose history Ukrainians and Belorussians can also see themselves). They shared a common language and faith, Orthodox Christianity, which created conditions for a common identity, but not as part of a single state. Instead a series of principalities made up what is collectively known as Rus, and much like Greek city-states, some might unite to face an outside foe. Too often, however, the enemy was to be found among their own, as internecine conflict was the norm. This virus, borne by princes' egos and avarice, would plague Rus until a more devastating force caught it by surprise and crushed it: the Mongols.

While foreign attacks had been a constant threat to Russia's ancestors, nothing matched the destruction wrought by the Mongols when they invaded in 1237. Medieval chroniclers describe them as a satanic whirlwind; resistance literally was futile. Every army fielded by a prince was destroyed; every city the Mongols attacked was left in ashes. The story of the first to fall, Riazan, offers a harrowing glimpse of "God's scourge": defenders slaughtered to the man, women raped and killed, children murdered, terrified survivors seeking refuge inside a church only to be burned alive.

Over the course of three years, most of the principalities of Rus suffered the same fate. A papal envoy who traveled through the region shortly afterward reported seeing "countless skulls and bones" strewn across the land. The invasion clearly carved a deep scar of trauma into the collective consciousness of those who survived it. Not only was the relative ease with which cities fell shocking, but equally terrifying was the seeming arbitrariness of destruction: what city would be razed, who would be slaughtered, who enslaved, who spared? Trauma even generated a legend, rendered centuries later, of Kitezh, a city that sank into a lake to escape destruction, thereby preserving its spiritual purity. It also led to accounts of attacks on cities that were spared, such as Smolensk, almost tempting one to classify Mongol assault as an expected rite of passage for any city of Rus.

For the most part, the Mongol overlords did not mix with those who survived. Tribute was regularly demanded by their khan, who resided in a city built on the Volga and to which princes regularly traveled to salute him as sovereign. Khans controlled the distribution of titles and land and played on that to ensure princes' obedience or, if tighter control was needed, summarily executed them. Cities continued to suffer from seemingly arbitrary assault, whether to punish or gain additional loot. (Riazan itself would be sacked and rebuilt several times.)

Rus in the thirteenth century

For the people of Rus, subjugation and humiliation by the infidel came to be their shared experience, in which, consonant with the mind-set of the medieval Christian world, one could see only God's wrath. Decades after the invasion, a bishop produced a series of sermons still lamenting the bodies "thrown to the birds as food" and blood "drenching the land." Equally punishing, though, was the blow to their collective ego. "Our greatness has sank, our magnificence has rotted, our wealth has become the enemy's spoils, our labor passed on as the unbeliever's inheritance, for our land has fallen into the hands of foreigners." Such was the Mongol Yoke, as it later became called, and it strangled Rus for almost two and half centuries.[1]

How did Christian neighbors, albeit Catholic, respond? With a stab in the back. Close upon the heels of the Mongol invasion, first Swedes, then Teutonic knights marched on Novgorod, in the northwest corner of Rus and one of the few principalities spared by the Mongols. This betrayal, however, produced the first rays of light, since it triggered the appearance of a hero who would become one of Russia's most enduring, virtually alone in his class: Prince Alexander Nevsky. He earned his sobriquet by defeating the Swedes at the Neva River in 1240; he cemented his legacy two years later by defeating the knights at Lake Peipus, known forever as the famous Battle on the Ice as captured by Sergei Eisenstein's 1938 cinematic masterpiece, *Alexander Nevsky,* made on the eve of yet another invasion from the West.

Nevsky never challenged the Mongols. Instead he paid obeisance and served as their agent and enforcer among his own, making sure to curb any rebellious inclinations. Yet for this service, far from tarnishing him with the title of collaborator, Russians have rewarded him with the gift of prescience, crediting him with understanding that it was too soon to strike back. Time was needed for Rus to regain its strength and for the princes to forgo their differences.

The first positive sign in this direction came in 1380 when Nevsky's descendant, Prince Dmitry of Moscow, led an army onto Kulikovo Field and, after a long, close fight, defeated a large Mongol force. Such a victory was unprecedented and earned Dmitry the title "Donskoy," or "of the Don," referring to the river he crossed to give battle. Equally significant was the constitution of his army; the list alone of fallen nobles is a veritable roll call of principalities in Rus, suggesting that a relatively unified fighting front was taking shape.

Though Donskoy's victory was not enough to deliver Rus from the Yoke—only two years after Kulikovo another Mongol force ravaged Moscow, and he was back in his vassal role—that period represents a new phase in the political evolution of Rus, signifying Moscow's increased dominance among sibling principalities. Such an outcome is not without irony because it was precisely the Mongol invasion that provided much of the circumstance by which the city, located in the geographic heart of Rus, also became its political, religious, and economic center.

Like so many other cities, Moscow was destroyed and made part of the Mongol Empire, but its princes, over time, turned out to be supreme opportunists. Misfortune opened the doors for them to make a fortune by serving their Mongol overlords as tax collectors and policy enforcers. Along with its position at intersecting trade routes, such servitude helped make the city rich—so much so that one prince during its rise was nicknamed "Moneybags." This wealth translated into land purchases, and power also accrued through no small supply of ruthlessness, such as when Moneybags joined with Mongol forces in order to crush Tver, a rival principality, in the early fourteenth century.

At the same time, Moscow's authority increased when the head of the church transferred there, making it the seat of Russian Orthodoxy. Victory at Kulikovo Field, several decades later, brought more prestige and, though the Yoke continued, it became clear that the tide was shifting. Torn from within by its own internecine fighting, the Mongol hold diminished just as Moscow rose higher by annexing, buying, or conquering other principalities—a process now called, as if it were inevitable, "the gathering of the Russian lands."

This power dynamic continued to tilt in Moscow's favor as more and more tribute began to flow in its direction. When in 1480, during the reign of Ivan III, a Mongol force attempted to reassert supremacy, a climactic showdown between infidel and Orthodox was in the making. It was not to be, however, as the confrontation sputtered into a skirmish across a river. The Mongols nevertheless retreated and the Yoke, as it is traditionally dated, was over.

With good reason Ivan is remembered as "the Great." Rus was free from foreign dominion and, simultaneously, under Moscow's fist had emerged as a unified state no longer beset with squabbling principalities. Though not every one of them was, as of yet, under its direct control, none could pose a serious threat to its hegemony. These two achievements alone would have been sufficient for Ivan to win his appellation, yet what cast Moscow's ascendancy in an even more special light happened offstage, as it were, even before he took the throne.

In the eleventh century, when Christianity split into Western Latinate and Eastern Orthodox wings, Constantinople, the capital of the Byzantine Empire, became the spiritual capital of Eastern Orthodoxy. It controlled the eastern Mediterranean and southeastern Europe, and with that power, it also exercised ecclesiastical jurisdiction over Rus. With time, however, that grip weakened. By the mid-fifteenth century, when Moscow became ascendant, the Byzantine Empire had shrunk to a fraction of its former size under the unrelenting assault of Ottoman Turks. Desperate for help, Constantinople turned to the Vatican, offering to submit to its authority. This decision met with a furious backlash in Moscow. Surrender to the heretic in order to save oneself from the infidel? There was no salvation in that, only a betrayal of spiritual purity. Moscow broke its bond with Constantinople and took sovereign control of its own church.

Was that bold action the right one? The answer came shortly after, when the Turks overran Constantinople in 1453, which, when combined with the lifting of the Mongol Yoke in 1480, changed forever how Russia could see itself. Precisely when—with hindsight—one could say the origins of modern Russia were coming together, God seemingly blessed it by elevating it to be the sole protector of the true faith. All other Orthodox realms were now in the hands of the infidels or the heretics save for this one with Moscow as its capital. Had not the Lord spoken definitively that now it was his chosen city, that only this land, free of spiritual contamination, was where salvation could be had, and that the Russian people themselves were his elect?

The idea that resulted is most famously known as the "Third Rome," following the logic that if the first, the Vatican, was controlled by Catholics and now the second, Constantinople, by Muslims, then Moscow was the new capital of Christendom itself. Other iterations of exceptionalism were that of the city as the "New Jerusalem" or Russia as the "New Israel," but under any name what occurred by the end of the fifteenth century constituted a watershed for Russian identity.[2] What Russians did in the world and in world history could be seen as nothing less than issuing from God's grace, and nowhere else was that idea more important than when it came to war. His elect had the formidable responsibility of defending the faith, but they also had a spiritually unassailable license to spread it—as was to be seen quite dramatically during the reign of Ivan's grandson, Ivan IV, known better to us as "the Terrible."

If the picture produced so far is that of Rus becoming Russia while under trial of invasion, it is equally true that Rus became Russia as an expanding power, itself attacking and invading neighbors. Under Ivan the Terrible, who ruled from 1547 to 1584, Russia grew to become one of the largest states in Europe. Spearheading that drive was the 1552 conquest of Kazan, the capital of a Muslim successor state to the former Mongol Empire, on the Volga some 450 miles east of Moscow.

The calls issued by the church to launch this campaign paint it as an Orthodox crusade inseparable from Russia's newly construed identity. Addressed directly to Ivan, they fold defense of the faith in with attacking the enemy and expressly compare him to Alexander Nevsky, who "defeated the Latins," and Dmitry Donskoy, who "defeated the barbarians," as if they were all part of an ongoing conflict of the one true religion against false ones.[3] The resulting siege of Kazan, the most famous in which Russians were the besiegers, ended with God's army savaging the city, where for seven days after, it is said, one could not drink from the river because of the bodies and blood.

This last detail comes to us from *The History of Kazan*, written a decade later, ostensibly by an eyewitness. The anonymous author describes the campaign in similar cosmic colors but with a rhetorical sleight of hand that presages a ploy favored many times ever since: how to turn a mission of aggression into its opposite. He does this by making the siege the final chapter in the story of Mongol oppression.

Kazan, in other words, had become the latest home of the infidels who, like their predecessors, continued to pillage, rape, and enslave Russians. This linkage elevates Ivan's task to one of even greater consequence than that of Nevsky's or Donskoy's. If the latter two campaigned to protect Russia from an existential threat, then Ivan strikes across the border to eliminate one. In a single stroke, the religious imperative of defending the Orthodox faith merges with the political one of defending the land and the people—all in the service of foreign conquest. Indeed, Ivan's retribution—impaling the defenders—was worthy of his sobriquet, which in Russian actually means to inspire awe of a dreadful kind.

The History of Kazan is more than a literary monument to conquest. It expresses full confidence in Russia's necessary and exclusive supremacy as a military power precisely under the aegis of being the "Third Rome." Expansion, therefore, is as much a sign of divine pleasure as the earlier subjugation to the Mongols was one of disapproval. After the siege, and presumably after the river was potable, the history describes priests cleaning Kazan with holy water, mosques being destroyed, and churches and crosses erected in their place. This transformation extends as well to the survivors (for there were some) who are liberated from "darkness" and enter the kingdom of "truth," which is also identified as the "Russian faith." And it concludes that for God's elect such campaigns are inevitable and just. If the conquest of Kazan has proven that the infidel is rightfully "destroyed by Christian might," so too then "the Christian faith spreads, the land of Russia grows and flourishes, and the people on it multiply."[4]

Kazan was a resounding victory in more than religious terms. Never again would the Russian state be what it was before. The city's conquest permanently altered Russia's geographic identity by delivering much of the Volga into its hands. This opened up the Urals and Siberia for exploration and annexation to occur over the next two centuries. It also spelled the end for another neighboring khanate, Astrakhan, which controlled the mouth of the Volga as it flows into the Caspian Sea. Four years after Kazan, it would fall to Ivan's soldiers,

Russia c. 1600

bringing them to the foothills of the Caucasus. The age of Russian empire-building had begun. In three quick centuries its imperial standard would fly over one-sixth of the world's land mass.

Yet before Russia reached that peak, it nearly perished in a chain of events that can also be traced to Ivan the Terrible—this time as the raging father who killed his eldest son and heir to the throne. While two other sons, Dmitry and Fyodor, survived Ivan when he himself died in 1584, by century's end they too were dead. First was nine-

year-old Dmitry, the younger sibling, who ostensibly stabbed himself
in the neck during an epileptic fit. Then it was Fyodor's turn in 1598,
by natural causes but having failed to produce an heir. The Riurik
dynasty, which had ruled the various principalities of Rus for over
seven centuries, was no more.

The calamity had no precedent and neither did the solution: elevate Fyodor's brother-in-law, Boris Godunov, to tsar though his own
blood, albeit noble, ran in the opposite direction back to the Mongols.
Shortly after his reign began, disaster struck. Snow fell in the summer
and a series of failed harvests left the population reeling from famine.
Entire villages succumbed or were abandoned as the starving wan-
dered, desperate for food. Those for whom desperation had passed
resorted to cannibalism. All told, up to a third of Godunov's subjects
died.

What might so displease the Lord, shattered survivors could ask,
since his assumed pleasure—or lack thereof—determined all in the
premodern world? Was crowning Godunov a mistake? What if he
wasn't God's choice? Fears over the new tsar's legitimacy quickly
mixed with suspicions over his past. Had he plotted the murder of
young Dmitry so as to seize power upon the older brother's death? Or
had Dmitry miraculously survived, meaning that Godunov's election
had violated the divine order of succession?

The last idea became fertile ground for much of the violence that
followed. A rival to Godunov emerged, claiming to be Dmitry. Provided with troops by the Poles, this "false Dmitry" also attracted Russians wanting to overthrow the unholy usurper and regain God's favor.
As this army of mixed religions, nationalities, and intentions marched
on Moscow in 1605, Godunov fell dead, a sure sign of the righteousness
of Dmitry's cause.

That impression lasted less than a year. Tsar Dmitry, with his Catholic Polish wife and retinue of foreign mercenaries, soon grated on
Orthodox sensitivities in the capital. He was murdered by Russian
nobles who again elected one of their own as tsar. What then befell
Russia defies imagination and conventional categorization. More

"Dmitrys" and other claimants to the throne rushed forward. As fighting ripped across the land, central power collapsed. At one point Russia had two tsars, two royal courts, and two patriarchs. This was its so-called Time of Troubles, and it only got worse.

The one constant during the conflict was chaos—the kind that marauding bands feasted on and of which foreign neighbors dreamed. From the south came the Crimean Tatars, vassals of the Ottoman Turks, who burned the environs of Moscow; from the north came the Swedes, first as allies, but who then began seizing Russia's Baltic territories. From the west, the Poles marched in and by 1611 would seem to have driven a stake into their longtime rival. They occupied the Kremlin and took the patriarch—there being only one at this time—prisoner. For that matter, there no longer was a tsar, and, as if to confirm that Russia's future was over, a group of nobles, some from quite prestigious families, had agreed that rule should pass to the Polish royal line.

What saved Russia was its religion, embodied in Patriarch Hermogen, held captive in the Kremlin. When he learned of the Polish king's plan to forcibly convert (future) Orthodox subjects to Catholicism, he spearheaded a campaign of missives and broadsides, with others joining in who called on all of the "pure faith" to rise and free their "great land" from the "rapacious wolves" and "Satanic hordes" that threatened its destruction on an apocalyptic scale.[5]

The Poles would have their revenge. They locked themselves in the Kremlin, burned the rest of Moscow, and starved Hermogen to death. The Russians, however, would have their victory. The campaign of letters worked, and in 1612 a national militia gathered under Prince Pozharsky and Kuzma Minin, a butcher in charge of its finances and logistics. It marched on Moscow and surrounded the Poles. Pozharsky and his men beat off successive relief attempts as the garrison itself began to starve and then succumbed to cannibalism. The wasted remnants surrendered in the fall of 1612, and though fighting would continue on and off for years, with the Poles reaching Moscow again in 1618, this generally marks the end of the Time of Troubles. The next year witnessed the quick election of a new tsar, Mikhail Romanov, whose progeny would make up the next—and last—royal dynasty in Russia.

Past as Present

Lake Peipus, Kulikovo Field, Kazan, and 1612 are the four most celebrated military events of Russia's premodern past, and they serve as bedrock chapters in the saga of how Russia came to be. Along with other battles and campaigns, they offer a panoply of inspiring examples of defiant resistance, stoic martyrdom, and even mass suicide to avoid enslavement. These are the archetypes through which the country's formative period is typically remembered, and Russians will never forget them.

Between these archetypes lies a lot more history—of the complex kind that myth generally shuns. If Moscow's use of Mongol rule to secure its political fortune offers one irony from this period, then another concerns the fate of Russian Orthodoxy. Though many churches were destroyed, especially in the initial years of invasion, overall it prospered quite well during the Yoke, since it was exempt from paying tribute and taxes. So too is the impression that the Mongols faced uniform defiance false; even contemporary chroniclers did not always cover up the fact that Russians sometimes allied and intermarried with them. In fact, much of Ivan the Great's success in lifting the Yoke in 1480 was due to an alliance with a rival Mongol successor state.[6]

Even the nature of Russia's other enemies, such as those Alexander Nevsky faced, can be debated. For Western scholars, the number and intent of the attacking Swedes and Teutonic knights remain in contention: large raiding parties or full-fledged invasions? That, for example, there is no record in Swedish chronicles of the battle at the Neva River might suggest its scale was smaller than the honorific title the prince claimed from it. Likewise, the relatively few casualties suffered by the knights at Lake Peipus—if non-Russian sources are consulted—have raised doubt about its epic pull.[7]

Similar questions can be raised about the forces fielded during the Time of Troubles. They were heavily dependent on mercenaries and thus were multinational and multiconfessional. Russians, in other words, fought alongside Poles, just as Tatars could be found in the Russian ranks. And most leaders played all angles of the political game, siding variously with Poles, usurpers, or other claimants. Even the campaign of 1612 was not that of a unified Russia but of a Russian-dominated and Russian-led army that succeeded in its mission.

In popular imagination, however, such questions have gained little traction. The victories of Nevsky, for instance, quashed true attempts orchestrated by the papacy to conquer the rest of Rus and kill or convert all, thereby eradicating Russian Orthodoxy. Eisenstein's *Alexander Nevsky* provides the requisite cinematic images of Germans tossing Russian babies into the flames, and, as is evident by the continuing consensus among Russian historians, nothing has dislodged this sentiment. By preserving the last remnants of a nominally free Rus, Nevsky laid the foundation for its eventual political and spiritual recovery. Put simply, as the Orthodox Church did in 2008, "without him there would be no Russia, there would be no Russians."[8]

Sentiments like these turn Russia's past into a heroic age that, alongside such dramatic tales, also passes on edifying lessons which with hindsight continue to speak to Russia's security concerns. As given in—to cite just one example from among many—*The Military History of Our Country,* a three-volume work published by the Defense Ministry in 2003, Nevsky's feats instill caution about Russia's neighbors, particularly those in the West, and Donskoy's victory underscores that national unity is the precursor to success. Ivan's conquest of Kazan demonstrates that sometimes the best way to neutralize a foreign threat is to swallow it up, while the campaign of 1612 wraps all of these tenets around the primacy of faith, the perils of anarchy, and the mystical power of the people.

These archetypes and lessons may skim over the rough waters of history, but they project a unified vision of a distinctly Russian experience of war that runs unbroken from the Middle Ages to today. It rests on a chain of interlocking themes and assumptions that, while fitted to match the political needs of the day, are not without a certain legitimate grounding—which is why they can be so powerful for a domestic audience.

It is best to begin that chain with invasion—the threat of, fear of, reality of—that colors so much of Russia's sense of engagement with the world. Long before its chapter on the Mongols, *The Military History of Our Country* dutifully preps the reader on how the early Slavs, "peace-loving" to be sure, were constantly tormented by outsiders from the east. In the fourth century came the Goths, en route to attack Rome; in the fifth it was the Huns, then the Avars and the Khazars in the sixth and seventh centuries. The Pechenegs, followed by the Polovtsy, bring one to the thirteenth century.

Following the Mongol Yoke and Nevsky's defeat of the Swedish and Teutonic attacks, Russia's history again can be traced as a century-by-century roll call of invaders. In the sixteenth from the south came the Crimean Tatars who burned Ivan the Terrible's Moscow just as they would do again at the beginning of the next century during the Time of Troubles. That convulsive period, as we have seen, also brought in the Poles and the Swedes, and in the eighteenth the latter invaded once more but were crushed by Peter the Great. In the nineteenth century, the Corsican "Antichrist," as Napoleon Bonaparte was designated by the Russian Church, marched his Grande Armée to its death in the Russian snows, and in the twentieth, a true devil bearing a swastika invaded again along the same roads.

Yet even these century-defining invasions do not constitute the whole of Russia's history. Before the Yoke, medieval chronicles give us a portrait of life soaked in blood at the hands of foreigners, and for hundreds of years after the Mongols disappeared Russia's borders were penetrated continuously. Of particular infamy were the aforementioned Crimean Tatars and their insatiable hunger for booty, the most valuable commodity being Russians themselves, sold as slaves at foreign markets. The constant fear of sudden attack was a defining part of life for those near the borders but, as seen, even the capital wasn't safe. Monasteries were built across Russia precisely as fortresses, and eventually five such structures ringed Moscow alone.

In short, it is not difficult for Russia to see itself as a unique object of invasion, not only because of their frequency but also because of their origin, literally coming from all points on the compass. They have differed in scale and intent, from extermination-enslavement to the seizure of land and other resources, but their legacy from the Russian perspective remains the same: a pattern of foreign attack in which the actors' names may change but not the primary action. Indeed, the very fact that one can chart Russian history around their occurrence has driven deep the impression that this is the nation's inevitable fate: always the target of aggression, caught forever in a cycle of foreign predation, peace as only a calm before the next storm.[9]

The acute sense of vulnerability led in the sixteenth and seventeenth centuries to the construction of an elaborate defensive system of fortified towns interspersed with ramparts and field obstructions that ran for over a thousand miles along its southern and southeastern frontiers, from the heart of present-day Ukraine all the way to the Volga past Kazan. While not equal to the Great Wall of China, the resources put into the system were pronounced, requiring at its height tens of thousands to maintain and man it. This need also produced a human counterpart, the Cossacks, a mix of freebooters, restless spirits, and runaway serfs who came to serve on the same frontiers as a buffer force. They were, however, prone to turn on Russia just as easily, until they were definitively co-opted by the empire in the nineteenth century.

Why this fate? Why has Russia earned the oft-cited appellation of "much-suffering," not just for internal woes such as the institution of serfdom or the grip of autocrats, but for external ones as well? Geography would seem a primary culprit, having conspired to make the lands of Rus so valuable yet so vulnerable a target. They lay across strategic trade routes both north-south and east-west, vital for millennia as the economic interchange between the Baltic and the Black

Seas, between Europe, Asia, and the Middle East. Russia came to be the crossroads both of continents and of great religions, the gateway of so many migrations from East to West. Yet it also has few natural defensive boundaries. There are no Alps to shield it or English Channel to hold marauders at a distance. Even its largest rivers freeze in wintertime—a fact the Mongols used to keen advantage.

Yet geography has never sufficed as an explanatory tool, especially for those who have borne the suffering. The exceptionalism offered by Third Rome–like ideologies imparted to the land itself a holy quality that elevated its defense to a sacred duty in the most literal of senses. This idea has lived on, even though the political borders of said land have been quite fluid. Sometimes it figures as metaphor, such as in Vasily Trediakovsky's aptly titled "Panegyric Verses to Russia," written in the early eighteenth century when its imperial might rolled west through the Baltic territories toward Poland.

> Who in the wide world does not know
> About your exalted nobility?
> You are yourself nobility's essence;
> In truth, the radiant work of God on high.
> In you the pious find all faith resides,
> To you the godless can no entry gain.
> In you there will not be divided faiths,
> To you evil dare not bring assault.
> Your people are all Orthodox in faith,
> And by their bravery known everywhere;
> The worthy offspring of such a mother,
> Always prepared to stand in her defense.

Elsewhere the belief's echo can be more prosaic, yet equally defiant, such as in the declaration by the commander of Russia's border guards, after the collapse of the Soviet Union shrank it back to pre-imperial size, that "faith and motherland are synonymous. Without faith there cannot be a motherland, and without a motherland no faith." Whether meant symbolically or literally, the bond between spiritual and physical dimensions looms large in the Russian collective consciousness. It is a thread that runs across centuries, and it is the thread from which many of Russia's war narratives are woven.[10]

The concept itself of motherland—perhaps no other word is so evocative of Russia and so dominant in its martial lore—reflects the depth of this sentiment. Its power even speaks from a pre-Christian past, when the pagan Slavs worshipped the earth as a kind of "divine motherhood." The word for "motherland," *rodina* (rohd'-eena), reflects this sense because its root, *rod,* is found in the verb "to give birth" and in associated words like "clan." This is why a more direct translation would be "birthland" or "land that gives birth," and, through no coincidence, that root also gives us the word for "people" or *narod* (na-rohd'). What might sound like a cliché for another culture—the inseparability of identity from the native soil—is semantically united and reaffirmed both as organic (born from the land) and spiritual (of one mother).

Conversion in the late tenth century cemented the connection even more. Central to Orthodox Christianity is the cult of Mary, whose role as Holy Mother far outweighs that of the Virgin. In Russian the common title by which she is known (and which is a calque from the Greek *Theotokos*) also employs the *rod* stem: *bogoroditsa* (bahgah-rohd'-eetsa) or "Birth-giver of God." In this capacity, she represents, as one theologian has written, "not only the Mother of God or Christ but the universal Mother, the Mother of all mankind," and this has given her a leading role in Russia's military heritage.[11]

As a mother, Mary protects her children. Therefore, while soldiers of Rus marched into battle with Christ's visage on their banners, chronicle accounts typically highlight Mary in heaven, directing the instruments of divine intercession. Her robe serves as a metaphorical shield, thus effecting a bridge for a military trope to pass from the classical age into the Christian, and also explains why so many Russian churches bear the name *pokrov* in her honor. (Literally from the word signifying "cover," it means "protection" and is translated as "intercession.") As Dmitry Donskoy prepared to give battle at Kulikovo

Field, an event that would take place on her holy day, it was in her church, we are told, that he summoned his "brother-princes," and it was to her icon that he prayed: "O, Our Lady, wonder-working Mother of God, Protector of all human creation for it is because of you that we know our true God, he made in flesh and given birth by you. Send us your aid and cover us with your invincible raiment." For believers, she did.[12]

Before the Kazan campaign, Ivan the Terrible offered similar prayers but with an expanded set of epithets. Here she is titled a "solid wall" and a "strong pillar" as well as a "powerful army" and its "undefeated leader." The tsar's piety was repaid not just with victory over the infidels, but with a miracle that duplicated military success for later generations of Russians. In the city's soil decades after its conquest, legend has it, there appeared an icon of the Holy Mother, entitled Our Lady of Kazan, which, as was believed, saved Russia during three subsequent invasions: the Poles in 1612, the Swedes in 1709, and the French in 1812.

The list alone of Mary's alleged intercessions covers much of Russia's military history and extends even into its Soviet-atheist period when, it has been claimed, she delivered victory at Kursk in 1943, the greatest tank battle of World War II, and saved Leningrad in the deadliest siege in history. Truth be told, however, her first appearance in this tradition is that of killing Russians when, according to the chronicles, as pagans they attacked the Orthodox Byzantines in 860 and were defeated because of her intervention. Needless to say, after their conversion a century later, her role flipped and she became the most powerful weapon in the Russian arsenal.

The ideational fusing of land and faith combined with the need to protect it permeates Russia's sense of war to the extent that it can function as a signature mark of national identity. Such, indeed, was the core message given by Metropolitan Sergii, the leader of the Russian Orthodox Church, on June 22, 1941, when Germany launched its surprise attack. His sermon, composed the same day and sent to churches around the country, takes as its rallying point the indisputable fact that this was "not the first time the Russian people have

Holy Mother and Child. Russian icon from the sixteenth century. Russian State Museum, St. Petersburg, Russia / Scala / Art Resource, NY.

endured such trials." Foreign invasion, in his recall of Russian history, is the pivot upon which it has turned. The Mongols, the Teutonic knights, the Swedes, and the French—all failed in their quest to conquer Russia, and "with God's help" this time too the people would "crush the fascist forces into dust." This past serves not just as precedent but as a decisive factor in what it means to be Russian. "Our ancestors," he stressed, "did not lose their spirit even when in the direst of circumstances because they thought not of their personal danger or welfare but of their holy duty before the motherland and faith, and thus emerged victorious. We—Orthodox and their kin by flesh and by faith—will not shame their glorious name."[13]

On the surface, Sergii's sermon operates like any religiously infused, patriotic invocation of national heroes, and, to no surprise, he singles out Alexander Nevsky and Dmitry Donskoy as exemplary models since both "laid down their souls for the people and motherland." That, at first, might seem an unusual step because neither died in combat. Yet this claim reveals yet another fundamental part of the defense-of-land dictum. The honorific of martyrdom does not hinge on death, as we might expect, but on service alone to Russia. In short, the sacredness of the land makes its defense a sacred act in and of itself.

Such a belief enjoys solid precedent. In medieval Europe, Rus stood out for canonizing princes outside of the typical path to sainthood. Instead of dying for their faith, which would apply to all Christians, many became saints just for defeating foreign enemies. Nevsky himself is a prime example, canonized shortly before Ivan the Terrible's Kazan campaign, and in no other European country was this path to sainthood so often employed. Even war heroes from legends, known as *bogatyry* and around whom fantastic folk tales of resistance were constructed, have earned this holy status.

The tradition invoked by Sergii still applies. Dmitry Donskoy, after a long period of semiofficial veneration, was formally canonized in 1988, the thousand-year anniversary of Russia's conversion to Christianity, and in 2001 so too was Admiral Fyodor Ushakov, undefeated in the eighteenth century commanding ships against the Turks bearing names like *Holy Trinity, Kazan Mother of God,* and *Saint Peter, Saint Paul,* and *Saint Magdalene.* Ushakov's canonization demonstrates how the defense of Russia's holy land can also extend to the sea and, in fact, into the air as well, for he is the patron saint of its strategic air wing, including nuclear bombers.[14]

Yet duty does demand the willingness to sacrifice oneself, and death, just as much as defense, also occupies a large—sometimes abnormally so—place in Russian war narratives. No military ethos, of course, can allow it to be in vain, which is why some variation of the famous line by Horace that "it is sweet and fitting to die for one's country" figures prominently in many cultures. Russia, however, prefers another injunction, that of John 15:13, when Jesus, before setting the ultimate example himself, declares, "there is no greater love than to lay down one's life for one's friends." In Sergii's sermon he recites it with almost incantatory effect, insisting that "if there is anyone who needs to remember Christ's commandment then it is precisely us." This call serves two ends. Not only does it honor the staggering losses caused by "all the enemy invasions of our motherland," it holds that solely because of Russians' willingness to shed their own blood have they persevered as a nation and people.

Echoing Sergii, in 2004 Patriarch Aleksii II pronounced John 15:13 the mantra of Russia's armed forces. For both church leaders, however, this was putting an official stamp on a cult of worship for Christ's injunction that already appears in medieval accounts, including those of Kulikovo and Kazan. From there it threads through Russian history, appearing by the time of World War I almost a mandate for soldiers to die, as given in a prayer book issued to them: "Military service is the direct fulfillment of the Lord's commandment: There is no greater love than to lay down one's life for one's friends." Millions would come to demonstrate the verity of those words. And for World War II, it is through John 15:13 that the Ninth of May is no longer just a secular holiday in Russia but, having shed its Soviet-era atheism, a church-consecrated holy day of memory for the millions dead from that war.[15]

Just as we can anticipate how a Russian war narrative might seem incomplete without soldiers dying, it is also important to recognize how John 15:13 can script an entire war. Indeed, Russia's image as a protector-liberator from the likes of the Mongols rests precisely on a sense of sacrifice for those beyond its borders. Such is the conclusion offered by *The Military History of Our Country*. If the Yoke did not extend into Europe appreciably beyond the borders of Rus, then Russians must have played the decisive role in containing it. How might that be? They "behaved like a shield," volume 1 declares, and in so doing "saved" Europe from destruction. Never would the descendants of Genghis Khan water their horses in the Rhine, the Seine, or the Thames, since they "could not continue west, leaving behind in their rear the indomitable Russians." Safe behind that human wall, it then reminds us, Europe would soon blossom during the Renaissance—which never reached the Russians who bled for it.[16]

On this point, John 15:13 writ large provides the necessary frame to map that event as precursor to and mirror of Russia's special role in defeating Hitler. In 2005, Patriarch Aleksii declared a jubilee year in honor of Kulikovo, fought 625 years earlier. His pronouncement, issued on September 8, the day of battle, began by citing John and then explained the battle's significance as one where "at the cost of a great many lives, Rus not only dealt a crushing blow to the Golden Horde, but also saved the states of Europe by shielding them from the threat of foreign invasion." Effortlessly, his attention then shifted to Russians in the Second World War, praising them for doing the same as their ancestors. As medieval sacrifice blended with the modern one, as September 8 entered the same orbit once reserved for May 9, it became clear why he chose that year for its jubilee. The sexquadricentennial of anything isn't particularly inspiring, but the sixtieth anniversary of 1945 made it so.[17]

A Civic Religion

Invasion, resistance, self-reliance, and self-sacrifice constitute the pillars on which Russia's grand narrative of war rests. Together they provide a sweeping view of the past which stands in contrast to that of many historians, particularly in the West, who would emphasize instead Russia's militant, expansionist nature. One of the most noted, Richard Pipes, has argued that its imperial impulse has been "unique" and offered the memorable analogy that from Ivan the Terrible to Peter the Great, that is, from the middle of the sixteenth century to the beginning of the eighteenth, it "acquired an average of 35,000 square kilometers—an area equivalent to modern Holland—*every year* for 150 consecutive years." Why Russia is exceptional in this paradigm, one that replaces foreign invasion with naked aggression at its apex, according to Pipes, lies in the convergence of precise historic, economic, geographic, and political factors.

Upon the rise of Moscow, its rulers "began to behave" as the Mongols "had taught" them, internalizing a ruthless possessiveness or sense of direct ownership of the lands they acquired. Those very same lands, however, while blessed with abundant natural resources, were incapable of supporting a large population—a condition that forced Russia into a cycle of conquest. Moreover, its strategic position astride Europe and Asia have fed this drive by "afford[ing] Russia opportunities for conquest enjoyed by no other power." ("Russian infantry can reach any part of the European, African, and Asian continents without getting their feet wet.") Finally, the land seized and the riches it provided were essential to pay off the elites who served the state and to finance the perpetual need for expansion in the first place.[18]

No one would deny the Russian Empire's record of fantastic growth by conquest, least of all those Russians for whom this martial feat is an enduring point of national pride. Other nations' foot soldiers, as it were, might just as well have marched across that length while keeping their boots dry; they just didn't—or couldn't. Yet Russia's war myth can even soften its imperial drive across two of the three aforementioned continents through the mantle of defensive protectionism. The conquest of Kazan, as we have seen, is a case in point; as stated in *The Military History of Our Country*, "it was absolutely necessary" for security purposes. And that same idea—Russian troops must march forth to protect the nation, the people, and others—can stand behind the push south in the eighteenth century, for example, culminating in the annexation of Crimea so as to put an end to the plague of slave raids by the Crimean Tatars. It too was a necessary conquest, we learn in its latest redaction, to save Russians *and* Ukrainians from an enemy who "considered it his inalienable right to traffic in the [Slavic] peasant and his wife." (With Russia's annexation of Crimea again in the twenty-first century, discussed in more detail in Chapter 7, a similar protectionist motive has been claimed, this time to defend ethnic Russians there from the ostensible threat posed by the Ukrainian government to their well-being.)[19]

A variant of this defensive expansionism can also cover Russia's conquest of central Asia in the nineteenth century—and was delivered as a point of policy while it was occurring. "[Once Russia comes] into contact with half-savage nomadic tribes," the foreign minister, Alexander Gorchakov, publicly declared in 1864, "the interests of border security and trade relations always require that the more civilized state have a certain authority over its neighbors." So acute were these interests, he continued, that they conceptually set expansionism on an infinite loop: "Once this result has been achieved the latter [neighbors] take on more peaceful habits, but in their turn they are exposed to the attacks of tribes living farther off. The state therefore must make a choice: either to give up this continuous effort and doom its borders to constant unrest . . . or else to advance farther and farther into the heart of the savage lands."[20]

Gorchakov's exemplary obsession with the line separating Russia from the (hostile) Other also helps shed light on some of the stereotypes through which it is often viewed. Acutely paranoid, fixated with its borders, paralyzed by anxiety over their violation, hobbled by a profound sense of isolation—these sins have long lain at its door. However, within the above vision of the Russian historical experience, each can find compensatory justification.

The toll of repeated foreign attacks is reflected in the fact that Russia has no myth of the citizen-soldier, the famous Cincinnatus of ancient Rome who leaves his plow and takes up arms when the enemy comes and puts them down afterward. It cannot afford the luxury, since the designs of its enemies make bearing arms a necessary, permanent condition. Survival, whether of nation, people, or faith, demands hypervigilance. As Boris Vasilev, a popular writer and veteran of World War II, once wrote, Russians are fated to be "eternal border guards"—a proposition enshrined by the Soviet practice of deliberately falsifying maps to confuse would-be invaders, of maintaining a nonstandard rail gauge to force any occupier to rebuild the entire network, or of institutionalizing the border guards as a separate branch of the Russian military.[21]

Yet innocence—the critical component of the Cincinnatus story—can still be asserted by focusing on the enemy and the actions and atrocities he commits on Russian land. Russia is attacked because they—whoever is on the outside—are implacable aggressors and bestial savages. Here the exterminating fury of both the Mongols and the Nazis seals the picture and means that "threat exaggeration" is something of an anomaly in the Russian vocabulary.

Belief in an exclusive spiritual quality for the Russian land and its people also fixates attention on borders. To be sure, just as its political boundaries have shifted, leaving Russians outside of that "space," non-Russians, whether defined in linguistic, ethnic, or religious terms, have always been inside it. Nevertheless, belief in exceptionalism, by its very nature, feeds a sense of isolation. That it yields this bitter fruit is a predictable outcome of its internal logic—and is not confined to Russia. If one is special, then separation from others becomes axiomatic. What is crucial in Russia's case, however, is that this sensibility can reach back once more to the fifteenth century, when, as a historian has observed, for the first time "*all* of Russia's neighbors were of a different religion from its own: they were pagans, Moslems or Catholics—i.e., pagan, infidel or heretical. In its world Russia was the only Orthodox, the only true Christian state."[22]

It should not be forgotten that these differences did not impede the crossing of that all-important border for diplomatic, commercial, and cultural purposes. Alliances and trade proceeded in the same compass directions from which came attack and invasion. But it does mean that any war with a neighbor, even if begun for clear political or economic reasons, could be recorded as a religious-cosmic one. To

Sixteenth-century depiction of the siege of Kozelsk in 1238. The town held out for an incredible seven weeks against the Mongols before it fell. All surviving defenders were put to death. Private collection / Sputnik / Bridgeman Images.

fight the Pole was, by definition, simultaneously a conflict with the heretical West; to fight the Turk or Crimean Tatar, one with the infidel South. For the devout, the step from this condition to seeing a threat by a neighbor as existential could be relatively small. To lose to the Catholic crusader, for example, could result in spiritual death if conversion followed, which was a fate worse than the physical loss of life. Centuries of hostility across these conceptual borders have thus dug deep and, at times, unbridgeable chasms between the key political players in Eastern Europe.

To push the point even more, when Rus became Russia it was also isolated to a degree that, one could argue, was virtually unmatched by any other major state in continental Europe. Neither the Pole nor the German at this time was surrounded by enemies of their faith, and neither was Spain in its struggle to rid the Iberian Peninsula of Muslims, since France to its rear was equally Catholic. And while the Reformation complicates this map, producing islets of Protestantism and Catholicism, the assertion could be made that no modern nation of Europe developed (or evolved) quite like the religious island that was Russia.

History has allowed this sense of isolation to persist, and even the Soviet period can be cast in this light by substituting ideology for religion. From 1917 until World War II, the Soviet Union was the sole country professing faith in Marxism. After the war, nations in Eastern Europe were forcibly converted, as it were, under the Iron Curtain, and Russia's role expanded to become the protectorate of the new ranks of the faithful. After the fall of the Soviet Union, the appearance of Orthodox-majority neighbors, Ukraine and Belarus, handicaps this line of reasoning. Yet the expansion of NATO east toward Russia's borders helps refresh the sense of encirclement whenever the need arises to tap into it, as has been the case most recently in the conflict with Ukraine. In sum, Russia can construe itself as a nation that, as a fact of its very existence and identity, has almost always been surrounded. To hypervigilance at the border, therefore, can be added hypersensitivity to those who live across it.

Outside impressions have played an equal role in drawing a cultural divide around Russia. The Catholic West and the Orthodox East, for example, operated along reciprocal fault lines in the Middle Ages. Papal-authorized crusades licensed violence against "heretical schismatics," the special category into which Orthodox believers fell. Other divides have arisen to define Russians that, when following ethnic prejudices, often reach back to the Yoke: Russians are not truly European; they're Asian or some kind of Mongolian half-breeds who have inherited their savage traits. Here Russia's image flips from savior of Europe to its menace and, as a telling result, has helped give the Poles their own myth of being the continent's protector from a Russified barbarous East.

That the same historical event can be invoked to distinguish Russianness underscores how powerful the medieval legacy can be for scripting its identity and reminds us that any special stature claimed from it can cut both ways. Fyodor Dostoevsky, one of the most passionate believers in Russian exceptionalism, recognized how the Yoke could serve equally as a point of pride or as fuel for outside prejudice. On one hand, he could write of his nation and people as having sacrificed themselves for "the common interests of humanity." On the other, using an alternative term to designate the Mongols, he shook his head that "the Europeans simply d[o] not want to acknowledge us as their own. 'Scratch a Russian,' they would say, 'and you will find a Tatar.' . . . We've become one of their proverbs."[23] Both for Russophiles and Russophobes alike, its assumed Asiatic infusion has remained a favored trope.

However spurious, reductive, and ahistorical these fault lines—who qualifies as "European" and thus not a "savage" has always been a question of who is speaking about whom and when—they can flourish in times of war, serving as engines, consciously or not, for so much of the hatred and civilian-centered violence that, on both sides of the coin, have marked so many of Russia's conflicts. They are powerful enough to infect peacetime, with neighbors harboring suspicions about likely Russian aggression and, conversely, with Russia seeing itself as their perpetual target.

While such perceptions have waxed and waned and their application has never been constant, they help seed another vital corollary to Russia's war myth: Russians are Russia's only guarantee for its independence. This is why for its patriots, trust—particularly toward the West—can seem a dangerous commodity. Other European nations, runs this impression, are always eyeing ways to take advantage of Russia, including, at the extreme, a desire for its destruction.

One need look no further, of course, than to German plans for a surprise attack and swift conquest, followed by the deportation of Russians to the West as slave laborers and then to be exterminated—precisely because of their inferior status. If, on this account, Hitler first comes to mind, then Russians can delve deeper into their past to find a precursor for such genocidal designs. In the sixteenth century Heinrich von Staden was a German mercenary who served in the *oprichniki,* Ivan the Terrible's terror-wielding domestic enforcers. That experience opened his eyes both to Russia's wealth and its vulnerabilities, and, in his scheme, the fault line he employed to justify its extermination was religion. With a proto-blitzkrieg in mind, he envisioned an amphibious invasion from the north, traveling rapidly down Russia's rivers. Because the populace was ruled by a "horrid tyrant," extensive collaboration could be expected, which is why, in his imagination, one hundred thousand troops, supported by one hundred chaplains, could take Moscow "without a shot being fired."

Von Staden addressed his work to the Holy Roman Emperor, but we do not know if it was received or reviewed. Nevertheless, variations of von Staden's "Christian enterprise" were seriously considered by a few Swedish nobles. At least we know its author was sincere—he even identifies by name experienced Dutch pilots to lead the ships—and possessed the ruthlessness to carry it out. In his autobiography he describes quite casually how, during a raid in service to the tsar, he buried an ax in a defenseless woman's back.

Von Staden's plan to erase Russia remained on paper in German archives until it was first published in Soviet Russia, and it has been reissued again for a post-Soviet generation. The dream was as delusional as it was murderous, but the fact that someone so minor would market it to those with the power to attempt it gives notional legitimacy to the country with, so it has been said, "the world's greatest persecution complex." Indeed, von Staden's fantasy reads as its perfect realization: an existential threat perpetrated by a conspiracy of nations motivated equally by fault-line hatred and old-fashioned greed and united across Catholic-Protestant lines despite the religious wars raging at that time in the West. Hitler, in sum, is not a lone wolf in the nightmares haunting Russia's historic imagination.[24]

The coalescing of these diverse traditions, beliefs, and experiences into a civic religion has proven indispensable for a resurgent, remilitarized Russia in the twenty-first century. It can mobilize public support for any current (or future) conflict by pulling it into the fold where just cause and self-defense reign. Wiped clean in the process is the image of Russia as preternaturally belligerent, a rogue nation with its sword forever unsheathed. Instead, it is forced to bear arms as a necessary, permanent condition; with such predators outside its borders, it can never afford to let its guard down. Moreover, this history helps reinforce the country's "great power" status—if "superpower" is no longer an option—by giving it a national narrative with considerable luster. Russia, in effect, has done things for the world that no other country has.

With World War II as its paradigmatic center, this religion also aims to bind Russian citizens together. If victory in 1945 was a "national awakening," we learn from a volume commissioned for its seventieth anniversary, then that legacy continues as the "foundation" of society's "moral and spiritual character." Shared commemoration of the war thus offers an unrivaled "sacred kinship," as noted at the beginning of this chapter, that stretches across political and social lines and the country's vast distances. To this degree, it transcends even Orthodoxy itself by uniting citizens "irrespective of their faith," including the atheist and agnostic. This is why when on May 9 all are invited into the streets to join a mass procession, bearing the photograph of a relative who was in the war, they enter the ranks of what is deemed the "Immortal Regiment." Regardless of age, participants become, symbolically speaking, siblings conceived by this victory since it teaches Russians, as another work intones, "who we are" as a people.[25]

Such triumphalism also illuminates the whole of Russian history. Nevsky, Donskoy, Pozharsky, Minin—they too are of that spirit, their names conjured up alongside those who marched on Berlin. It is omnipresent and so powerful, as we will see, that it can even turn defeat into victory so that Russia's past can return as one of unbroken pride. And it rises today as an irresistible—and so far irrepressible—rallying point in the current conflict in Ukraine and broader confrontation with the West by proving to those in the choir that isolation and self-reliance are Russia's true and noble destiny. This is mythic history at its best, doing just what one expects it to do by leavening a majestic spirit with sufficient historical grounding to make it feel right.

This is why in its temples, such as the Central Armed Forces Museum in Moscow, and through its scriptures, like the publications sponsored by the Academy of Sciences and Defense Ministry, the religion's high priests declaim that studying the nation's military heritage—more so than any other subject—is necessary in order to cultivate the sense of what it means to be a true Russian. For here is to be found, several of their treatises extol, what Russians have perpetually chased: a "national idea" for their time and place.

However one encounters this network of belief, ritual, image, and word, two caveats should be kept in mind. First, today's propagandists did not invent it. In linking the Mongols with the Nazis, for example, some might recognize an inheritance from the Soviet period. Indeed, reading the experience of the Yoke through the legacy of World War II was de rigueur during the twentieth century, as was the notion that Russia saved Europe from being overrun in the Middle Ages. In 1980, for instance, on the six hundredth anniversary of the Battle of Kulikovo Field, Yevgeny Yevtushenko, a poet who could fill stadiums, let France know—in verse—that the Eiffel Tower's "roots"

A procession of the Immortal Regiment in Sevastopol, Crimea, on May 9, 2015, after its annexation by Russia. © Larina Elena / Cliparto.

grew out of the Russian soil watered then with Russian blood. If not for that distant sacrifice, Paris would not be Paris.[26]

Yet it would be mistaken to stop in the Soviet period. All of the foundational tenets of Russian exceptionalism—its essential vocabulary, catechismic rhythm, premise of providential destiny, and tying of salvation to the sacrifice for others—predate 1945 and, for that matter, anything Soviet. It has a deep history, as we will see, extending back at least two centuries, when it first flourished as a touchstone to project an exclusive national identity.

The second caveat issues from the first. While institutions of power have favored and propagated this brand of myth, its echo is heard in countless venues, shaping fiction, history, and film—and not necessarily because authorities might dictate it that way, even during periods of heavy censorship. Just as one could say regarding the expression and influence of exceptionalism in America, in societies permeated by such a belief, greatness—both the search for it and articulation of it— is easily the default topic of national narratives, no matter who or what occupies the producer's seat. And while it may be the scholar's job to dissect that myth, to expose how it distorts or ignores events in the past, popular imagination—just as much as politics—tends to thrive on it. How this might be so can be found in a short personal letter from nearly two hundred years ago in which was written:

> We have had our own special mission. Russia, with its immense expanses, was what absorbed the Mongol conquest. They did not dare to cross our western frontier and leave us in their rear. They withdrew back to the desert and Christian civilization was saved. And for achieving that goal we have had to lead a completely unique existence.

The source is not a general or church official. Neither is it an ideologue or autocrat. Rather it was someone who disparaged central authority and who was censored and exiled by the state. That someone would also become Russia's greatest writer: Alexander Pushkin.[27]

What gave Pushkin this conviction, seconded by a battery of his contemporaries, be they conservatives or radicals? What galvanized for their generation images and ideas from Russia's distant past into the materials for modern myth? The answer, we might predict, is simple. Yet another invasion.

2

A Myth Comes of Age

Having rid itself of a tyrant bent on world domination, Europe in 1815 wasted no time finding someone else to play that role. With Napoleon Bonaparte in permanent exile, suspicion promptly fell on Russia for harboring similar designs of conquest. Evidence would seem clear to any Western observer. Possessing the largest army in the world, Russia sat upon half of Europe; no one after the defeat of Napoleon could rival its power on land. Expansion to the east was no longer possible, since its imperial border had reached the Pacific long before. The only paths that remained for conquest were to the south and the west, and here Russian intentions were already known. A century earlier, its first emperor, Peter the Great, had bequeathed an actual plan detailing how its "ferocious Asiatic hordes" would devastate the rest of Europe, massacre thousands, enslave still more for deportation to Siberia, and ultimately rule the world.

This nightmare was far worse than anything Napoleon had posed. At least his armies had marched under the banner of Enlightenment. But Russia was different. It was a false friend of Europe. As the seat of "oriental despotism," it loomed like a Genghis Khan for the modern age. And how could it not? Power and enslavement were the only words Russian autocrats knew, because that was the Mongols' parting gift. Four centuries later, that savage inheritance threatened to lash out again. Whatever pretenses of peace this giant might offer, no one could ever trust Russia. "Its methods, its tactics, its maneuvers may change," Karl Marx warned mid-century, "but the polar star of its policy—world domination—is a fixed star."[1]

Though no stranger himself to ideas of global hegemony, Marx's alarmism was not without cause. To be sure, he was looking through the wrong end of the telescope when discovering a star in Russian plans. Like most, he didn't know that Peter's legendary testament was precisely that: a forgery concocted by the French in the eighteenth century. Yet even without such "evidence," decisive actions in Europe stoked the perception of Russia as an imperial ogre. For many, at the top of the list was Poland, which had been extinguished as an independent state in 1794, after a series of partitions and annexations, with Austria and Prussia joining Russia as fellow conspirators. However, Russia, glutton that it was, grabbed the largest portion, and when Poles rebelled in 1830 and again in 1863, its imperial wrath crushed any hope for independence.

Also traumatic for Western liberals in the post-Napoleonic age was Russia's desire to hold, as much as possible, the rest of the continent under autocratic rule. Earning the sobriquet "gendarme of Europe," its troops seemed permanently mobilized as watchdogs against social and political progressivism. And following the 1848 revolutions that rocked Europe, they marched, striking a fatal blow, the defeated insisted, against liberty. No matter the cause, Russia—the belief hardened—would always be found on the side against freedom, against civilized values, against the future. This was when the cliché of the Russian bear received its claws, fittingly intractable for both beast and empire.

Yet this era could offer another role for Russia, one equally compelling and globally significant. After all, would be the counter question, who actually rid Europe of Napoleon? The climactic battle of Waterloo in 1815 may dominate our imagination and certainly has ensured Britain's permanent claim to that title. But what if Waterloo was the final scene of the French emperor's denouement, as Lev Tolstoy would describe it in *War and Peace*? Who then inflicted the mortal wound?

We need not have waited until the novel's publication fifty years later for the answer. The 1812 invasion of Russia by Napoleon and his Grande Armée unfolded as if history had tired of previous conflicts and needed to pull out all the stops. Greatest general, largest army ever known, a victory that would ensure French supremacy over the continent, if not the world—all combined to create a scenario worthy of an age of titans. For Russia the stakes rose even more as the conflict was wrapped in existential colors. Napoleon was no ordinary threat, as if just the latest in a line of Western invaders. As the ruler of France, he was the heir to godless revolutionaries who executed their king, Louis XVI, in 1793. He overthrew Europe's political order by not only placing himself but members of his family and generals on several royal thrones around the continent. To many who believed in the divine origins of that system, such moves were a direct assault on God's plans for the world. In certain eyes Napoleon, the Corsican upstart who once sought to fight *against* the French, was nothing less than the Antichrist.

This sentiment played well in Russia, where the Orthodox Church officially made that claim five years before Napoleon even set foot on its soil. Once he did, others rushed to the same conclusion, such as a professor from the University of Dorpat—present-day Tartu in Estonia but then part of the Russian Empire—who assigned a numerical value to each letter in the title "The Emperor Napoleon" and discovered that, if rendered in French, the sum was "666." He promptly passed his findings on to the government, where Tsar Alexander I himself spoke of the war as a holy one. And when foreign troops in outlandish uniforms and speaking many tongues crossed the border and began ransacking Orthodox churches, many Russian peasants came to believe that the invasion literally was an assault on their faith.

Equally impactful were secular variants of this epic mentality as best expressed by two brothers, Fyodor and Sergei Glinka, who wore the uniform and also wielded the pen. The fight against Napoleon, the first declaimed, was "an unprecedented struggle of freedom against aggression" and "of virtue against vice."[2] Hyperbole became the norm; reality demanded it, given the scale and scope of conflict. The invading army was awe-inspiring not only for its size, exceeding six hundred thousand, but also for its composition, drawing on so many nations and peoples. The French, as compared to the combined numbers of Poles, Prussians, Austrians, Bavarians, Croats, Italians, and so forth who served alongside, were actually in the minority. For Russians, it seemed that Europe—or the non-Orthodox West—had united against them. Alone, Russia would decide its own fate and in so doing change the world.

As if by history's command, the campaign itself yielded to even bolder dramatization. Half by design and half by weight of circumstance, the Russians retreated, turning the alien host, as Fyodor Glinka deemed the Grande Armée, into "a terrible thorn driving into the healthy flesh of Russia." Yet while they marched back to Moscow, that flesh was willingly sacrificed as Russians put their own homes, villages, and fields to the torch. "Russia burned," he lamented, "our days were enveloped in smoke, our nights lit bright by flames." But in this self-immolation they sowed the first seeds of victory by denying Napoleon's massive force what it needed most: food. Sergei Glinka could thus see in these flames an echo of Horace's claim about the nobility of death in battle, except that this time it was the land itself suffering a beneficent death. "The country's smoke," Sergei declaimed, "is sweet and pleasant to us."[3]

Russian soldiers themselves also bore the ultimate sacrifice. After their commander, Mikhail Kutuzov, chose to face Napoleon in a showdown at Borodino, a village outside of Moscow, tens of thousands of Russians remained forever on the surrounding fields. To Fyodor, who fought there, their feat was "Homeric"; soldiers remained steadfast before a murderous cannonade, as if their "legs had grown into the earth, for how could it not be, since this was their native soil!" Tradition tends to remember Borodino as a French victory, but hindsight also conditions it as a truly Pyrrhic one, since tens of thousands of invaders also lay there, further blunting the thorn.

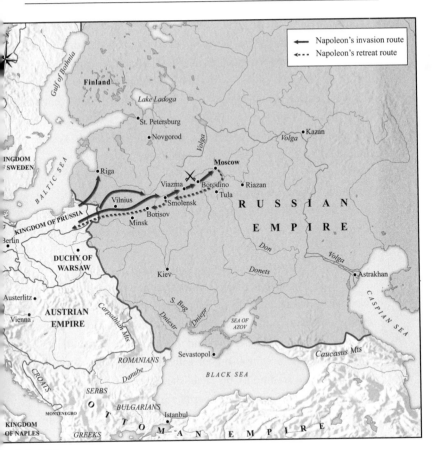

Russia in 1812

The true climax came a week later when the greatest sacrificial role befell Moscow itself, "the Mother of Russian cities," "the heart of the empire," and "the Jerusalem of ancient Russia," according to the Glinka brothers. Abandoned to the French, it would burn like so many villages and towns before. But here too its ashes signaled another martyrdom, and thus another harbinger of victory. For Russians, who blamed the French for the city's destruction, a war of righteous defense now erupted into a war of vengeance, unleashing, in Fyodor Glinka's words, "the spirit of our great people." As the Grande Armée began its inevitable retreat from Moscow—since Tsar Alexander would never surrender, even with the loss of one of his empire's capitals—that spirit united regular soldiers with Cossack raiders, militiamen armed with pikes, and ax-wielding peasants, including women. With avenging fury, all fell upon the fleeing remnants; only a pitiful few thousand escaped. The destruction of the foreign beast, along with Russia's salvation, made Sergei proclaim 1812 "a miracle year."

Yet wonders did not cease there. The next year, Russian forces crossed their border, uniting with Austrian and Prussian armies in a crusade for continental liberation, not conquest, as given in Alexander's proclamation to his troops, just as they prepared to enter France:

Soldiers! . . .

We are crossing the Rhine, to enter the boundaries of the land with which we are engaged in bloody and cruel war. We have already saved our country and covered it with glory, and we have restored to Europe her freedom and independence. It remains to crown this great accomplishment with the much-desired peace. May calm and tranquility be established over the whole globe! May every kingdom live in prosperity under the sole power of its own government and laws! May faith, language, arts, and trade flourish in every country for the general welfare of the people! Such is our intention—not the continuation of war and ruin.[4]

The crusade ended in Paris in 1814. Never again would Napoleon threaten Europe. His hundred-day return in 1815 was but a last gasp, and while the Duke of Wellington and other allies would join Alexander for a victory celebration less than two months after Waterloo, the day was given to Russia. The Prussian king and the Austrian emperor wore Russian uniforms, its army commanded the parade ground, its ruler led the prayers, and its faith determined the calendar. For the date chosen to celebrate Europe's victory over tyranny was August 30 (O.S.), the feast day of Saint Alexander Nevsky.[5]

This unrivaled epic of triumph unfolded precisely when nationalism was sweeping Europe. The French Revolution and Napoleonic Wars inflamed this sentiment more than anything else, and in Russia the effect was volcanic. Inflated rhetoric like that favored in official proclamation and by the Glinka brothers was to be expected, and voices from the era brim with patriotism that often slides into jingoism. Yet excess was also wedded to a genuine sense of pride, which came to define that generation. "I consider myself to have been born solely for the fateful year of 1812," declared Denis Davydov, the flamboyant cavalry leader who pioneered the lightning strikes against Napoleon's rear. His daring exploits earned him fame throughout Europe as the "black captain," extending all the way to the doyen of romantic nationalism, Sir Walter Scott, whose wall bore Davydov's portrait.[6]

In less than two years, from Borodino to the fall of Paris, Russians' ability to define themselves had pivoted. If this was the age when European nations searched for the roots of their respective greatness, Russia need look no further. Its lay in a feat of arms, as if destiny had singled it out for a special test in 1812—one that it passed with flying colors. No other country had, by itself, repelled an attack by Napoleon and no one else had utterly crushed his army, once seen as invincible. If read as a contest of peoples, in which, as Russians were always keen to point out, the opposing side had marshaled forces from nearly the whole of continental Europe, only one had an exclusive claim to superiority. "Now my head rises with pride," Davydov exclaimed, "knowing that I am Russian."[7]

To attribute such a defeat to the bitter cold, as Napoleon did in public bulletins sent home as his army disintegrated in retreat, was for those like Davydov an unpardonable insult, especially as that argument took hold years after the war in the imagination of others outside of Russia. Its soldiers, of course, experienced the same weather, and Davydov published a retort, mocking this as a victim's face-saving maneuver, and underscored again that only his country "had taken upon its shield the blows" not just of the French but of "the whole of the West that rose with her." Russians earned their victory "without any allies whatsoever, except a wounded national pride and fiery love for their country." (The insult was also a personal one because Napoleon had been dismissive as well of the effect of partisan attacks.)[8]

Of all the wounds that summoned this pride, first and foremost—besides invasion itself—was the burning of Moscow. Assuming, as was the case then, French culpability (though now the belief is that Russians bore initial responsibility), it was seen in terms of what we would call a war crime, and it struck at the very core of national identity. If St. Petersburg was the capital of a multiethnic, multiconfessional empire, Moscow was that of the motherland itself, where, in the words of the renowned poet of the time, Karolina Pavlova, "all Rus awaits us." So strong was the association that a contemporary song anthropomorphized the city as the divine mother in both Christian and pagan terms:

> Who, brothers, destroyed Moscow?
> Destroyed Moscow an evil foe.
> Evil foe, a Frenchman young.
> The Frenchman rolled out cannons of brass,
> The Frenchman raised shining gunbarrels
> He shot and fired at mother Moscow.
> From that Moscow caught afire,
> Mother moist earth shook,
> All God's churches collapsed,
> Cupolas of gold set a'rolling.[9]

In death, Moscow earned special merit, subject both to poetic lament and adulation. Tears for the loss, pride in its sacrifice. No other European capital that fell to Napoleon was burned, and the city itself was never surrendered. (We recall Napoleon waiting impatiently for its keys to be brought to him.) Thus Moscow became a symbol of resilience, mirroring the Russian soldier himself, known for his legendary quality to persevere through anything, and also beholden to a never-surrender mantra seen just before on the field at Borodino.

Napoleon was astonished since, unlike in a "normal" contest, Alexander I had refused to bow despite the loss of his nation's spiritual heart. Such defiance reinforced the notion that things were different in Russia and also embedded it in an unmistakable Christian parallel: destroying the physical does not destroy the spiritual. Sergei Glinka even claimed to have foretold the fate of the war through that of the city. In the initial weeks of the campaign, when the Russians were retreating, he attended a heated council discussion in Moscow where he dampened fears of the city's impending loss by holding it up as a necessary, almost Christlike sacrifice. "Giving up Moscow," he argued two months before it actually happened, "will be the salvation of Russia and of Europe."[10]

As much as 1812 was both the catalyst and conduit for Russians to see themselves and their country in an exceptional light, the voices where we find it belong to the educated classes. How the average villager understood the war, especially when it left Russian soil, is difficult to tell, though a rare glimpse comes from Pamfil Nazarov, a peasant conscripted that year who went on to fight all the way to Paris and, having learned to read and write in the army, produced a short account much later in life after he became a monk. Not surprisingly, what draws more attention than the world of politics and patriotism is a smaller one consisting of personal experiences. Battles with doctors over the treatment for his multiple wounds trump those with the French, and the impression left by two days spent in Kiev, where he got lost in caves containing holy relics, outweighs the more than two months he spent in Paris. This does not mean that Nazarov never thought of himself or his service in a special light, but his dispassionate remembrances, published decades after the war, add a prosaic counterweight to romanticized versions of a nation aroused.[11]

Nevertheless, in the public sphere exuberance reigned and spread equally to the more liberal elements of Russian society. In fact, it helped fuel the passions of the Decembrist revolutionaries, made up of officers who hoped that the political liberties enjoyed by other Europeans would be applied to their own country. With the failure of their coup following Alexander I's death in 1825, Fyodor Glinka himself was exiled for suspicion of harboring sympathies with the revolutionaries. So too would that fervor continue, for example, with Vissarion Belinsky, the literary critic and influential future socialist who wrote a review of Glinka's memoirs on Borodino. He urged readers to "hold sacred" the memory of that epoch and could not contain himself when describing the importance of accounts like Glinka's for the development, in his words, of a "national self-consciousness." The defeat of Napoleon, Belinsky wrote, "revealed a great destiny" to the Russian people. The nation's strengths, once "lying dormant," had been "awakened," and the stories of soldiers like Glinka, this political radical observed, can only cause the people's blood "to burn" and their hearts "to beat stronger."[12]

Written in 1840, such feverish rhetoric was typical of the Romantic Age, but it captures how the patriotism unleashed by 1812 still fired the imagination, even as that year drifted further into the past. The poet par excellence of that spirit and Belinsky's contemporary, Mikhail Lermontov, summed it up best in a line from a play: "Didn't we prove in the year 1812 that we are Russians?"[13] The question remains rhetorical, suggesting how its meaning was growing. If initially that year defined the achievement of a single generation, now it had begun to encompass an overall sense of what it meant to be Russian, that is, a unique spirit coursing through all their veins. In as many words, both Belinsky and Lermontov—the first an infant during that fateful year, the second not yet born—revealed that this turning point had already been reached. A writer from the next generation, the Age of Realism, would step forward and make that connection immortal.

The People's War

Tolstoy's *War and Peace* overwhelms all that preceded. As a novel, as a philosophical tract, as a historical study, ever since its publication in the 1860s it has become for all subsequent generations Russians' primary source to remember, to relive, and to understand 1812 as a majestic ordeal. Nothing the poet writes can rival it as epic; nothing the scholar

Monument to the "Heroes of Borodino" located in the Great Redoubt (or Raevsky Redoubt) at the center of the Russian lines. Author's personal collection.

produces can displace its scenes and characters as the icons of that age. And nothing to this day, even from the Second World War, can hope to dethrone it as *the* statement of Russia at war.

Yet the irony in this achievement—and with Tolstoy we are never far from one—is that he devoted so much of the novel to undercutting

the conventional ways in which the war with Napoleon was celebrated. It seems that for every positive, *War and Peace* turns the reader's head to something less glorious. Some characters offer portraits of
cowardice and self-interest that counteract the legend of ubiquitous
heroism and self-sacrifice. Scenes of suffering, of the human costs of
leaders' mistakes, or of witless bravery, challenge the idea that death
in war is always ennobling, as Horace would have it. The more we
read, the more the novel's details accumulate to de-romanticize war,
as with the flash image toward the end of dogs eating bodies—unclear
whether of just horses or humans as well. (Born in 1828, Tolstoy knew
firsthand the subject of war, having fought in the Caucasus and the
Crimean War.)

All of these diversions from the norm were by design, including the
most controversial: portraying commanding officers on both sides as
fools, besotted with their own egos, which have them believe that they
control events and thus deserve the laurels. Tolstoy's insistence on
this, often delivered in a withering, Dickens-like satiric tone, brought
rebukes in the press from veterans. Even those officers born after the
war took offense because Tolstoy's point was that this is always the
case, regardless of the war.

Tolstoy's subversions stemmed from his desire to unseat the Great
Man Theory of historical agency. No single person, no matter how
highly placed, the writer believed, can determine the outcome of
an event—all the more so, the greater its size and scope. A myriad of
factors shape, for instance, why a battle turns out a certain way, thus
dwarfing the plans of any one participant, be he of a general's rank or
not. To think otherwise is to blind oneself with hubris and likely
cause the death of many by fatally misreading a situation.

While Tolstoy's principal target in this regard is Napoleon, his
blanket refusal to exalt any leader (except for Kutuzov, who in the
novel acknowledges the forces greater than he) daringly set *War and
Peace* against the Russian government's version of events. That message
put Alexander I at the center, leading Russia to victory because all
members of society performed according to their place in the political

hierarchy: first came the tsar, then the aristocracy, and then the people, many of whom were serfs, being either the property of landowners or of the state itself.

Even the war's official title, *Otechestvennaia voina,* proclaimed already in 1812, bore the stamp of this rigidity. Its usual translation as the "Patriotic War" is misleading, since the descriptor is actually from the term for "fatherland." A more accurate title for 1812 would therefore be the "Fatherland War" or "War for the Fatherland," which should not be confused with the concept of the motherland. The two are not cut from the same cloth, referring instead to separate entities. If "motherland," as we have seen, conjures up a land connected with faith and people, then "fatherland" speaks to Russia as a political state. Coming into widespread usage during the imperial age, when the first emperor, Peter the Great, was designated "Father of the Fatherland," it reflects the language of authority.

The "War for the Fatherland" resonated favorably for those in power in two ways. First, it presumed a unity of effort across class, rank, and institution. If the monarchy led and inspired, then towns and churches donated funds and supplies, while nobles put on the uniform and donated their serfs to the militia. Second, the title underscored that the force unleashed by those efforts deployed in only one direction, against the French, thereby preserving by the same token the given political and social order. The essential point in all this was that while the French Revolution unleashed populist fervors across Europe, there was no peasant uprising when Napoleon invaded— something authorities greatly feared when weapons were issued to thousands in hastily formed units. Master and serf did just as master and serf should.

This was not the story Tolstoy could bring himself to repeat. Russia would still triumph, of course, but its hero would be someone else: the Russian people themselves. In *War and Peace,* they are a David before the Goliath of "two-and-ten European nations" that "has burst" onto their land. Unlike bombastic leaders, their strength lies in a "hidden patriotism" stoked by hatred of this foreign foe as flames consume their fields and homes. The power this bestows on ordinary Russians is unquantifiable and, for Tolstoy, unnameable. It is an "unknown X" that grows and grows. It is what sweeps through the Russian soldiers at Borodino and holds them in their ranks while French artillery tears them up; it is what Kutuzov intuitively recognizes and what Napoleon never can. It is what saves Russia and changes the course of history.

Tolstoy calls this the "People's War," or *Narodnaia voina*. If the fatherland / patriotic designation ties the nation to the crown that the people serve, this title sidesteps that hierarchical distance by identifying the nation directly with the people and calling forth the mystical soil of the motherland *(rodina)* which gave birth to them *(narod)*. Both the official title and the one favored by Tolstoy underscore the conflict's scale and scope: the fate of the country is at stake; its salvation demands a total mobilization of resources. Yet the People's War invokes a different dimension by elevating the saga of their suffering and achievement above all else. Even though fatherland / patriotic remains the war's canonical designation, Tolstoy's title defines their experience of it.

Tolstoy did not coin the term, but no one has produced a more compelling testament, due both to his creative genius and conscious avoidance of conventional panegyrics. Compared with all that preceded, his account is a radical refashioning of the war, and it opens a door that leads directly onto a classic image of Russia. Our invitation to follow comes in a celebrated digression sometimes overlooked by foreign readers, perhaps out of fatigue (it appears in the last volume after a thousand pages of text) or because they may not recognize the network of cultural significances embedded in it. However, it is one every schoolchild and scholar in Russia knows. Tolstoy, as usual unsatisfied with historians' traditional explanations for why the Russians won in 1812, drops his discussion in favor of an analogy:

> Let's imagine two men coming to a duel with rapiers, according to all the rules of the art of fencing. The contest continues for quite a long time when suddenly one of them, realizing he's

wounded, understands that this is no joke but his life is at stake. He throws down his rapier and grabs the first club he can find and begins waving it.

"According to all the rules," the duel would have stopped there, but the possibility of that happening had long passed. This war had become like no other. With fields and villages scorched and a capital in ashes, only a club could defeat the rapier. Maybe that's not how it should be done—the French officially complained to Kutuzov about peasants attacking their foraging parties—but in this unconventional war only an equally unconventional force could save Russia. Tolstoy discovers that power in the people themselves, turning them into the duelist's club and completing the digression with an image forever wedded to Russia's victory:

> The club of the people's war rose up in all its awesome might and majesty, indifferent to anyone's rules or preferences, with numbing simplicity but right for the task; it rose up as if blind to all around and then rained down and down upon the French until the entire invasion force was wiped out.

The club is Tolstoy's symbol of choice because in Russian it derives from the word for "oak," suggesting how the instrument of victory comes from the living land. Plain, yet solid, methodical and unstoppable—it is something everyone instinctively knows how to use. These are also the stereotypes that define the Russian peasant, whether in uniform or not, and in Tolstoy's world it is precisely these qualities that make them collectively an optimum vessel for the "unknown X" to grow. No weapon forged by man—be it rapier or, one can anticipate, tank and plane—can defeat this power when it rises in just defense of the land.

Tolstoy's "people" are as mythic as those produced by state-sanctioned formulas, but he has bequeathed portraits of them that live to this day as colorful archetypes of a quintessentially Russian character. Just pages after the club digression, we are introduced to peasant-turned-partisan Tikhon. Something of a super soldier, he prefers to hunt the French at night "like a wolf" and none of their "puny swords"—even four at once—can defeat his ax. But he is also simple and modest, someone who will do any task put before him, and also a jester in the ranks.

Tikhon is undeniably Russian. Shot in the back by a French prisoner, he heals himself with vodka, applied "internally" as well as "externally." Key, though, is that his killing prowess is not tied to some innate aggressiveness. Absent an invasion, the same hardiness and dependability would be applied elsewhere. After all, we are informed, this is the same ax with which he chops wood, carves toys, and crushes lice. With such characters, Tolstoy brings the poetic excess of previous generations' encomia on 1812 down to earth, while giving us the fullest sense of the Russian people coming alive, in the words of his narrator, to "free their own land from invasion."[14]

The place of *War and Peace* as a national treasure is such that almost anytime Russia waxes triumphant, one senses its influence. A typical example comes in Sergei Eisenstein's 1938 *Alexander Nevsky*—Russia's greatest contribution to war cinema—which plays out both as medieval legend and as Tolstoy's novel, all in anticipation of an upcoming war with Nazi Germany. An innocent nation, invaded by demonic forces, literally rises out of the ground while a chorus sings of the "People's War." And though Nevsky remains the hero, he shares center screen with another Russian who bashes German heads with an oak beam. Victory against all odds is assured when Russia itself joins the battle, swallowing the enemy knights whole as they crash through the lake's ice.

Tolstoy loved his country, but his phenomenal success in providing an unsurpassed tale of Russia at war should not be mistaken for a claim on his part for any innate superiority of the Russian people. He always sought universal truths in observed patterns of the real world, whether concerning individuals or events. The "unknown X" for him was not a secret power in Russians' sole possession, but a way of accounting for why some armies defeat others despite what military science might dictate. As a case in point, the novel explicitly contrasts 1812 with 1805, when Napoleon routed a combined Russian-Austrian army at Austerlitz on Austrian soil. In other words, while Tolstoy devotes his novel to an exceptional year of Russian history, one can imagine him, obsessed with the elemental forces that shape events, writing a similar saga of a different people. (For the sake of blasphemy, the unexpected victory of France's revolutionary armies over Austrian and Prussian invaders in 1792 comes to mind.)

Nevertheless, *War and Peace* could not escape an undertow of patriotism that has turned Tolstoy's novel precisely into such a testament. In fact, its grip on the Russian collective imagination is so strong that it transcends itself as fiction. Not only has it inspired belief in a special "X" known only to the Russian military, but it is seen as providing the key to understand Russians themselves. When introducing *War and Peace* in translation to French readers, Tolstoy's fellow writer, Ivan Turgenev, informed them that more than "hundreds of essays on ethnography or history," this work was the "faithful representation of the character and temperament of the Russian people." It served, in a sense, as a living document of what constituted "true Russia." And so the novel has endured, leaving it difficult not to agree with Konstantin Simonov, a novelist of World War II, that "it is unthinkable, indeed impossible, to imagine Russia without Tolstoy."[15]

The March of Time

When modern Russia awoke under the light of 1812, it did so with one eye on its past. Already at Borodino, General Kutuzov had observed Russian soldiers comparing themselves with Dmitry Donskoy's men at Kulikovo Field, the largest military engagement on Russian soil until then. Another of the battle's veterans, Fyodor Glinka, recalled the same kinship as well since they, like their medieval "forefathers," had also faced an attacking "horde of twenty nations."

That past loomed large. Too large, in fact. Help was needed to bridge the centuries of history in which Russia could see its roots. It required a scholar to pore over the numerous chronicles and other documents that medieval monks had laboriously produced in a language bearing a distant resemblance to nineteenth-century Russian. It required a judge to decide what events and people deserved special attention, and it required a fabulist to wrap them around a story line worthy of a country destined to change the world. Just when Napoleon burst onto Europe at the beginning of the century, Russia found all three in one man, Nikolai Karamzin, whom contemporaries dubbed both their "Columbus," for discovering the grand arc of Russian history, and their "Homer," for telling it.

Already an accomplished writer of fiction, essays, and poetry, Karamzin had just turned forty when he upgraded his position and became the official court historian under Alexander I. Written under the shadow of war, the resulting twelve-volume *A History of the Russian State* seized the public's imagination. This was not, as one might suspect, strictly because of the emperor's sponsorship; indeed, despite its length Karamzin's masterpiece became one of the century's most widely read works. The first volumes, while finished before Napoleon's invasion, appeared in 1818, right at the peak of patriotic euphoria. Riding that wave, the initial print run of three thousand sold out in less than a month—a phenomenal record for the time—and it was also designated an official textbook for schools. With a dozen editions published over the course of the century, it entertained, instructed, and frankly absorbed all of lettered society, regardless of generation or political orientation, and had continued impact as the inspiration for numerous novels, operas, ballets, and works of art.

From Karamzin's pen the past came alive through tales of epic battles and historical figures that together provided the narrative scaffolding to raise Russia to unrivaled heights. No matter what corner of history he recovered, a lesson could be gained to instill pride. Even tragic downturns like the Time of Troubles could serve this end since his self-imposed directive was that while "great peoples and nations" can stumble, "in that very misfortune they display their greatness."[16] Not for nothing, in fact, has Karamzin's own work returned to prominence as if never suffering with age. The opus has been reprinted several times and even shown on television as a computer-animated documentary. Debuting in 2007, it cut the content of the original's twelve volumes into four-minute segments in order to provide a daily dose of useful history that, were it to be consumed in one sitting, would run for sixteen hours.

Dostoevsky was not alone when he claimed that he "grew up on Karamzin"; virtually all of Russia back then did—from radicals like the Decembrists, Belinsky, and Alexander Herzen, the so-called father of Russian socialism, to fellow writers such as Pushkin (who had bestowed on Karamzin the "Columbus" moniker), Nikolai Gogol, and Tolstoy himself.[17] Karamzin's telling of the Mongol Yoke, for instance, set the standard: invasion is catastrophic, and, no matter how brave the Russians, they cannot match the Mongols' numbers. Resistance cedes into a series of heroic last stands, while princes' disunity ensures a prolonged "enslavement" of the populace. That darkness is temporarily broken at Kulikovo, where "Russians awakened from a deep slumber." The West steps in as Judas, but its treacherous plans are thwarted by Nevsky. Deliverance finally comes with Ivan the Great when "Russia, crushed and oppressed by all its woes, healed itself and rose to a new greatness such that History would hardly be able to offer us another two examples of this happening. If we believe in Providence," he concluded, "then we can flatter ourselves with the thought that it has destined Russia to be long-lived."[18]

Flattering his history assuredly is, and it serves an unabashedly political purpose as well. Only autocracy, Karamzin believed, produced the conditions for such a rise, and only autocracy—benevolent, not tyrannical—could preserve it. For this reason he, unlike those who suffered invasion in the thirteenth century, could find a silver lining in the Mongol cloud. Subjugation forced Rus to re-create itself as a centralized power under Moscow's hegemony, which put the country on its proper path to empire. In making this argument, replete with a series of leadership do's and don't's, he acutely demonstrated why institutions of power, then as much as now, prefer this brand of myth. The rules for achieving national greatness inevitably favor the very power such institutions assume.

Karamzin's voice was also instrumental in seeing the Mongol experience as a decisive element of Russians' collective identity. The triad of invasion-subjugation-liberation gave them a special claim on history: only to us, it effectively runs, came the Yoke, and only by us was it lifted. His poetry reinforced the idea that this past presaged future eminence. In "The Liberation of Europe and Glory of Alexander I," Mongols prefigure Napoleon as the scourge of the world, with one exception: the French version is worse, since he is the product of the Enlightenment yet behaves as a savage by threatening to upset the God-given political order. Only the "legions of Russian heroes" can stop that "ferocious tiger" because they are as strong as a "wall of diamonds." And because they have not "bowed their heads under the [French] yoke," they alone can lay claim to being "the one, blessed people in Europe." (Presumably Britain was disqualified from that honor since the tiger never touched its land.)[19]

This distinction gave Russian identity a performative aspect: to be Russian was to defend the nation, to protect the faith, to save the continent. To be Russian was to be the beneficent warrior in the world. Threats to civilization march here and there, conquering and destroying, until they step on Russian soil and meet their end. National identity, in short, anchored itself in the idea of destiny fulfilled. Or, as Gavrila Derzhavin, the aging court poet famous for odes and hymns under Alexander's grandmother, Catherine the Great, put it in one of his last poems,

> What an honor from generation to generation
> For Russia, its glory indelible,
> The universe saved by her
> From the new hordes.[20]

Such lines would be expected, of course, from those like Derzhavin and Karamzin, who were essentially propagandists for the state. But, as noted before with Pushkin, belief in this exceptionalism transcended ideological differences. Further to the left of Pushkin and a generation removed, the same could be heard from Nikolai Chernyshevsky, a radical who spent copious time in prison and inspired Lenin. "It's not as conquerors or pillagers that Russians appear in history," he announced, "but as saviors, serving like a wall between Europe and the Mongol Yoke."[21] On both ends of the political spectrum rose a sense of national superiority, especially at the expense of the French. If burning cities was the calling card of Mongol barbarians, then, given the fate of Moscow in 1812, what might one conclude about those in the West who claimed to be the epitome of civilization? "Such strange people!" Nadezhda Durova observed of the French for burning "our beautiful city." Her voice, by no means alone, was certainly the most distinctive. Her fame was unique, for she served in the cavalry—and was wounded at Borodino—as a man, Alexander Alexandrov, with the express permission of Alexander I, who also gave her that name. Her story became known thanks to the intervention of another Alexander, that is Pushkin, who published her memoirs in his journal, *The Contemporary,* in 1836.[22]

Virtually no opportunity was missed to celebrate the past as presaging the present. The coincidence in 1880 of the five hundredth anniversary of Kulikovo and the four hundredth anniversary of the lifting of the Mongol Yoke proved especially irresistible. Already by then the next generation of historians after Karamzin had elevated Kulikovo's status to history changing, that is, on par with the Battle of Chalons in 451 AD, where Attila the Hun was defeated by a combined Roman-Visigoth army; or that of Tours (also known as Poitiers) in 732 AD, where the Franks stopped the Muslim incursion into western Europe, thereby ensuring the survival of Christianity. Further honors were bestowed on Kulikovo itself, fewer than two hundred miles southeast of Moscow, which became the site of one of Russia's first battlefield monuments, a hundred-foot column adorned with a massive cross. It was paired with a church dedicated to Mary—and there could be no other since the date of the battle, September 8, was the day when her birth was celebrated.

On that same day in 1880, over twenty thousand people, led by officials from the state, church, and military, came to Kulikovo to commemorate the battle with a mass procession, a parade of soldiers, an artillery salute, and a requiem for the "holy blood of Russian heroes." In the speeches and commentaries surrounding the event, all boxes were duly checked off: war as the window onto a nation's character; Russia as exemplary in that regard by defeating the "dark forces of Asia" and saving Europe; the unbroken link of the past with the present because at every turn Russian troops were willing to die "for faith and fatherland."[23]

If this ceremony was purely symbolic, the sentiments expressed were not necessarily so, given that Russia two years earlier had won a major war that could be seen in a similar light. If the Russo-Turkish War of 1877–1878 is little remembered today, for those at the Kulikovo celebrations—and, indeed, across the country—it was, militarily speaking, the event of their generation. More to the point, it confirmed their role as a beneficent power yet again, though this time the recipients of their largesse were the Slavic, Orthodox-professing Serbs and Bulgarians for whom Russia had long assumed the mantle of protector.

The war began in 1876 when Serbia, acting independently, turned on the Ottoman Turks. In Russia, thousands rejoiced and streamed south to assist their "little brothers," with a Russian eventually commanding the Serbian army. Popular support was immense, yet what pushed Russia to officially declare war in 1877 was an event that stunned all of Europe: the systematic slaughter, rape, and torture of thousands of Bulgarian civilians, including women and children, by Turkish irregulars following a feeble uprising against their Muslim overlords.

Russia's war—its fourth with this enemy in the nineteenth century—initially proved costly and indecisive. However, it ended in dramatic fashion when the Russians finally broke through the Turks' mountain defenses in Bulgaria and drove all the way to the outskirts of Istanbul—the closest they would ever come to what was once Constantinople. Some were tempted to take the Second Rome in the name of Orthodoxy, but more pragmatic minds prevailed, not wishing to completely destroy the balance of power in so volatile a region, which would likely have spurred a greater conflict on the continent. Nevertheless, with Turkey defeated, Bulgaria got its independence and Serbia was saved.

In Russia, victory handed yet another generation a fresh example of their distinctive role in history. As rendered in the 1880 Kulikovo celebrations, for instance, the victory even earned something of a dual legacy: the Russo-Turkish War was one part crusade for liberty, just as the campaign against Napoleon had been, and one part crusade for Christendom, as with Donskoy. Upholding the first was the bond between French and Ottoman tyranny; cementing the second was that in 1380 and 1877 Russians had marched against a common Muslim foe to save their "brethren from the same barbarian yoke," making both "holy wars."

In marshaling the past, the Time of Troubles also offered ample fare to hone the Napoleonic themes of Russia betrayed, Russia with its back to the wall, and Russia versus the world. After the French crossed its border, Tsar Alexander I issued a proclamation urging his subjects to behave like Minin and Pozharsky, heroes of 1612. It was a prescient call. Not only did Poles help swell the ranks of the Grande Armée, the two campaigns shared the same highlights as if to match their precise bicentennial coupling: Western invasion, occupation of Moscow, popular uprising, expulsion of the invaders.

Once more, Karamzin played a central role in codifying the Time of Troubles in precisely these terms. Yet his death mid-work in 1826 prevented him from completing the story. The final volume of *A History of the Russian State* reached 1611—just shy of the glory year. Others, inspired by him, dutifully completed the task, such as Mikhail

Zagoskin, also known as Russia's Sir Walter Scott, who penned the century's best seller, *Yury Miloslavsky or the Russians in 1612*. Patterned less on actual history, the novel delighted readers with a swashbuckling tale that feasts on the villainy of the Poles and the gallantry of the Russians. The title character rises up, vowing to die "for Orthodoxy and Holy Rus." He succeeds in helping stir a national awakening (without shedding his blood), while the narrator joins in with side commentaries pillorying their Catholic opponents.

A special reverence attached itself to the Time of Troubles. Around the same time readers were devouring Zagoskin's novel, a statue to Minin and Pozharsky was raised in Red Square, and they remain the only Russians so honored there—Lenin's tomb notwithstanding. And for the three hundredth anniversary Patriarch Hermogen, martyred for launching the liberation movement, was canonized a saint (and in 2013 honored with his own statue in a garden alongside the Kremlin walls).

The reasons why the Time of Troubles earned this attention in the nineteenth century were twofold. One was political: it gave birth to the Romanov dynasty that currently ruled the Russian Empire. The other, however, was more organic and dug deeper into nationalist sentiments. Looking back into the past, many could find in that ordeal the seeds of Russian pride, inseparable from Orthodox Christianity, that would sprout in the Napoleonic Age.

What helped give rise to that feeling was the written legacy of the Time of Troubles. Unlike conflicts in the Middle Ages, this one was closely documented—even in real time—and the language employed, as nineteenth-century historians readily gleaned, reflected an emerging sense of a collective identity wrapped around the belief of being God's chosen. Victory over the Poles, it was clear, deeply affected Russians in the seventeenth century following a simple, yet almost unimpeachable logic. If everything derived from a divine plan, as was believed at that time, then how could their success and deliverance—just like their initial punishment—not all be part of the same scheme? In other words, if Russians began the Time of Troubles as God's victims, wallowing in famine, civil war, and social turmoil, then did they not end it, a participant in the 1612 militia thus wrote, as his agents, comprising "the forces of the Higher One?"

These words belong to Avraamy Palitsyn, a member of the clerical elite, who produced a historical tract, appearing around 1620, that circulated widely and was readily embraced by the likes of Karamzin. Indeed, he was something of a precursor to the great historian by anchoring a gripping tale in Orthodox-based nationalist triumphalism. His focus was the siege from 1608 to 1610 of the Holy Trinity–St. Sergius Monastery, located forty miles northeast of Moscow, and destined to become a battle of iconic significance.

While the Time of Troubles was witness to many sieges, there was none more consequential in a symbolic and, literally speaking, spiritual sense for the Orthodox faithful. In terms of religious prestige and authority, the Holy Trinity Monastery was unrivaled since its founding in the fourteenth century by Sergius of Radonezh, who would become one of Russia's most legendary saints. For contemporaries, in the words of a historian he represented a "symbol of faith," and according to the chronicles was a key moral force behind Donskoy's campaigns against the Mongols, blessing him before he marched to give battle at Kulikovo.[24] As a model of asceticism, Sergius's lifelong devotion and piety inspired nothing less than the reformation of Russia's monastic system, and his monastery became one of the richest, most powerful and largest in terms of land ownership. Such was its influence, which carried on this legacy in Sergius's name, that the Holy Trinity Monastery has served ever since as the spiritual capital of Russian Orthodoxy. Therefore, when a large Polish-Lithuanian force surrounded it in 1608—that is to say, an army predominantly of heretics—something of a cosmic showdown was in the making.

Palitsyn casts his narrative in precisely these terms. Inside the monastery walls stand "Christ's flock," "Christ-loving warriors," or simply "the lambs." Arrayed outside are "Satan's hordes" or "the wolves." Russians who joined the attacking side (and some did for purely mercenary reasons) become "vile apostates" or, indicatively, "Russian traitors."

The Holy Trinity–St. Sergius Monastery showing its dual role as a fortress. It withstood an eighteenth-month siege during the Time of Troubles in the early seventeenth century. © svic / Cliparto.

For eighteen months, the faithful hold out against innumerable assaults while rebuffing overtures to surrender. St. Sergius rewards their pious fortitude by descending from heaven to warn of nighttime attacks and to boomerang foes' arrows back on themselves. Exhausted by the defenders' perseverance and, so it would seem, divine intercession, the enemy finally withdraws.

If on these notes Palitsyn's account reads like standard fare from a devout Christian of the time, it also diverges sharply from such conventions with its unprecedented attention to detail and elevation of commoners to the role of heroes. He himself did not participate in the siege, but he was the monastery's representative in Moscow and wrote his history afterward based on its records and eyewitnesses' testimonies (some of whom he names). The result is, arguably, Russia's first truly realistic war narrative.

Its short chapters—forty-five of them in total—typically feature a dramatic episode effecting a you-are-there flavor. Enemy cannonballs rain down on the defenders, including women and children, tearing off limbs and heads. Hunger, scurvy, and, most devastating of all, "non-stop diarrhea" follow. Below ground, enemy tunnels snake their way unseen to the monastery walls. Sorties capture "tongues"—enemy soldiers—who are tortured to reveal their locations. Russian peasants blow themselves up inside one tunnel. Tellingly as well, not all the defenders are "lambs"; some steal bread, shirk from duty or, shockingly, given the stakes, desert to the side of the Antichrist.

However, unlike in medieval texts, "the people" are not just warriors in the abstract. In fact, no prince dominates these pages; the focus is just as much on those from the lower castes and who are identified by name, such as Shilov and Slota from the village of Klementevo who blew themselves up in the tunnel, or a peasant nicknamed "Restless" who in almost cinematic fashion rallies fellow Russians with his pole ax aloft. Palitsyn presents these individuals as if they are worthy of identification because they belong to a common cause, a connection between land and faith that he entitles "Great Russia." The joining of the terrestrial and the spiritual allows him to offer illuminating passages such as that the enemy has "suffered defeat from the Russian people, that is, rather from God."[25]

In reality—and with supernatural indulgences aside—things were not as clear-cut as Palitsyn described. He, like many others, worked multiple sides during the Time of Troubles, until the rise of the national militia to liberate Moscow. Yet it is not difficult to see why the story he left resonated strongly in the nineteenth century, becoming the most popular to emerge from that conflict. For Karamzin, basing his account on Palitsyn's, the monastery's defenders—"simple people, low in rank but extraordinarily high in spirit!"—provided for posterity an unsurpassed example of the valor and patriotism that ultimately saved the country. Another scholar, a contemporary of Tolstoy, proclaimed Palitsyn's history "a favorite book of our ancestors" and, in the light of *War and Peace,* this perhaps brooks no surprise. If anything, Palitsyn anticipated how the Time of Troubles could just as equally be a "People's War" *avant la lettre,* as if it and 1812 were two sides of the same coin—which is precisely the meaning the former took after the defeat of Napoleon.[26]

The enduring power of Palitsyn's saga of the Holy Trinity–St. Sergius Monastery lay not just in its narrative flair or historic resonance but in the symbolism one could draw from it. Distilled down to its core, it taps into the primary vein of Russia's war myth: a sacred land surrounded and attacked by heretics, traitors, and apostates. As of this writing, the image of a nation besieged has gripped Russia once more as it suffers from—and also, to a degree, revels in—a newfound isolationism. And just such a siege took center stage in a 2007 blockbuster release, sponsored by the government, *1612,* which featured Polish invaders in near-genocidal colors.

Yet already in the nineteenth century this idea proved irresistible and was best captured by a poet, another of Tolstoy's contemporaries, who equated the whole of Russia with a besieged monastery under continuous foreign assault from the Mongols to the Time of Troubles. As the narrator wanders around its scarred, dormant walls, they wake up and speak directly to his "soul":

> Stand firm! . . . and you withstood,
> Holy Rus, all the Lord sent you—
> All the blood and burden,
> Slaughter and pain.
>
> A heavy hammer has forged you
> Into one people—the pounding lasted for centuries.
> But you know that God, out of love,
> Punished you, and by that you are unbreakable.[27]

Thus arose an image embraced ever since as Russia's destiny with two factors in continual play: the pounding would not stop as long as it faced a hostile West, and the blood shed forthwith would always be marked by John 15:13 exclusivity. As Sergei Glinka, the brother of Fyodor who had fought at Borodino, concluded, it "runs crimson" like everyone else's, but Russia's reigned as "the blood of the only warriors in the world who have so faithfully defended the borders of others and fought for the protection of fellow countries."[28]

Transcendent Heights

As the nineteenth century went on, the insistence that Russia's suffering was of another order, both in terms of scale and purpose, became a mainstay of its elect status. It grew more mystical and, under the curatorship of the likes of Fyodor Dostoevsky, broke from the moorings of mere national pride and entered a different orbit of exceptionalism. For him suffering and altruistic sacrifice defined what it meant to be Russian and, on his terms, held a positive charge, since they drove a wedge between Russia and the rest of Europe, enmeshed as it was in materialism, self-interest, and a host of other vices. That division was unbridgeable and absolute because of the simple reason, in his words, that God had assigned Russia a "special mission" for which it was "predestined and created"—nothing less than the world's salvation.

Though the mission was concrete, Dostoevsky preferred to think of the Russian people in the abstract. Prone to their own vices, namely alcohol and violence, as Orthodox Christians they nevertheless bore God within themselves, both embodying and preserving the true faith. What made them the purest of vessels was that very same suffering, the accumulated centuries of serfdom, poverty, and misery. What they lost in the flesh, they gained in spirit which, as God's word, eventually would fill the world, turning it into a "blessed and genuine union of all humanity."

Until the mid-1870s, Dostoevsky's eye was generally off the battlefield. By that time, as he entered his fifties, his career was already established with the publication of three of his four major novels, *Crime and Punishment, The Idiot,* and *The Possessed.* But with the clouds of the Russo-Turkish War gathering, he became relentless in tying that conflict to his vision of Russia redeeming the world. Did not its altruistic intentions behind declaring war in 1877—for those were the only ones he would recognize—demonstrate its unique capacity to sacrifice on behalf of others? No other European nation could do this, he believed; they could never fathom "taking up arms to save the oppressed" because it was a gift God had bestowed upon Russia alone.

While the language sounds familiar, Dostoevsky was imagining war of a different kind, of which this latest one with the Turks was a subset. His was an existential contest with the West, since it was the seat of all that this consummate Slavophile hated. In no particular order, his targets ran from rationalism and secularism, to Catholics and Jews, to capitalism and socialism. Russia needed to be free from all those poisons, threats, corruptions, and heresies, since it was God's true land, he would argue endlessly, after it threw off the Mongol Yoke and entered history as the protector of Orthodoxy. This is why for him even the 1812 campaign had turned out the way it did. The European way of fighting, based on "money and scientifically organized six-hundred-thousand-man invasions," ran into a "new and unknown power," Russia itself, whose "unconquerable" strength lay in two entities over which no one else could ever have claim: "the endless Russian land" and "the all-uniting Russian spirit."

This is also why Dostoevsky was beside himself as war in the Balkans unfolded before his very eyes. The fact that thousands of Russian volunteers poured south to fight with the Serbs and Bulgarians and that popular sentiment goaded a reluctant tsar to declare war prompted Dostoevsky to declare it yet another "People's War." This time, however, the stakes might even be greater than in 1812. Could war with the "Mohamedan Barbarians" be the first step in the ultimate realization of God's plan? A Russian victory would lead to the union of Orthodox Slavs and deliver Istanbul into their hands. Then they could lay down their arms and from that city, resurrected as the Second Rome, pronounce the "true exaltation of Christ's truth," and this "new word" would lead to "the universal reconciliation of nations" founded on a principle already embodied by Russians themselves: "universal service to humanity."[29]

Or so it might be. Dostoevsky logged these thoughts in *A Writer's Diary,* a compendium of fiction, political commentary, current affairs, and philosophy crafted as a kind of correspondence with readers. It sold extremely well, but he abruptly—and to the disappointment of many—stopped working on it before the war's end. The reason he publicly gave was illness, which was true, but it was also to devote himself to rewarding those very same readers with his last and greatest novel, *The Brothers Karamazov.* In 1881, shortly after its completion, Dostoevsky died with his Slavophilic prophecy not so much unfulfilled as untested, given that Russia, in victory, kept its hands off the ultimate prize, the city from which it received God's word.

The grandest expression of how 1812 permanently altered the meaning of war in Russian consciousness can still be experienced today, a short walk from the Kremlin. The Cathedral of Christ the Savior is the country's largest and dominates the center of Moscow with its gleaming cupolas. It was completed in 1882, marking the seventieth anniversary of the war, and opened its doors accompanied by the sounds of Tchaikovsky's *1812 Overture,* also written for the occasion. More than any other artistic or architectural monument in Russia, the cathedral brings into one sacred space all of the war's historic and mythic dimensions. Over 170 massive marble plaques adorn its walls, each dedicated to a major battle from 1812 to 1814, listing the officers killed and the number of regular soldiers lost. The cathedral is both a shrine to and showcase of their sacrifice, be it in defense of nation or liberation of the continent.

Complementary art and icons inside the cathedral link the soldiers' struggles to Russia's defenders of the past, such as Nevsky, Donskoy, Minin, and Pozharsky, and then elevate all of its wars into the biblical realm by depicting battles of the Old Testament (David versus Goliath) and related events. Just as Moses led his people to freedom, the heroes of 1812, again enacting God's will, saved their own country from a new pharaoh, Napoleon, and then liberated those he had enslaved. Images of Exodus yield to those of Christ's birth, crucifixion, and his victory in resurrection, thereby completing the Judeo-Christian cosmic cycle. Here in this immense structure, the epicenter where the power of faith, the state, and the military merge, one might be convinced that Russia knows only one kind of war: just, defensive, under God's eyes and against his enemy, always a foreign aggressor, and all for the goal of peace.

To a certain degree, Russian exceptionalism projected through a martial lens reminds us of the images and themes favored by other Western powers in the nineteenth century: a land touched by providence; the nation's history framed as fulfillment of a glorious destiny; sacrifice ennobled as a necessary step on that march; warriors of a heroic age mobilized as spiritual antecedents, taking their place in the ranks alongside their flesh and blood counterparts in the present. England, for instance, would raise its cult of Alfred the Great, who defeated the invading Danes in the ninth century. France, besides Joan of Arc, would claim as a national martyr Vercingetorix, the chieftain who led the Gauls in their last, futile attempt to stop Julius Caesar's legions; and America, always at a chronological disadvantage in such matters, would import Cincinnatus from ancient Rome into its pantheon of iconic warriors.[30]

Russia, however, pushed beyond the usual arsenal of metaphor and analogy favored by writers, politicians, artists, and philosophers. Its drive to enthrone a sense of exceptionalism penetrated the military itself, leading by century's end to its reemergence there as a doctrine, operating on firm postulates. An illuminating example comes from the highest of sources, the General Staff Academy, an institution on par with West Point and Sandhurst.

In 1898, General Nikolai Sukhotin became the academy's director and published *War in the History of the Russian World.* The title is significant: not a military history of Russia, but rather of the role war has played in the centuries-long shaping of its national identity. If a besieged monastery could make the poetic argument for a nation

The Cathedral of Christ the Savior, Moscow. Built to commemorate the seventieth anniversary of the victory over Napoleon, it was destroyed by the Soviets in 1931 and rebuilt during the 1990s. It is the largest church in Russia. Its height is over 330 feet and it can hold up to ten thousand people. © Iakor Filimonov / Cliparto.

forged in war, Sukhotin preferred an empirical one, arming himself with numbers and dates to chart Russia's steady diet of conflict. Since Donskoy's time in the fourteenth century to his, it had spent "two-thirds of its entire life"—353 years out of 525—waging war. Following this with a barrage of tables and graphs in linear, bar, and circular fashion, he flattens Russia's past into a catechism of principles that turns his study into a veritable handbook of the country's war myth.

Invasion, self-reliance, and self-sacrifice are at the core. Regarding the first, Sukhotin's emphasis on quantitative data reaffirms the qualitative shift that Russian identity was undergoing as the unique victim of foreign aggression. While he makes clear that a primary reason behind this condition was due to Russia's place astride strategic crossroads without natural defensive boundaries, he almost dares the reader to conclude that being attacked is what makes Russia what it is. His insistent use of the present tense suggests that it will never escape this predicament, as if to make that fate a permanent feature of the nation's identity. Not every engagement with the outside world results in hostilities, but with every engagement, his argument would hold, Russia must be on guard for that possibility.

This proposition flows logically into the second, self-reliance, which he easily fleshes out with what were by now the canonical examples. During the Middle Ages, Russia "could not count on the West's assistance." On the contrary, because of the behavior of the Germans and the Swedes, "the Mongols and their hordes could always count on finding allies, by intention or not, in the very same West." As for the Time of Troubles, "Russia's salvation could only come from within its own people, led by Avraamy Palitsyn, Minin, and Prince Pozharsky."

The third component, self-sacrifice, Sukhotin raises as the banner of Russian exceptionalism by invoking John 15:13, which, also by this time, had become so ingrained it could operate in purely secular terms: "It is in the Russian people's willingness to lay down their lives for others," he emphasizes in the original, "that one finds the key to understanding *the special nature of Russia's experience of war* which so acutely distinguishes it from the experiences of countries in the West."[31] Like many soldiers born mid-century, Sukhotin could even claim firsthand knowledge of this distinction, since he was a decorated veteran of the Russo-Turkish War.

Nothing escapes Sukhotin's encyclopedic attention, including wars of expansion. Pressed through his mythic filter, all of Russia's major conflicts function as sacrifices "to provide a better life for others, no matter who they may be—even the enemies of yesterday or tomorrow." On his pages one can follow this pattern in all directions. In the east, beginning with the conquest of Kazan in the sixteenth century and extending in the nineteenth to Central Asia, diverse racial, ethnic, and religious populaces were "delivered from slavery and barbarism." In the south, Russia helped liberate "Christians, Slavs, Greeks as well as peoples of the Caucasus." To the north, Nevsky's victory over the Swedes followed by Peter the Great's in the eighteenth century stopped them from establishing a hegemony there; and in the west, Russia served as the necessary bulwark halting, in reverse chronology, Napoleonic, Polish, and Teutonic expansionism.

Although reprinted in the 1990s as a "forgotten classic," *War in the History of the Russian World* never became a cultural phenomenon like Karamzin's *A History of the Russian State* or Tolstoy's *War and Peace*.[32] Nevertheless, its significance lies in showing how what was once the product of the romantic imagination had hardened into a precept, turning the nation's destiny into a seamless narrative defined through its experience of war. More to the point, while poets, historians, and philosophers made connections between wars past and present, Sukhotin showed how *all* of them could be assembled under a single banner. In short, General Sukhotin did not create the myth. Rather, *War in the History of the Russian World,* just like the Cathedral of Christ the Savior, signaled that it had reached full maturation and gained the essential ability to go anywhere in history—which is why, in a sense, it didn't really need to be reprinted. In Russia, today's generals still carry the same baton.

*   *   *

As with any apologist for imperialism, Sukhotin was eager to crown his nation as a benevolent power. For most in the West, however, Russia's demonic horns were growing even more as the century continued. Writing at the same time, Friedrich Engels saw nothing in Russia except designs for the "mastery of Europe." Its addiction to expansion was all the more evident in its post-Napoleonic, self-congratulatory posturing. "Conquest—under cover of liberation" is how he termed it. Any contribution to protect Slavs in the Balkans, for example, was in reality the result of Russia's desire to seize Constantinople from the Ottoman Turks and gain access to the Mediterranean. Russian megalomania ran so deep that even its story of saving Europe was a sham. Though not denying the destruction of Napoleon's army in 1812, Engels turned the liberation chapter of 1813–1814 on its head. Instead of leading Austria and Prussia on a crusade against France, Russia left the brunt of the fighting to them, finishing the war with "relatively slight sacrifices" but stealing the laurels of victory.[33]

Engels proudly announced that he was continuing "the work of my dear friend," Karl Marx (who had died over a decade before), and repeated the warning that Russia's "polar star" was "world domination." What had it been up to ever since the rise of Moscow? After all, he noted, by the end of the sixteenth century it was the largest state in Europe, stretching from the Baltic Sea to the Urals. In the seventeenth century, it crossed those mountains and marched through Siberia to the Pacific, and in the eighteenth it reached the Black Sea. With the simultaneous dismemberment of Poland, Russia gained most of its land, plus the territory making up present-day Belarus, western Ukraine, and the Baltic States. In the nineteenth century, the insatiable empire absorbed Finland, the Caucasus, and completed its grab of large swathes of Central Asia—all under the pretext of a "civilizing mission." By century's end, this "colossus," this "fortress of reaction," ruled more of the world's landmass than any other. Peter the Great's apocryphal testament of conquest—which Engels did not fail to cite—was no doubt coming true.

Whatever their radical political theories, in excoriating Russia Marx and Engels were quite mainstream for the West. Similar fears and accompanying hyperbole swept across the ideological and cultural spectrum. The conditions and causes of Russophobia, as it is commonly known, were manifold. For some it stemmed from the empire's threat to become a continental or global hegemon; for others, from its suppression of nationalities and basic liberties within its borders. With authoritarianism reaching its height under Alexander I's successor and brother, Nicholas I, the Russian Empire loomed large in the imagination of many as the largest prison in the world, which is when the Czech historian cited in the Prologue called it an "infinite and inexpressible evil."

Where that charge would have been most fitting was in the conquest of the Caucasus, which spanned the first half of the century. Here the scorched-earth policy that had saved Russia in 1812 was turned into a weapon of terror, resulting in forced famines among mountain populations such as the Chechens. "It was necessary to exterminate half," observed Nicholas's son, "to compel the other half to lay down its arms."[34] However, Eurocentricism on one side and Russian censorship on the other tended to blind the West to such inhumane policies. Ironically, it would be Tolstoy—late in his life when he had become a pacifist and, in the state's eyes, dangerously subversive—who exposed the exterminating force of Russian imperialism against the Chechens in his novella *Hadji Murat*. So damning was the indictment that the book would not be published until after his death in 1910.

Ever since the nineteenth century, Russia's image has been torn by these irreconcilable forces, one emanating from inside, the other from without, mobilizing around examples drawn from the same historic well. If for Russian patriots the Mongol experience signaled their debut as continental savior, then for others it heralded their rise as continental pariah. Far from defending against an eastern scourge, Russia's ancestors inherited its worst traits, becoming, in the words of a French traveler, the Marquis de Custine, a nation of "regimented

Tatars." So great could be the assumed contamination of Russian-ness by Mongol blood that some Poles, enraged at the loss of their country, denied that Russians were even Slavs.[35]

Russia's victory over Napoleon served as the catalyst for opinions to polarize. As long as Russia was a peripheral force, no one painted it as an existential threat. Barbaric and bloodthirsty, to be sure, but not something out to destroy civilized Europe. Yet after it emerged from the Napoleonic Wars unrivaled as a land power, its reputation has never been the same. Custine's impression, provoked by a visit to Russia in 1839, proved an early and influential one. What drove him there as a French aristocratic was, by his own admission, politics: the logical de-sire to find an argument *against* democracy. What he found there left him so aghast that he returned in favor of it. From an audience with Nicholas I to encounters with everyday Russians, nothing could per-suade Custine that anything positive, progressive, or inspiring could come from them. They were "inept in everything" save one matter: the "wish to rule the world by conquest." Why this was their dream and in their grasp were no longer mysteries. "Asia stomped the earth," in his brusque conclusion, "and out of it came the Kremlin."[36]

Custine's account, which consisted of letters he wrote during his visit but feared sending before he was safely out, was banned in Russia—a move that only helped prove his point. In the West, it enjoyed wide-spread success and helped shape the canon that transcended politics. Lord Curzon of Britain, Engels's contemporary but, like Custine, his ideological opposite, announced after his own visit to Russia that it was "as much compelled to go forward" in its imperial ambitions "as the earth is to go round the sun." So too did Theodore Roosevelt de-clare that Russians were "huge, powerful barbarians, cynically confi-dent that they will in the end inherit the fruits of our civilization."[37] None of the other great imperial powers that rose in this period—from Curzon's Britain and Roosevelt's America to Custine's France—was subject to such continuous charges and verbal attacks, even though some of their expansionist practices exhibited a similar ruthlessness at times.

Of course, the twentieth century only gave more ammunition to those convinced that Russia, now under a Soviet flag, was morally retrograde and an abomination—always and everywhere savage, murderous, and enslaving with the "avowed objective," as a CIA report declared in the 1950s, of "world domination by whatever means and at whatever cost." Three decades later, after the bear invaded Afghanistan, it earned the appellation "evil" once more from President Ronald Reagan, and, as if on cue, Peter the Great's testament was dusted off again—though not by the president—as evidence of Russia's true nature. Even when the hammer and sickle came down, the specter of being a menace to others did not. In the 1990s, one could hear from a noted American columnist that "expansionism is in Russia's national DNA." And even before the annexation of Crimea in 2014, a British journalist posed, in his words, the "unavoidable question": "If Russia gets what it wants in the Caucasus or the Baltics, the Balkans and Central Europe will be next. And what then? The Arctic? Western Europe?"[38]

Whether arch-conservative, radically revolutionary, or authoritarian nationalist, Russia has remained in the eyes of observers a consummate aggressor in world affairs, leaving Russians themselves tarred as unstable and dangerous, paranoid and untrustworthy. Yet against these charges, Russians believe that history has dealt them a trump card that—at least on domestic tables—always wins.

3

The Burden of Victory

The Second World War offers Russia the greatest of war stories. If crushing Napoleon did not convince others of its indispensable role in the world, then destiny would bring out the script once more just over a century later. A seemingly invincible demon invades from the west; again Russia is pushed back to the wall; again its lands and cities burn; again the fate of the nation is decided in a titanic struggle on its own soil; again the war ends when Russians, at the head of a coalition of liberators, enter the enemy's capital; again civilization is saved. This time, however, the scenario plays at a truly earth-shattering pitch. From every angle—the scale of fighting, the scope of destruction—the twentieth-century version shatters what humankind had experienced before.

What is more, if seen in this superlative light, nothing in the war contradicts the tenets that matured in the nineteenth century. If anything, it provides an incomparable demonstration of their verity. Russians' capacity to withstand anything at any cost; their tenacious refusal to surrender no matter the odds? What else does the epic struggle at Stalingrad prove, when in the course of five months, whole units were slaughtered to the man in the most vicious block-by-block, house-by-house fighting known to history? Yet never would they give up, even when pushed to the very banks of the Volga, where literally yards separated them from its waters and the enemy. "The Russians are not men," a German soldier there bitterly realized, "but some kind of cast-iron creatures."[1] The same iron courage drove civilians too, like in Leningrad, trapped in a nine-hundred-day vise of death in which over a million perished, mainly from starvation. Yet inside the worst siege ever, one survivor declared in her diary that "hungry, lice-infested, suffering Leningrad holds on and doesn't think of surrender."[2] No more convincing example exists of why there the Cincinnatus legend gains little traction. The Russian does not fight and then return home; he and she fight to save their home because foreign invasion has forced it onto the front line.

The decisive marker of why this war must surpass all of Russia's previous ones is what made it history's deadliest. Perhaps alone, it truly was an existential one. Though in 1812 the same rhetoric was applied to Napoleon, conquest and extermination were certainly not the French emperor's intent. Indeed, his aims were somewhat muddled even to himself, and the official title he gave his invasion, the "Second Polish Campaign," underwhelms with its ordinal back-seating and spotlight on an ally instead of the enemy. One might even place the Mongol invasion outside the existential category as well. After all, they stopped their mass destruction at a certain point because to erase Rus in human and physical terms would have eliminated its value, put dryly, as a perennial revenue base. (Certainly this idea can only be entertained with hindsight; Russians in the thirteenth century assumed the apocalypse had come.)

With Hitler no speculation beckons. Erasure of the Slavic presence in Eastern Europe was to be total, excepting a minority condemned to slavery. In the Nazi mind-set, the fault lines of history, geography, and ideology, carved ever so deeper by implacable bigotry and hatred, converged like never before, as captured by a German corps commander:

> The war with Russia is a vital part of the German people's fight for existence. It is the old fight of German against Slav, the defence of European culture against the Muscovite-Asiatic flood,

and the repulse of Jewish Bolshevism. This war must have as its goal the destruction of today's Russia—and for this reason it must be conducted with unprecedented harshness. Every engagement, from conception to execution, must be guided by the firm determination to annihilate the enemy completely and utterly.[3]

For those on the receiving end, to surrender one's home, therefore, was to sign a death warrant. The struggle in the East was to be unlike anything in the West, including its outcome. Of all the nations Hitler invaded, only the Soviet Union, the one at the heart of his Lebensraum fantasy, repulsed him.

Yet the war can also be framed from a different perspective—one that makes its legacy unique. Unlike those of its victorious allies, Russia's story of World War II has not settled firmly on the "good war" pedestal; instead, it can show cracks and fissures that almost threaten to topple it. To be sure, America's version must contend, inter alia, with the internment of Japanese Americans on U.S. soil and the controversies surrounding the atomic bomb, but rarely do they challenge the sense of triumphalism. In Russia the list is incomparably longer and is inseparable from its Soviet legacy. In fact, the factors complicating its remembrance and commemoration even predate the war itself with, for example, the purge of the Soviet military command during Stalin's Terror in the 1930s and his nonaggression pact in 1939 with Nazi Germany.

From there, it only gets worse. In September of that same year the two allies invaded Poland, followed by a separate Soviet attack against Finland. In 1940 the Soviet Union annexed the Baltic States and unleashed a wave of deportation, imprisonment, and execution in all of these newly acquired territories. The German invasion of 1941 brought the collapse of the Red Army and its near destruction, and even up to the end, its soldiers suffered from pitiful conditions, including acute shortages as well as repeated leadership failures that took the lives of thousands, if not millions.

Away from the front lines, national minorities suspected of collaborating with the Germans, such as the Chechens or Crimean Tatars, were forcibly deported to Central Asia, which cost more lives. And what of the sheer number of Soviet citizens who did collaborate, either through coercion, the need to survive, or anti-Soviet sympathies? Even the war's end does not put a stop to this counter perspective. Can one separate the defeat of Germany from the mass looting and rapes inflicted by Red Army soldiers there and across Eastern Europe? Finally, one must wrestle with the cruel tragedy of the war's outcome: though the Red Army liberated millions from Nazi tyranny, victory in 1945 ensured that not only would the tyranny of Stalin endure, but that it would ensnare the newly liberated territories as well.

Where is Russia in all of this if the above actions and experiences pertain, more accurately, to the Soviet Union? This creates another challenge. Can Russia claim the laurels of victory as the leading nationality in the country, both in terms of population and power, while evading its shadows which, at their darkest, constitute crimes against humanity? Though "Soviet" and "Russian" generally refer to two separate entities—the first, a political state lasting from 1917 to 1991, the second, a national-cultural identity spanning centuries—in common practice the two are often hopelessly entangled and confused. Such interchangeability and slippage occur not only in Russia but equally so in the West. It can happen in the positive, such as when Winston Churchill announced to Parliament in 1944 that "the guts of the German Army have been largely torn out by Russian valour and generalship," and in the negative, as with a British historian's recent charge that on the Eastern Front the "Russian" military "was a barbarian army, which had achieved things such as only barbarians could." Whatever the sentiment, "Soviet" would have been correct in both cases.[4]

Even history, it would seem, has joined the conspiracy to make matters more complex. Usually in a nation's biography, greatest triumph and greatest tragedy constitute separate chapters. For Russia

The Soviet Union on the eve of the German invasion, 1941

such is not the case, which leads us to the war's burden. It cannot forgo victory, since to do so would be to erase the crown jewel from its national heritage. However, how might it—or should it—close the door on a bevy of skeletons? Within World War II there are simply too many stories, too many potentials for burnishing and tarnishing Russia's reputation. One direction pulls to its unrivaled role in ridding the world of its greatest villain; the other turns inward to the staggering cost of that deliverance—with so much of it self-inflicted.

This duel of incompatibles distinguishes Russia from the other combatants and also helps keep the war at the center of national attention. Its presence is inescapable, whether reflected by the endless shelves it consumes in bookstores, or by the numerous programs on television and a bounty of movies devoted to it year after year. Only in Russia does the war continue to dominate popular culture and consume the energy and attention of so many at all levels of society. More than any other event of the past, it also plays a defining role to articulate a collective identity for Russians in the twenty-first century.

The Soviet Canon

To be sure, the war's legacy was not always like this. For forty years after 1945, the Soviet Union succeeded, for the most part, in upholding a triumphalist narrative. Its main tools were censorship and the Communist Party's monopoly on public expression that ignored, downplayed, or, as in the case of the 1939 secret agreement with Nazi Germany to carve up Eastern Europe, flatly denied the negative side of the historical ledger. Only top-ranking commanders were allowed to publish memoirs, and those were heavily filtered through the same lens. So too was the writing of history reserved for those who toed the party's line, which paired freshly minted Soviet formulas with traditional ones. The official title of the war, the Great Patriotic, was an upgrade from that of 1812 with a few requisite changes. It still rested on the notion of society united behind a strong leader; only this time the "people" was a multiethnic, multinational Soviet collective. The role of infallible, ever benevolent monarch was taken over by the party, and victory in 1945 was not a sign of God's blessing but of the superiority of one system, socialism, over another, fascism, which itself was presented as the worst manifestation of capitalism.

Yet for all its fortitude, the Soviet version showed weaknesses from the very beginning. Its transnational Marxist ideals might have inspired some, yet for many Russians, the war was not a clash of ideo-economic systems, but a life-or-death struggle for their motherland.

The unequivocal source for inspiration, a Leningrad survivor asserted, was Tolstoy's *War and Peace,* for only that novel gave authentic voice to the idea of the people summoned by an internal drive to defeat the invader.[5] Party authorities realized as much, and purely Soviet propaganda often gave way to evocations of Russia's military greatness as embodied by Dmitry Donskoy, Alexander Nevsky, and Mikhail Kutuzov. Here they were more on track since the most popular work among those on the front line, for example, was an epic poem, *Vasily Tyorkin,* that essentially ignores the party and, for that matter, anything Soviet. Instead, it is an anthem to the common soldier, a Russian peasant who reminds us of Tolstoy's Tikhon, who once again is called to defend his land.

> The hour has struck, our turn has come.
> Now we are to answer
> For Russia, for the people.
> For all that is on Earth.
>
> Every Ivan, every Alyosha
> Whether dead or still alive,
> All of us together—that is we,
> The people, we are Russia.[6]

And like Tolstoy before, though this time in verse extending for hundreds of pages, *Vasily Tyorkin* turns foreign invasion into a paean to "much-suffering" Russia, focusing on the violence done both to its land and people. This is not to say that its author, Alexander Tvardovsky, was ignorant of other Soviet nationalities fighting and dying to save the country; after all, he became a party member before the war and served as a Red Army correspondent throughout its duration. Rather, his poetic vision remains within the parameters established by Tolstoy and thus resistant to ideological co-optation. Tvardovsky's narrative horizon is also realistic and offers details typically absent in the Soviet canon. Readers in the trenches could appreciate the earthy humor woven among references to the cold, frontline tedium, lice, friendly fire, problems with adequate food, and the absence of sex.

Tvardovsky's love for Russia is also like Tolstoy's in that it feels organic without nativist sentiments. For the poet's Vasily, the land is his mother, but he is a son with a conscience, expressed most daringly for that time through his profound sense of shame that soldiers like him have betrayed her by abandoning so much and so many to the horror of German occupation. This love-guilt is what steels his heart, awakening in him a similar "hidden patriotism" that will lead to victory.

> Mother—my native land,
> Suffering so in captivity.
> I am your son of the same blood,
> I will deliver you.

Works like *Vasily Tyorkin*—and there were others—not only underscored the challenges the official version faced in securing legitimacy among its intended audience. Today they serve as reminders that Soviet culture was not as monochromatic as is sometimes remembered. Nothing proves that point more than what transpired after Stalin's death in 1953 and the atmospheric shift that followed, known as the Thaw, when censorship was partially softened and the Soviet Union underwent a de-Stalinization campaign.

While the canon of triumphalism remained dominant during the Thaw, which ran until the mid-1960s, a new contingent broke into the literary scene: veterans who survived the front lines and found safe haven with Tvardovsky, who was chief editor of the period's most provocative journal, *New World*. In a number of hard-hitting, quasi-autobiographical novels and stories (because memoirs were still off-limits and literature allowed for more flexibility), they shed the first light on the real conditions soldiers experienced. In so doing, they also gave primacy to the people's ordeal over the party's role, but with a twist that threatened Soviet authority itself. Why they suffered so grievously could no longer be pinned solely on the Germans; Red

Army commanders and their political henchmen from the Communist Party bore that blame as well, whether through idiocy and ineptitude or through sheer sadism and malevolence. Of all the examples that abounded, one headed the list: penal battalions comprising soldiers convicted of petty offenses, disobeying orders, or political disloyalties. Often innocent, tens of thousands were sentenced literally to die as fodder, whether leading frontal assaults against impregnable German strongpoints or force-marched through minefields in order to clear them.

If *Vasily Tyorkin* was, to an extent, a-Soviet, then works from the Thaw tending in this direction were to hard-liners almost anti-Soviet, since they brushed closely with the ideas emanating from dissident political circles that painted the state and the party as the enemy of the people. This alone ensured that their run was short-lived, and by the 1970s, the doors had closed on the war's unsettling issues.

By that decade, with Stalin a taboo at one end and the army's criminal malfeasance at the other, the official version of the war entered its mature and, some would say, stagnant phase. The party reasserted its essential role in leading the Soviet Union to victory, and fidelity to it and to the state's ideals served as the anchor around which a collective identity based on war commemoration was formed. Professed exceptionalism—of the Soviet people, their socialist system, their communist beliefs, and the cost paid to deliver the world from the Nazis—constituted the banner under which all citizens were to unite.

As with official productions before, some Soviets found inspiration in this streamlined version, but its overt ideological designs, lies, and cover-ups repelled even more. It whitewashed the war's controversies and deliberately flattened the people's personal experiences of it, since individuals' trials, achievements, and losses were shunned in favor of a party-approved cult of heroes and ritual platitudes. Nowhere else was such brazen manipulation evident than at the very top in the guise of Party Secretary Leonid Brezhnev, who had served as a political officer during the war, far from frontline danger. When he assumed power in the mid-1960s, a move that signaled an end to the

Thaw, he began awarding himself the highest military order, Hero of the Soviet Union, akin to the Medal of Honor or Victoria Cross. Three more times in fifteen years the insult was repeated, making him the war's most decorated veteran in this regard, and no doubt more would have come his way had he not died in 1982.

Not long following this pinnacle of vulgarity, the Soviet edifice collapsed thanks to Mikhail Gorbachev, who came to power in 1985 and instituted reforms aimed at prying open the clamp of censorship. This policy, known as glasnost, was intended as a top-down exposé of Stalinist excesses in order to revitalize the party's legitimacy among the general population by regaining its trust. However, the push from below, once the first moves were made, exploded beyond control and helped bring down the Soviet Union itself.[7]

The Revisionist Turn

Of all the revelations that poured through the floodgates of glasnost, some of the most divisive and fiercely debated concerned the war and, for some, forever changed its meaning as the sense of triumph was upended. The key role in this revolution was played by many of the same veterans whose writing had first appeared during the Thaw, and who now faced no censorship. Their attention, however, was less concerned with larger controversies over Soviet policies, such as the non-aggression pact. Instead, what drove them, as they entered the final years of their lives, was the need to share their personal experiences, leavened with the moral seasoning only fiction could afford but with no limits on its expression. This cohort aspired to nothing less than the "holy truth," as Viktor Astafev put it, since Russia had never seen anything "more falsified, tossed together and made-up" than Soviet histories that bound the war to such a narrow, triumphalist script.

Along with memoirs and remembrances of other frontline veterans whose voices were being heard publicly for the first time, writers like Astafev brought readers once more into the trenches, though this time they were now full of broken bodies, filth, hunger, fear, and despair—as well as a rage that still burned decades after soldiers put down their rifles. Yet this visceral anger was not unleashed on Germans but on the Soviet system that had treated the entire population, in their eyes, as if it were a single, massive penal battalion—human material, in short, to be deployed, abused, or eliminated as the power apparatus saw fit.

Such is the driving force behind Astafev's 1994 novel *The Damned and the Dead,* which is arguably the most devastating take on World War II in Russian literature. Its centerpiece is the 1943 forced crossing of the Dniepr River, which led to the liberation of Kiev, capital of Ukraine and the largest city in the USSR occupied by the Germans. In so doing, he took on an icon of Soviet remembrance, second only to Stalingrad as a tale of epic and enduring feats.

Due to the decisive advantage offered by the river's breadth and steep banks, the German defensive position there became known as the Eastern Wall, a counterpart to its Atlantic Wall protecting the French coastline, and behind which Hitler was determined to stop the Soviet advance after their victory at the great tank battle of Kursk. Red Army commanders, moving quickly, decided to strike directly from the march which meant—unlike in Operation Overlord eight months later at Normandy—there was little preparatory bombardment and an acute absence of proper transport. The only things available were some fishing boats, hastily constructed rafts, or just boards on which to paddle.

At night and under direct fire, Soviet troops, aided by "unprecedented heroism" according to the official version, carved out two bridgeheads, north and south of Kiev, and successfully defended them against repeated counterattacks. While losses were inevitably high, so too was the number of troops, 2,605, who were awarded Hero of the Soviet Union. No longer would the Dniepr be just the greatest river in Ukraine; Soviet history would also crown it as the "River of Heroes."

Or, on Astafev's pages, the river of hell. If in the official version facts such as the minimal preparation only bolstered the pride one could take from the operation since it raised the degree of difficulty, for him it was act of idiocy that cost thousands of lives. In *The Damned and the Dead,* the nighttime crossing disintegrates into chaos. Exhausted soldiers drown in the river's strong currents as their flimsy rafts fall to pieces or are blown to bits. The absence of artillery cover gives German machine gunners free rein to slice apart the soldiers as they desperately try to paddle under the glare of illumination rounds. Succeed nevertheless they do, though the morning reveals the river has turned crimson, its shores blanketed with corpses and body parts that in short time become food for rats. With most of their supplies lost in crossing, the surviving soldiers huddle near the bank, drawing water and eating fish from the Dniepr, with bodies floating about or tangled in its weeds. Subject to unrelenting artillery fire, they nevertheless hold on, and the ghastly stalemate ends only when subsequent crossings, no less difficult and bloody, allow for the scattered bridgeheads to link up and push the Germans back.

Astafev knew of what he wrote. As a radio operator he was in the first wave, and his eyewitness fiction highlights facts of the battle that failed to appear in Soviet accounts, such as the simultaneous dropping of thousands of paratroopers behind German lines, the largest airborne operation for the Red Army during the war. The fate of those who came by air, however, was essentially the same as those who came by water. Inexperienced and ill-prepared pilots scattered the troops over a vast area. Many came down right on top of a panzer corps or fell directly into the Dniepr and drowned. Still others were accidentally dropped behind Soviet lines, which did not result in the safe outcome one might assume, since they were promptly accused of desertion and shipped off to penal battalions.

Astafev turns the Dniepr crossing into a metaphor that can stand for the whole of the war as personally experienced by him and millions of others in the Red Army. Though they ultimately won it, his novel insists, it came at so great a cost that pride in sacrifice should become shame in carnage. In other words, there has to be a point—moral, ethical, and semantic—where pyrrhic victory is no longer victory.[8]

Literature by the likes of Astafev, seconded by a new generation of historians free of the censor's whip, has empowered a revisionism that calculates the war dead differently. If the Soviet standard held sacrifice and triumph in a symbiotic relationship—the greater the former, the greater the latter—then here it is reversed. The more blood that was shed meant the waste was that much greater. Whether so many had to die remains the unanswered question for the revisionist line.

So immense was the loss of Soviet life that no accurate count can ever be made. Like a festering wound, the debate still continues because estimates are a historian's only recourse. Rosters of those killed were sometimes falsified or disappeared when units were overrun. Moreover, soldiers were not always issued identity tags and were often hastily buried in mass graves on the battlefield. Others fell deep in forests and swamps, their bodies lost forever. In the first months of the war, when catastrophe loomed, civilians by the tens of thousands were formed into militias and, sometimes unregistered and without weapons, sent to plug holes in the line. Even before glasnost, when the official toll was twenty million, it was believed that of those men born between 1923 and 1924, like Astafev and thus of draft age when invasion came, only 3 percent survived. While empirically this demographic cannot be proven, it was no doubt the case in many instances when classmates gathered after the war and it still operates as a truism, particularly for Russians today.

To add to the military toll, how can one ever know how many Soviet civilians perished on German-occupied soil, invisible to the rest of the world, whether starved, shot, gassed, or burned alive in mass executions to retaliate against partisans? So staggering was the overall loss of life that it also became a pawn of political manipulation. Under Stalin the number of claimed dead was seven million—an absurdity that placed it below Germany's and helped preserve his reputation as brilliant wartime leader. With the Thaw it "grew" to twenty and with glasnost to twenty-seven million. However, as a continuing sign of its negotiable immensity, it was later reduced by four hundred thousand.

Nevertheless, that number alone, if divided by the forty-seven months of fighting Germany (and minus an additional one hundred thousand killed in the war with Finland, 1939–1940), means that almost twenty thousand Soviets died *each day,* every twenty-four hours, for 1,418 consecutive days. How many in that unrelenting slaughter were specifically Russian, as opposed to Ukrainian, Georgian, and so forth, also remains unknowable.

Revisionists often question official claims (Astafev believed the toll surpassed forty million). Yet what is not in dispute is that a large share of that loss was self-inflicted. In any military the soldier's lot, particularly at the lower ranks, is rarely an easy one. In the Red Army, however, the very conditions of service, from inadequate or absent shelter and equipment to pitiful medical and sanitary conditions, could be as lethal as enemy bullets. Whether found in memoir or fiction, what united recruits, besides diarrhea and lice, was constant, irrepressible hunger. Vladimir Tsvetkov, a three-percenter who was wounded four times, recalled one ravenous soldier who, upon finding a chicken in an attic, ate it raw on the spot, spitting out the feathers. Desperation drove Tsvetkov himself, he admitted, to wallow in cow manure searching for scraps or to make soups out of rats, mice, and frogs. Cannibalism in besieged Leningrad (a fact suppressed until glasnost) was not a unique phenomenon but also came to Tsvetkov's native Orel when the Germans occupied it and, with grim predictability, occurred among Soviets in prison camps. Ironically, for some soldiers, the only time they received adequate food was in 1945 from captured food stocks in Germany.[9]

Even proper uniforms and clothing could be rare commodities. Stripping corpses was necessary, quite widespread, and continued into the war's last year. Sometimes it was done en masse; Tsvetkov also wrote of burying corpses just in their underwear in order to save their outer garments for others. Sometimes it was done in ghoulish, à la carte fashion, as another reflected on their lieutenant, killed by a sniper.

Plaque marking the collective grave of soldiers of the Thirty-Second Rifle Division, killed fighting the Germans at Borodino in October 1941 on the same battlefield where the Russians fought Napoleon in 1812. Author's personal collection.

His corpse was dragged over to the woods and lay for a long time in the snow. He was gradually undressed. First he lost his pistol, coat and boots; then his shirt, pants and underwear. The naked body turned yellow and for several days served as my signpost, letting me know the exact spot where I was.[10]

In *The Damned and the Dead,* Astafev also highlights this practice to foreshadow the fate of soldiers at the Dniepr. The novel begins in training camp, where recruits are inducted wearing the uniforms of those who have already been killed, yet no attempt has been made to cover the clothing's bullet holes or bloodstains.

Crueler, though, than the system's failures and breakdowns, were those who ran it. From tactical ingenuity that rarely graduated beyond frontal assault to outright contempt for soldiers under their command, the revisionist portrait of officers is harrowing. During glasnost many of the rank and file revealed that they feared their own superiors more than the Germans. After all, the former were closer at hand and enjoyed a dangerous latitude to beat, bully, and summarily execute subordinates. The power this conveyed was often intoxicating—all the more so when alcohol was involved—and bred a callous viciousness that typically increased the higher up in rank one went.

The Damned and the Dead presents this abuse in frank terms, describing officers who can be distinguished by the severity of their punches, and who ultimately beat to death a private who wets his bed. The recruits' experience of their Siberian training camp reminds us of the Gulag, and they are even identified as "goners," prison slang for those near death in the labor camps. (There is something to the fact that in Russian a good share of army jargon comes from prison life.) So malnourished, unkempt, weakened, and incapacitated are the recruits by the end of training that their officers refuse to present the regiment for review. And so stark is Astafev's picture of a broken, violently abusive military that he felt compelled in an afterword to take off his fictional mask and cite exact names, places, and units involved lest he be accused of exaggeration.

For those in the trenches, officers away from the battlefield, the so-called rear rats, were particularly despised. Comfortable in their huts and sated with food and vodka, they were parasites, many recalled, who stole from the soldiers' already deficient supplies and who issued the kinds of orders that bore little correspondence to reality but for which the common soldier would pay the price, often with his own life. To the women who served as nurses, doctors, snipers, machine gunners, and pilots, they appear in revisionist texts as unrepentant and nearly unstoppable predators. Whether raped or threatened into having sex, for many of the eight hundred thousand women who wore a uniform, service in the Red Army meant systemic, serial sexual assault. In a glasnost interview with the journal *Motherland,* Astafev inadvertently gave the publication's title new meaning when he stated that "the political leader of our brigade never once set foot on the front line. Though he did knock up seven girls during the war. There's his victories for you."

The further one follows the revisionist path, the more the story of the war turns to tragedy. No longer can be it just that of good defender versus evil invader. Instead, it gains another, more chilling layer: that of Soviet state power, manifest in the combined military-party-police complex, at war with its own people. Only if framed in this way could someone like Astafev make sense of what so many endured, whether as a civilian on occupied territory or as a starving child in Leningrad; as a prisoner in the camps or as the common soldier in the trenches. All suffer "there," wherever that might be, but because of circumstances they do not control. Instead, that power belongs to a shape-shifting wraith bearing either a swastika or hammer and sickle.

This path also leads to what is the most divisive and controversial revisionist proposition: the degree of separation between Nazi and Soviet tyranny. The closer it comes to zero, the closer one gets to the heart of Russia's predicament in remembering the war. Can it be done without recognizing the killing potential of the Soviet system itself—and not just during the war, but before, such as in the collectivization campaign of the 1930s, when millions in the USSR starved to death in man-made famines, or in the Great Terror that followed and consumed millions more, including Tsvetkov's father? At the raw level of the victims' point of view, the two decades run together, since they bookend when German and Soviet power converged and, for a time, conspired to make this the bloodiest period in Russian history—which also holds true for Ukrainian, Belorussian, Polish, and Jewish history as well.

Yet even if for revisionists "Nazi" and "Soviet" tend to operate as synonyms, the tyranny of the latter is still seen as qualitatively distinct because its crimes include one of a different order: betrayal. It betrayed everyone in the Soviet Union by turning them into an inanimate resource to be disposed of at will. There was a betrayal of trust in the soldiers to fight, manifest most lethally in the deployment of heavily armed troops, so-called blocking detachments, behind the front line to shoot any of their own who retreated. There was a betrayal after the war, such as in the callous treatment of veterans, especially the disabled, who were cast away to fend for themselves, or in the Communist Party's theft of the laurels of victory by insisting that its leadership, more than the blood and sweat of soldiers, defeated Germany. And there was a profound betrayal of those who believed their collective sacrifice would result in a freer, more humane society. In 1990, on the forty-fifth anniversary of VE Day, Viacheslav Kondratev, another three-percenter turned writer, solemnly reflected, "All our hopes that something would change were destroyed."

Futility, waste, betrayal—these are the words that more commonly define the legacy of the First World War, which is where the path of Russian revisionism for the Second World War ultimately leads. To Kondratev, who out of despair committed suicide in 1993, his was a "lost generation," when the "flower of the nation perished." To another fellow writer, their war was a "harvest of corpses," and Viktor Astafev, after he came home to Siberia, was haunted by "the impression that we were the defeated ones."[11]

Restoration

In the twenty-first century, Russia has climbed up from the depths of those sentiments along two paths. One is a journey tinged with Christian motifs to offer redemption for the suffering uncovered by revisionism. Its horizon, characteristically, lies in past traditions. The other is more of a forced march, driven by political imperatives emanating from the present and leading directly to the Kremlin.

Exemplary of the first would be the phenomenal success of the 2004 miniseries *Penal Battalion,* which reignited the fierce debates that first erupted during glasnost. With its focus on the unit that by its very design suffered the highest mortality rates in the war, nothing better epitomizes the people's victimization by their own government. The condemned range from the political criminal to the common one, from the urban intellectual to the impoverished peasant, and so serve as a stand-in for the whole of Russia, whose collective experience runs the full gamut of the system's betrayals. One soldier sentenced to the battalion, for instance, as a boy survived the prewar famines caused by forced collectivization. The source of his good fortune? His own mother, who killed her two other sons and fed them to him—an act nearly impossible to contemplate even in fiction, not to speak of reality, where we know such things did occur during those years of starvation.

The battalion is repeatedly decimated in frontal assaults against enemy strongpoints or across uncleared minefields. (It can easily be replenished by importing replacements from the regular ranks.) Yet the Germans are, for the most part, off-screen. Taking their place are the terrifying agents of the military police and Communist Party who hover nearby, thereby reinforcing the impression that they bear primary responsibility for the war's carnage, leading all the way up to Stalin, whose hands, the series informs us, are "bloodier than Genghis Khan's."

Over the course of ten episodes a simple question arises: why do the condemned continue to fight for a regime guilty of mass murder before the war and continuing its homicidal practices during it? The answer, given by the battalion's commander and fellow political prisoner, returns us to the very foundation of the war myth. True Russia is not a political state but more of a cosmic entity born of the organic connection between the land and the people. Whatever government rules it and how it behaves is, in this regard, immaterial. Even if that temporal power, whether Soviet or not, sends its own to their deaths, the land, he declares, "remains theirs forever"—but only if they are willing to die for it.

The prisoners in the battalion uphold that bond, perishing on a bridgehead across a river in 1943, as if retracing the steps laid out by Astafev in *The Damned and the Dead*. Yet if the latter is a descent into hell, in *Penal Battalion* the direction is reversed with the help of a priest who joins them midway through the series. That the work is fiction helps hold historical accuracy in check as he begins blessing the prisoners, picks up a rifle himself, and elevates their struggle into a holy mission to save Russia with those who suffer the most at its fore. Their last stand turns into a literal confirmation of their exalted status. Soviet commanders, safe in the rear, deny them reinforcements when the Germans attack, but they receive aid from a higher source as an image of the Holy Mother and Child grace the sky at the end. Victory is theirs, and the enemy is stopped, though only two remain alive to enjoy it in this world: the priest and the battalion commander.

The screen is the preferred medium for productions of this nature. They run the gamut from B-grade pieces involving blocking detachments to blockbuster efforts such as *Burnt by the Sun—2* by Nikita Mikhalkov, currently the most powerful person in Russian cinema. Their common approach is to apply conventional formulas to the war's darkest recesses, especially where it involves Soviet-on-Russian violence. This makes for a powerful tool in reclaiming the war as the people's ordeal yet in reverse direction. Once applied, religion can redeem bloodshed and accommodate the war's unprecedented horrors, no matter the cause or culprit. (German bullets, after all, still take their toll.) Therefore, no matter what fact or historical reality is thrown at it, no matter what a future revelation may bring, this template can find a place for it by turning the unconscionable and incomprehensible into the familiar and spiritually fulfilling. The people will suffer—grievously, sometimes gratuitously—but in that will be Russia's salvation.

The combination of a Tolstoyan-like vision projected through an Orthodox lens does not mean that these works always succeed, at least in terms of audience appeal. *Penal Battalion* was *the* television event for its time, with heated discussions over it ensnaring journalists, talk show hosts, bloggers, and even historians. However, *Burnt by the Sun—2*, the long-awaited sequel to Mikhalkov's Oscar-winning takedown of Stalinism from the mid-1990s, *Burnt by the Sun*, bombed at the box office when it was released in two parts in 2010 and 2011, collapsing under the weight of its own pretensions. Nearly every scene is designed to extract as much symbolic importance as painstakingly possible: a bomb accidentally falls on a church, but an icon of the Holy Mother and Child survives; a young woman is saved by a dying soldier, a defrocked priest, who baptizes her with his last breath; secretly armed with his cross, she becomes an angelic nurse who in turn gives her breast to a dying soldier—a battlefield reprisal of a famous icon of Mary nursing Jesus in Moscow's Tretyakov Gallery.

In short, from this sequel we learn that Soviet atheism can never erase the Christian spirit that lives in her veins as a true Russian. This proposition extends to her father as well, played by Mikhalkov himself. His character once was an instrument of Soviet terror (gassing rebellious Russian peasants after the 1917 Revolution), but he rediscovers his soul after a stint in a penal battalion, where he realizes that violence should never be directed against one's own but only against the real enemy. Daughter and father end the film together as a combat team on a tank—the perfect pairing of military might and Christian grace in order to repel the foreign invader.

The second path to restore triumph faces no box-office test since it is the civic religion, the cult of 1945, nurtured by the state. It follows the Soviet precedent of aligning the government, the party, and the people as a united whole but also tackles some of the bitter truths that can no longer be denied or ignored. In so doing, it also reminds us of Nikolai Karamzin's type of history by flipping any event into a reflection of national greatness that, fittingly, has received its own canonization in an epic twelve-volume history, sponsored by the Defense

Ministry and completed in 2015, *The Great Patriotic War.* As if its nearly twelve thousand pages were not enough to pull off the feat, it joins a sibling of similar heft, this time sponsored in part by the Foreign Ministry, *The Great Victory,* that runs for another fifteen volumes.[12]

The war, we learn from the latter, is a "sacred" event of Russian history marking when it led the Soviet Union in "defending the planet from the forces of evil." As such its memory is sacrosanct as well, which means the full resources of the state, across all points of society and all media angles, must be deployed to preserve and protect it from six primary heresies.

One heresy festers on the domestic front as the darling of revisionists: command decisions by the Communist Party and the military that caused so many losses. The modus operandi favored by the state to tackle these controversies—one abetted by an ongoing flood of similarly directed pulp histories—is to turn 1945 into a teleological lens looking backward. From the perspective of the war's outcome, virtually all of them can be revisited in a new light.

Fiascoes can be nudged aside as distractions from that triumph. The first year of the German invasion, for instance, was not a chain of defeats that brought the Germans to the outskirts of Moscow and Leningrad, but the first step to victory because their blitzkrieg did not succeed. Penal battalions and blocking detachments can likewise be claimed as unfortunate but necessary measures dictated by the fact that the country's life was hanging by a thread. This lens can even see before the war, offering a tame picture of the early 1930s, when millions died during collectivization and the resulting state-induced famine. *The Great Patriotic War,* for instance, presents this drive strictly by the numbers—not the human cost but the statistical change in industrial output that turned the Soviet Union into a powerhouse. In this vein, others have retroactively justified those deaths by turning the victims, in effect, into the first casualties of the war, since only by diverting resources from the countryside to help build factories could the Soviet

Union acquire the industrial strength to defeat Germany. That the war ended in Berlin and not Moscow proves these were the correct choices.[13]

The five other heresies, as listed in *The Great Patriotic War,* consist of the following: (1) placing blame on the Soviet Union for helping start the war through its 1939 alliance with Nazi Germany; (2) equating Nazism and Communism; (3) rejecting the Red Army as on a liberating mission; (4) distorting the character and conduct of its soldiers; and (5) downplaying or ignoring the decisive role Russia played in defeating Germany. Collectively, they take us across the border into the former republics of the Soviet Union and its satellites, where memories of the war are still at war.

Until glasnost, the Communist Party's suppression of truths about the war also kept the experiences of those in the Soviet sphere of influence tied to the singular narrative of the Red Army as a benevolent force. That, in no uncertain terms, is not how Poles and Balts, for example, tend to see it. For Poland, the joint German-Soviet invasion in 1939 was a replay of the eighteenth-century conspiracy by Prussia, Austria, and Russia to carve it up. This time, however, the results were far worse. Russians came in accompanied by the Soviet secret police, known as the NKVD and made up of homicidal maniacs intent on decimating Polish intellectual and professional elites, as attested by the mass execution of thousands at sites like Katyn.

The trajectory of the Lithuanian, Estonian, and Latvian experiences follows a similar course. Like Poland, they gained independence following the collapse of the Russian Empire in 1917. In 1940, they lost it once more when the Red Army entered and the NKVD began its inevitable cycle of imprisonment, deportation, and execution. A year later the Wehrmacht pushed it out and became the new occupier, with the Gestapo taking over where the NKVD had left off. In 1944, the Red Army returned and the cycle continued. Therefore, from the perspective of the Baltic nations, the war—defined as foreign occupation from either side—ended only in 1991. Poignantly capturing this is Lithuania's Museum of Genocide Victims, which opened in Vilnius shortly thereafter and is located in a real house of horrors: the building was used first by the NKVD as its headquarters, the Gestapo then put it to the same purpose, and, when the flags changed once more, the KGB kept up the tradition.

Russia's Soviet inheritance has, in short, kept its reputation locked in a vise. Did Russia win the war as the liberator, attacked in 1941 yet rallying to slay the Nazi giant? Or did it win as an aggressor conspiring with Germany in 1939 to divide Eastern Europe and, by war's end, coming to dominate all of it? Both stories conclude in Berlin, yet with conflicting images to mark the occasion: should it be the red flag raised in victory over the Reichstag in 1945 or that of the Wall raised in 1961? What date should Europe, indeed the world, commemorate so as never to forget the war's horrors? For Russia it is unequivocally May 9; its neighbors, however, now champion a new one: August 23.

For many outside of Russia, this is the day that will live in infamy, since it marks the signing of the Nazi-Soviet pact, whose secret protocols became the chronological ground zero for all that followed, beginning with the invasion of Poland one week later. In 2008 the European Parliament officially declared it the "European Day of Remembrance for Victims of Stalinism and Nazism," and members of the European Union followed suit by ratifying it. The Russian Federation, for which in the context of the war "Russian" and "Soviet" are nearly synonymous, took that move as a shot across the bow.

The declaration identifies the Soviet Union with Nazi Germany as partners in crimes against humanity, but it is the former that gets first billing throughout. This shift in emphasis is deliberate, since attention to Nazism "has long obscured the influence and significance of the Soviet order and occupation on and for citizens of post-Communist states." Language such as this assumes that crimes first committed in the 1930s lasted, in effect, until 1991 and, what is more, implies that the aftereffects still continue. The declaration twice notes that the statute of limitations does not apply in such cases and thus in theory extends to Russia as the legal inheritor of Soviet treaties and positions (for example, its seat on the UN Security Council). That this action by the

European Parliament speaks as much to the present as to the past comes in the added insistence that the annual remembrance of August 23, also known as Black Ribbon Day, serve as an instrument for "rooting democracy more firmly" on the continent.

Nowhere is Russia mentioned in the declaration; however, there is no way it could not see itself as the explicit target. The official response came the next year in 2009 from the president himself, Dmitry Medvedev, and his convening of the Commission to Counter Attempts to Harm Russia's Interests by Falsifying History. Headed by his chief of staff, it included blue-ribbon politicians, leaders in the military, and historians from the Academy of Sciences, and it sent a commensurate jolt through society with its contention that speech contrary to its version of history could be criminalized. Though no prosecutions occurred during its three-year tenure, this group helped initiate the writing of *The Great Victory* in order to eradicate the alleged heresies on this front as well.

If there is to be talk of crimes, it declares, then to conflate the Soviet Union with Nazi Germany as co-aggressors is a crime against "objective history." Instigator of the war? Western accusers should look to themselves, since in the 1938 Munich Agreement England and France signed Czechoslovakia over to Hitler and showed the world it would not fight him. That cowardly betrayal, repeating a standard line of Soviet history, disqualified the West as a reliable ally against Nazism and forced the Soviet Union into a deal with Germany in order to protect itself. And this necessity, buttressed by teleological hindsight, also justified the subsequent occupation of eastern Poland and annexation of the Baltic States. The move bought the Soviet Union time and space, pushing its borders hundreds of miles west. Without that added buffer, Hitler might have taken Moscow in 1941, ending the war right then and leaving all those nations under permanent Nazi occupation.

Nor should the two be linked as villains. While it is true that "many innocent people" died in both countries under twin dictatorships, the crimes were categorically distinct. Germany's were racist and genocidal, paralleling its ambitions to world domination; Soviet "repressions"—using the Russian term for executions—followed Stalin's personal hunger for unrivaled power in the government. Indeed, no one should forget that the war culminated in a death match between the two countries, the "butchers" versus the "victims," and the Nuremburg Trials proved that the right side won.

That verdict carries over to the fate of Eastern Europe after 1945. From the Russian perspective, the war consisted of two fundamental, interconnected, and simultaneous operations: "defending its own land" and liberating "the other nations that had fallen under the yoke of German fascism." Having succeeded in both, one cannot speak of a postwar Soviet occupation of the latter. Rather, its interests lay in establishing loyal partners, which coincides with what America and Britain "did in those countries which their armies entered"—that is to say, France, Belgium, West Germany, and so forth.[14]

Regret can be extended—reluctantly, one might add, since it passes in a just a few lines in *The Great Victory*—to what some of the Red Army soldiers might have done on those liberated lands. "No historian can deny the very fact" that they committed "murder, robbery and rape." But those cases cannot stand for the entire army, allowing it to be painted as the sword of "Asian barbarism" as is swiftly done in the West, or take away from its core mission. Moreover, such "atrocities"—the word is given in quotes—unfortunately follow in any war and perpetrators can be found among all the ranks of the allies.

As upheld here and in virtually all similar rebuttals, these charges against Soviet Russia are seen as sharing a common goal: to steal its victory away. And the most brazen invitation to thievery, the last heresy so to speak, is when others fail to give Russians due credit for defeating Hitler. Downplaying their role, disparaging it, ignoring it—whichever one applies—there is no greater affront, since it effectively writes them out of the greatest moment of their history.

The anger occasioned by these perceived insults is not entirely without merit—particularly if one looks to the United States and its culture's penchant for scripting the war as an exclusively American, or

American-led, affair. Most often one encounters this in commemorations of D-Day that paint the Normandy landings as the war's turning point. On its fiftieth anniversary in 1994, for instance, President Bill Clinton traveled there to proclaim the beaches "sacred soil," the "place a miracle of liberation began." Russia pointedly was not invited to participate; a united Germany came instead. The same year a similar message was parlayed by one of the war's best-selling historians, Stephen Ambrose, who declared that on those beaches was where the "outcome of the war" was decided, and four years later he served as the consultant for Steven Spielberg's *Saving Private Ryan,* which to many in Russia (and also in Britain) enshrines the assertion that the United States, essentially by itself, delivered Europe from Nazi hands.[15]

Russian historians, however, would be quick to point out that by June 1944, when the Western allies landed, the war's turning point had long passed. The Battle of Stalingrad, which broke the back of the German offensive machine and forever ended its dreams of conquering the Soviet Union, had occurred a year and a half before. So too might the result of the Normandy landings have been different if the Red Army had not simultaneously launched Operation Bagration, a million-and-a-half-man offensive that brought it to the outskirts of Warsaw by August, just when Paris was liberated. Eight months later the Red Army was in Berlin. The war was won, first and foremost, where the Russians fought it, as borne out by the statistic, which Western historians do not dispute, that at least 80 to 85 percent of all German casualties, if not more, occurred on the Eastern Front.

What stings even more on the road to victory is when Western allies put their sacrifices before Soviet, especially Russian, ones. If the backstory of *Saving Private Ryan* concerns the death of three American brothers, then as a counter to that *fictional* tale, *The Great Victory* reminds us that in the Dniepr operation alone, seven brothers of the Korolev family were killed. Such rebuttals inevitably lead to comparisons of each country's aggregate war losses—which may seem callous to some but are unavoidable in the official Russian narrative, particularly if claims are made on individual contributions to defeating Hitler. It can be stated, for instance, that during the siege of Leningrad, in such a relatively compressed space, more people perished than the 866,000 total for America and Britain combined, across the entire globe, from Europe to the Pacific. Or, if June 6, 1944, was the bloodiest day for the American military in the war, when 2,500 of its soldiers were killed at Normandy, then the Soviet Union suffered the equivalent of eight of them every single day from June 1941 to May 1945. At a base level, one could say that for every American who was killed, almost sixty-five Soviet citizens perished.[16]

What sometimes lingers in the wake of such comparisons is yet another way of contemplating the war's losses. Why did so many Russians die? If revisionists point fingers at their own, others, especially those bearing arch-nationalist credentials, point to the West—but not just at the Germans. Did the United States and Britain act so as to ensure that the Eastern Front would be soaked in blood? To be sure, they shipped thousands of tons of supplies and munitions to the Soviet Union through the Lend-Lease Act, but their move to open up a second front was painfully slow. If Western historians attribute that delay to issues of training, experience, buildup, and logistics, conspiracy theorists can see it as a calculated decision to let Russia bleed. What is more, this camp even has its smoking gun, provided by a U.S. senator who declared in Congress on June 23, 1941, the day after the German invasion, that "if we see that Germany is winning, we ought to help Russia, and if Russia is winning we ought to help Germany, and that way let them kill as many as possible." The words were Harry Truman's, soon to become the first Cold War president, and if they are forgotten in America, in Russian history books they often appear in bold print.[17]

Amid the ranks of those defending Russia's side, anger is doubled when mixed with a sense of historical déjà vu. To depose the continental tyrant with designs on the world only to be mounted in his place on the pedestal of villainy—was that not Russia's fate after 1812? By no means alone, Alexander Pushkin certainly believed so and

dedicated his poem, "To the Slanderers of Russia," to that idea. It remains infamous outside of Russia, since he addressed it to those enraged by Russia's suppression of the 1830 Polish uprising, but its core
message still rings true on native soil. Why do you hate us, he asks of
the West?

> Is it because amid the ruins of flaming Moscow
> We defied the insolent demands
> Of the one, to whom you bowed?
> Or because we struck down
> The idol who loomed over nations
> And by our blood restored to Europe
> Freedom, honor and peace?[18]

By invoking sacrifice, Pushkin extends the key that then, just as
now, locks up the argument about Russia's place in history. In the end,
The Great Patriotic War concludes, any "sin" committed against other
countries' property or people was "paid for by the blood of Russians
on the field of battle where they broke the back of the seemingly invincible Wehrmacht."

Such are the battles Russia wages in a conflict it deems the "Infor-
mation War." The stakes are real, according to those who believe in it,
since the foreign assault against its history has the aim of isolating it
once more. If, *The Great Victory* asks, during World War II the "whole
of Europe, in essence," was deployed against Russia, then what is the
real goal of the 2008 EU edict against Stalinism and Nazism if not
"an attempt to form a new pan-European identity" on an "anti-Russian
basis" and "at the expense of Russia"? If Soviet actions are crimes to
be pinned on Russia, one can hear, then would not the next logical
step be a demand for material or territorial compensation by the alleged victims? Would this not be an assault against Russia itself? To
impugn it in such fashion so long after the war can have only one
objective, the eighth volume warns: to destroy "the most important

foundation for the construction of a new Russia and its ability to move forward."

As this last statement reveals, the risk of material loss is not what is truly at hand. The more profound blow is against national prestige, that is, the acute sense of collective belonging and pride cultivated by the state. Nothing is more "sacred," politically speaking, than its version of the war, which is why the wall of sensitivity thins the higher one gets. Even the notion of a "version" is something of a misnomer that only an outsider would use; this memory of the war always and only performs as the "truth," and nothing so far has proven stronger as a binding agent for the Russian Federation. What other experience can every citizen lay claim to that, in this packaging, is more inspiring? "We are history's makers," the popular historian Vladimir Medinsky wrote before he became the minister of culture in 2012. "Just as we broke the back of a continental Europe united behind Napoleon," he explained, "we did it again to a Europe united behind Hitler."[19]

This is why the real target of massive productions such as *The Great Victory* and *The Great Patriotic War* is not so much a foreign threat, real or imagined, as it is Russians themselves. They were not released in simultaneous translation, which means that their power of persuasion essentially erodes outside Russia's borders, and they often read less as history than as a catechism with the pretext of a loyalty oath. Accepting Victory on its (typically capitalized) terms means to embrace in similar fashion the whole of Russia's "thousand-year history" and its "centuries-old values," and taking that step, the twelfth volume of *The Great Patriotic War* instructs, is the "main criterion in the Russian Federation" to prove "the sincerity of one's patriotism."[20]

Yet as a real measure of what World War II means in Russia, even that statement doesn't exhaust its potential. Revisionist and counter-revisionist are, to a degree, used here provisionally in order to outline overall trajectories that have sub-corollaries too numerous to engage in depth. Under the revisionist lens, for instance, one can find truly provocative twists, like the *Icebreaker* series by Viktor Suvorov, the pseudonym of a Cold War defector who has planted the hypothesis—with many devotees, it would seem—about how Stalin was planning to attack Hitler, which is why the German invasion was (justifiably) preemptive. Dismissed by real historians, Suvorov's books, after first appearing in Russia in the 1990s, nevertheless continue as best sellers.

In a different vein, but just as needling to many, is counterfactual speculation such as in *Occupation: Truth and Myths* that in 2002 floated the idea of how a German victory over the Soviet Union could have been an unexpected blessing by removing the Stalinist regime. Mindful of the charge of being pro-Hitler, the author immediately adds that in this scenario Germany still loses the global war with Britain and the United States. Eastern Europe is then occupied by Anglo-American forces, which bring the gifts of democracy and capitalism and save the world from continued darkness.[21]

Regarding the infusion of religion, if *Penal Battalion* and *Burnt by the Sun—2* present miracles on-screen, for believers such occurrences were not the product of fiction. During the war itself, for instance, the story arose that Mary's visage appeared in the sky over the tanks battling at Kursk in 1943. In today's church-sponsored literature, one now encounters a full litany of such claims, extending from grand interventions—such as her role in saving Leningrad as well—to divine grace protecting individual soldiers on the battlefield.

Alternatively, those who favor a strong-armed Kremlin can easily find several paths beyond the official line to embrace Stalin. While *The Great Victory* touts his brilliance as a military leader, it also admits, albeit briefly, a few sins, such as the prewar purging of the officer corps. Others, untethered from the need for even an appearance of balance, fall into rhapsodic worship. For them his role is invariably that of a righteous hammer, whether raised against Jews at home or Germans on the battlefield. In the latter capacity, his military brilliance goes without saying, but perhaps less known, as several works purport, is that he was "a great humanist," "a true son of Russia who dedicated his intelligence, talents and life" to it, or simply a "titan of humankind."[22]

As a sign of his intractable presence, Stalin's invocation defies consistency and bridges the incompatible. He can serve as the Soviet Union's savior for pro-communist nostalgists or as Russia's for anti-communist arch-nationalists. In one cringing example, a 2008 film touted as a documentary, *The Third Reich versus the Third Rome,* Stalin leads Russia, spiritually pure and God-chosen, against the whole of the materialist West and the seat of "world evil." His natural ally in this clash of civilizations is, we learn, none other than the Holy Mother.

Neither should these two trajectories be seen as mutually exclusive since they describe overall tendencies and not rigid domains. Though on-screen Nikita Mikhalkov rescues Orthodox Russia from Soviet demons in *Burnt by the Sun—2,* that in no way has hampered his political rise as a member of the governing party, United Russia, which has the most to gain from a pro-Soviet imaging of the past. So too Viktor Astafev, nearly unmatched in the cynicism of his revisionist fiction, was at his death in 2001 not a pariah but the recipient of numerous state awards, with that recognition crowned by President Putin laying flowers at his grave.

Finally, these two trajectories do not even begin to cover the war as a magnet for traditional fare. There is always ample room for action-tale fodder or even for flights of silliness, such as introducing flying saucers and time travel to its cache. (Three movies so far have demonstrated that today's young slackers, after being transported back in time to the front lines, return to present-day Russia with a newfound respect for their elders and love for country.)

When all is put together, the result sometimes makes for cacophony. In bookstores, volumes by the likes of Astafev stand firm alongside Kremlin-sponsored histories, both of which are in turn flanked by Stalin-loving treatises. Across cinema and television, the sanitized and the chilling chase one another. A movie that idealizes the agents of SMERSH, acronym for "Death to Spies," the military's counterintelligence wing, can be purchased in the same gift collection with another vilifying them as insatiable sadists. *The Third Reich versus the Third Rome,* in which one also learns that Russians were called by God "to bring light" to all on Earth, can be watched alongside a miniseries, *Life and Fate,* based on Vasily Grossman's once-banned novel from the 1960s that presaged glasnost revisionism by presenting the war instead as a struggle for Russians, Jews, and others to survive the satanic fury wrought by two homicidal tyrants.[23]

What does the future hold for these trajectories? As the cult of May Ninth grows and the state's threshold for intolerance lowers, the cacophony might be silenced. Yet for the time being, despite this pressure, cinema remains a vibrant area that can pose challenges to officially sponsored scripts. Likewise, while the production of revisionist fiction has come to an end with the passing of frontline veterans, the most talented members of that cohort are serially reprinted and the torch of revisionism is carried on by a new generation of historians—though their numbers are not as strong as in the halcyon days of the 1990s. Still others transcend the debates and finger-pointing by focusing on what the war meant on an individual level, as in the 2014 collection from survivors, primarily children, of the Leningrad blockade, aptly subtitled *The People's Book of Memory.* A starving eight-year-old girl is forced to lie for days in the same bed with her dead brother, neither she nor her mother having the strength to move the body. Another girl barely escapes cannibals on her way home. Or an eleven-year-old overhears her father, driven crazy by hunger, tell her mother that they should let the children starve to death; use their ration cards to survive; and then have new children after the war. Her mother refused. These too are the experiences from the war but whose shadows no myth can dissipate.[24]

One suspects that something of this nature will continue. The war is too big, too demanding to be contained in any single version—more so, perhaps, in Russia than anywhere else. Conflicting impressions and legacies—whether clothed as fact, fiction, or fantasy—were present under Stalin, and are likely to continue, especially when one steps out of the official chambers of celebration and encounters the myriad, quotidian ways its memory is being preserved. It has become the platform for the historic grounding of nearly all of Russia's mythic identities, whether flattering or damning, and empowers them with images never to be surpassed. The war will remain greater than any single diktat, making it forever inescapable and unavoidable as a touchstone for national identity. The losses alone ensure that—no matter the story behind each individual one.

4

Halo of Blood

Death plays the lead in nearly everything written, imaged, and imagined about the Second World War in Russia. Put simply, there is no way it could not. For Russians, death constitutes the obligatory template for scripting both the horror and the triumph of those years. It permeates the land and defines the people by marking the common condition—the shared threat faced by all and shared fate for those who perished—no matter their age, their gender, or how far from the frontlines they might have been.

Outsiders can feel the nation's obsession with the war's losses to be excessive, almost as if another idiosyncrasy of its character, such as when newlyweds place flowers at the Tomb of the Unknown Soldier. Yet it is a ritual that enacts the poet Olga Berggolts's famous declaration on the war—"no one is forgotten, nothing is forgotten"—which adorns Leningrad's Piskarevskoe Memorial Cemetery, one of the world's largest, where the remains of around five hundred thousand siege victims lie, or approximately half of the total who perished there. It also signals a new family's debt to the fallen. They owe their ability to live and love to those who were denied that by the war. The ritual thus preserves the conflict in the ever-present. All subsequent generations of Russians can trace their lineage, in effect, back to those who didn't return in 1945.

This obsession, however, is not just a symbol of reverence. It is inseparable from the character of those who served. Of all that has shaped Russian soldiers' reputation, nothing remains more persistent, legendary, and yet compelling than a distinct fearlessness of dying. In studies commissioned by the United States from German veterans, the one universal regarding their Eastern Front opponent centered on his "contempt of death." That premise invariably led to other observations that, taken together, set the Russian apart from the norms of "modern warfare" and made him almost otherworldly.

"He can suffer without succumbing."

"He endures cold and heat, hunger and thirst, dampness and mud, sickness and vermin, with equanimity."

"In defense he develops an unheard-of tenacity, right to the bitter end."

"Tank crews whose tanks were burning, continued firing with every available gun as long as there was life in them."

"For them the word 'impossible' is non-existent."

The Russian was a "first-rate fighter" who could only be overcome, came their grim conclusion, by his physical extermination: "Our success was never secure until we could be sure that no living enemy was left in the position."[1]

This impression ran so deep that it could turn Nazi racism inside out. To explain Germany's defeat, one Waffen SS corps commander surprisingly sidestepped the usual culprits. It was due neither to Hitler's blunders nor Stalin's ruthlessness, nor to overwhelming Soviet numbers, nor to crippling German shortages. Not even the Soviet Union's colossal expanses with their foreboding swamps, deep forests, and dust-choking steppes; not even Napoleon's favored answer, the unforgiving climate, was the primary cause. All that might more easily excuse German failure—and provide an SS general who lost to the *Untermensch* a face-saving out—took a backseat to something more formidable: "the resistance offered by the Russian infantry which, supported by the Soviet armored formations, fought fanatically for every inch of Russian soil."[2]

Leaving aside for the moment the fact that not all Red Army soldiers were Russian (or male, for that matter) and that these German veterans might want to indulge their American patrons who now were allies facing a common enemy in the Cold War, this was not the first time Russians were singled out by their opponents with a mix of apprehension and admiration. Such sentiments, in fact, crystallized centuries before—precisely when Russia emerged as a continental power and shocked the West.

The Russian Soldier

Russia recovered quickly after its near death during the Time of Troubles at the beginning of the seventeenth century. The Romanov dynasty that ascended the throne not only restored stability, but led the drive that ultimately would push the empire to its greatest extent. Early victims of this expansion included Poland, a onetime powerhouse now in decline, and Sweden, whose final invasion of Russia was crushed by Peter the Great at the Battle of Poltava in 1709. As the Russian Empire—officially christened as such by Peter—grew, it swept aside these neighbors, and by the middle of the eighteenth century its troops were campaigning on the plains of central Europe, embroiled in the struggles between the great powers of France, Austria, Prussia, and Britain. There they shed their reputation as exotic savages, the descendants of Mongol warriors. Instead, the rank-and-file Russian infantry earned itself recognition, in the words of a French military expert of the time, as "one of the finest in Europe." "It is a veritable wall," he concluded.

This impression came, first and foremost, at the expense of Frederick the Great, king of Prussia during the Seven Years' War from 1756 to 1763, when Russia was ruled by Peter's daughter, Elizabeth. Before it began, the Prussian announced that "the Muscovites are a heap of barbarians. Any well-disciplined troops will make short work of them." After he met them at the Battle of Zorndorf in 1758, a bloody stalemate in which the "barbarians" refused to quit the field despite suffering nearly 50 percent casualties, his opinion reportedly changed: "It's not enough to kill the Russian soldier; he must be knocked down as well." A year later, after the Battle of Kunersdorf—where Frederick suffered his worst defeat ever and was nearly captured—that sentiment spread across the continent as well. "Experience has proved," wrote a British historian when the war ended, "that the Russian infantry is far superior to any in Europe."[3]

What steeled this infantry with such tenacity? Why did Western observers, loath at the time to bestow a positive value on anything "Russian," share a near unanimity of respect for something that was the product of such a backward, tyrannical realm? Some would suggest that that last fact explained more than anything why the Russian peasant, once in uniform, made for a different breed of soldier. Did not the desperate, slave-like conditions of being a serf inure him to hardship and deprivation? Did not the oppressive fist of the autocratic system as well as the rigors of the climate scar him with a fatalist approach to life that held little consequence for death? And in the army itself, was not the discipline so harsh and the officers so ready with their knouts that violence was also commonplace off of the battlefield? On his own, each soldier might seem an uncaring, unthinking brute, but when arrayed side by side and rank behind rank, they turned into the bricks and mortar of that formidable "wall," which, as Frederick learned, seemed immobile. Shot and shell could bring it down, but few could ever break through.

Historians today would not underestimate the impact of such conditioning on a soldier, but, they would also add, in its cruelty the Russian socioeconomic system produced something relatively unique for its time: a homogenized professional army. Its building blocks were the serfs, that is to say, the property of the militarized state and the nobility that served it. As a consequence, only autocratic Russia could claim such a ready supply of bodies and in such tremendous numbers.

According to annual need, quotas were placed on each village or series of households to deliver a certain number of men for military service. Each conscript was placed in irons as the prisoner of the state and his sentence was for life. Military service by itself, in other words, bore the certainty of death, which was reflected in the funeral rites conducted by a conscript's family upon a soldier's induction. Even if not killed in battle or construction projects in peacetime (which could often prove just as fatal), never would the man come back. And even when the term was reduced to twenty-five years at the end of the century, the funeral rite continued, since it was still likely to be a killer sentence and, even if not, in most circumstances the soldier would not be allowed to return home.

This practice ensured the empire a ready supply of manpower to deploy huge armies, yet it also professionalized Russia's fighting forces since its soldiers were dedicated, permanently, to one purpose and were always and only among their own—unlike the typical continental army of the time, which was usually a multinational, multilingual, multiconfessional hodgepodge of mercenaries, militias, cheap levies, and impressed lowlifes. The cohesion and continuity of Russian ranks were further enhanced by their division into individual groups of approximately a dozen men who for the length of their service shared everything in common, from food and money to other possessions, and thus lived, in effect, as a surrogate family. Whatever they did, be it in labor or battle, they did as one, united by the same language, faith, and fate that bred the bonds of small-unit loyalty now seen as crucial to military discipline and effectiveness.[4]

A combination of these factors helps explain why at battles like Zorndorf and Kunersdorf the Russian infantry astonished its European counterparts and forged its distinguished reputation. Yet in the Russian imagination virtually no memory of either engagement has survived beyond the ledger of military historians. This gap extends to the Seven Years' War itself, whose uninspiring name sounds more like a Soviet industrial plan. From the Russian perspective, it was fought for indecipherable reasons, in faraway places and for no appreciable gain. Even its ending was perverse, in an almost comic way. When Empress Elizabeth died in 1762 with her armies pressing Frederick, the throne fell to the fervently pro-Prussian Peter III, who pulled Russia out, gave Prussia back all the territory it had gained, and then proposed to reenter the war as Prussia's ally. (His penchant for flipping Russian foreign policy was, just like his reign, short-lived, thanks to his German wife, Catherine, who helped plot his murder and succeeded him as "the Great.")

That war and its battles would not do. Instead, Russians save such devout reverence for another place, not a village ending in *-dorf* a thousand miles from home, but one just a few days march from Moscow, where they turned to face Napoleon in 1812: Borodino.

Russian soldiers forever made their name on the gentle heights surrounding this unassuming village. The decision to give battle there was by moral necessity as much as for tactical reasons. As Napoleon's juggernaut drove deeper into their heartland, they could never let Moscow, known as the "Mother of all Russian cities," be taken without a fight.

For the French, the stakes were equally momentous. Borodino offered Napoleon the opportunity to destroy his adversary and put an end to its Fabian-like elusiveness. A decisive victory in the field, he believed, would force Tsar Alexander I to come to terms, since this had been the case with previous opponents such as Austria and Prussia. Alas, in the bloody marathon that followed—Napoleon admitted it was his toughest battle ever—the intentions of both sides were, in a sense, defeated. Nevertheless, until World War II nothing would rival Borodino as the showcase of Russians' willingness to die for their country.

The battle took place in late August 1812, two months after Napoleon's invasion began, which meant that his Grande Armée, while still seemingly invincible, was not the same as when it crossed the border. Massive as it had been, its numbers shrank as forces peeled off for other targets, as garrisons commanded more troops, as the

summer heat exhausted his men, as the impact of scorched-earth policies further ground them down, and as the safety of their supply lines
grew ever precarious. Thus at Borodino the Grande Armée barely outnumbered its Russian adversary, both within the range of 120,000–
130,000 men. (This slight advantage would refer to regular troops mus-
tered. Several thousand peasants, hastily pressed into militias and armed
primarily with pikes, would—thankfully for them—see no action and
are typically not counted as actual combatants on the Russian side.)[5]

The first day began with a sharp engagement that forced the Russians to reposition their left flank a mile back on a small rise. The next
day, Sunday, both armies adjusted their lines while the Russians
on the left hastily prepared a series of V-shaped earthworks, called
fleches, to protect their new ground, as if already knowing that this
sector would see some of the hottest fighting. Trepidation, of both the
anxious and excited kind, gripped both armies, yet for the Russian
soldiers it was tempered by the calming ritual of changing into white
shirts, the customary vestment with which to meet death. That sentiment would not be disappointed.

The morning of the third day erupted with one of the greatest cannonades ever heard until the twentieth century as over a thousand
artillery pieces on both sides let loose. The roar was so deafening and
continuous, veterans like Fyodor Glinka and Nadezhda Durova (aka
"Alexander Alexandrov") recalled, that it drowned out the sounds of
tens of thousands of muskets firing simultaneously—not to mention
the screams of those men and horses pulverized by solid shot, exploding shells, and canister balls. The French attack fell primarily on
the Russian left wing, and throughout the morning the fleches were
lost and regained as assault was repeatedly met with counterassault.

Midday, with the fate of the fleches still undecided, Napoleon
launched a second wave concentrating on the Great Redoubt that
dominated the Russian center. It too exchanged hands as he committed all his reserves, with the notable exception of the Imperial
Guard, which he dared not risk, he later admitted, so far from Paris
lest no troops remain. Only in the evening, as darkness and exhaus-

tion settled in, and as ammunition stocks dwindled, did the blood-bath come to an end.

So many men died at Borodino on that third day that we can never be sure of the precise numbers. The conventional total of Russian casualties—killed, wounded, and missing—hovers around fifty thousand, which would be between one-third and one-half of the army, with Russian tradition holding to the higher percentage, since earlier estimates of battlefield strength were lower than is now assumed. Correct math aside, that number astounds even more when one factors in that losses were not distributed evenly. Thus a commander of one division that fought over the fleches discovered at evening roll call that only three hundred soldiers answered muster—out of four thousand who began the day.

French casualties were less grievous but not by much. Their combined total is estimated at around thirty-five thousand, which was between one-third and one-half of the army's battlefield strength. Together, this makes that day at Borodino the single bloodiest in all of the Napoleonic Wars and, in this estimate, of all modern wars up to and including the first day of the Battle of the Somme in 1916, which claimed over seventy thousand casualties on both sides. Moreover, unlike that later carnage, which was spread along miles of trenches, at Borodino most of the men died and bled in a hideously compressed space of just over two square miles. To put this difference in a grislier perspective, there were no machine guns or long-range artillery to produce such casualties en masse or at a remote, invisible distance. Soldiers' limbs and heads were torn off, their bodies disemboweled, their chests run through with bayonets—all within sight, sound, smell, and reach of those both doing and suffering such physical destruction. As summed up by General Petr Bagration, the fiery commander of the Russian left wing, "the battle was the most savage, desperate and murderous that I have witnessed." It was also his last, for he died two weeks later from the wounds he sustained that day.[6]

Yet precisely because of its murderous outcome, Borodino became one of Russia's proudest battles, and its laurels were won by what

Bagration's men didn't do. Despite the tremendous cannonade—often mowing down soldiers as they stood in ranks awaiting the French—despite the continuous assaults on their line for hours, they did not break and they did not run. And even though Bagration's left wing had been pushed back, it stood in good order at day's end—in some places merely a few hundred yards behind its initial entrenchments. (The right wing, relatively untouched, still held to the same position as it had at daybreak.) Nor did Russians allow themselves to be captured. Incredibly, given the size of the two armies and the ferocity of fighting, Napoleon's adjutant counted at day's end a mere eight hundred prisoners. "These Russians let themselves be killed like automatons," the French emperor snapped, "they are not taken alive. This does not help us at all."[7]

What might one call the courage, resilience, and defiance on display at Borodino that have long exasperated opponents and which have made Russians themselves such legendary fighters? The language itself, fittingly, has a single word to sum up these attributes: *stoikost* (stoy'-kust), deriving from the verb "to stand." For Glinka, as he wrote in his memoirs of the battle, this quality united their ranks against unrelenting French blows, and to this day it remains the favored term to describe when a certain fanaticism takes over. Its power allows Russians to absorb casualties that would cause others to flee or compels them to suicidal behavior, like that shown by Alexander Tuchkov, one of twenty-nine Russian generals killed at Borodino.

Tuchkov was at the fleches, where the fighting was worst. When summoned to counterattack, he seized his unit's colors and rushed forward at the head of his men. The charge succeeded, but Tuchkov died, reportedly taking a blast of grapeshot full in the chest. Given the carnage of that day, his feat was, one could assume, not the only of its kind, but in Glinka's view his choice of near-certain death is what made him a "genuine Russian soldier," echoing once more how 1812 imparted to Russian identity a performative aspect. For Glinka, in no uncertain terms, to be an authentic Russian was to behave a certain way when facing the enemy, and death, if we take him at his word, would be the crowning achievement.[8]

Tuchkov's legacy doesn't end there. Two months later his wife, Margarita, came to the battlefield to recover his body (most of the corpses were still unburied). According to one version, she couldn't find it; according to the other, she discovered just his finger—the one, to be sure, bearing his wedding ring. In either case she sold their family possessions to build a chapel amid the fleches, thus consecrating the field of battle, and changed her name to Mary as she took a nun's vows. The chapel came to include a convent, still functioning to this day (after an enforced shutdown during Soviet times), where prayers are said in perpetuity for the "Christ-loving warriors" who "laid down their lives" for their country (and who also include Tuchkov's brother, another general killed that day).

Champions of Romanticism feasted, as it were, on the carnage of Borodino. What better could capture the organic connection between the people and the land than their willingness to sacrifice for it? Where else did Russians prove themselves in such distinctive—if paradoxically terminal—fashion? On the battle's twenty-fifth anniversary, Mikhail Lermontov, in a poem simply titled "Borodino," delivered its signature lines: "we gave our vow to die / and kept that oath / not batting an eye." Karolina Pavlova, in turn, invoked the dead as a positive, regenerative force—almost as if Borodino were the nation's Golgotha. For this is "where the people came to lay their heads," she wrote, and their blood, a "testament of their love" for Russia, planted a "bountiful seed" that would always protect it.[9]

Yet, as with virtually everything concerning 1812, Tolstoy gave the battle its definitive treatment by devoting over twenty chapters to it in *War and Peace*. It serves as the novel's climax and, always the historian, he makes us witness to it from all perspectives. First, the omniscient narrator warns of the errors made in previous accounts and how they have misled popular perceptions. Then extended pre-battle scenes of the commanders, Napoleon and Mikhail Kutuzov, highlight the former's arrogance and the latter's humility, especially before the incalculable and unpredictable factors that war presents. Moving down the ranks, we meet Russian soldiers who are neither

The Spaso-Borodinsky Monastery, Borodino. Actually a convent, it was founded by Margarita Tuchkova, wife of General Alexander Tuchkov, killed in battle there in 1812. It is located amid the earthworks where the heaviest fighting occurred. Author's personal collection.

the automatons who enraged Napoleon nor flat, propagandistic cut-outs. They remain nameless but are brought to life as they quietly and calmly go about their business, which includes donning clean white shirts. What stirs them, bringing tears to the eyes and knees to the ground, is an icon of Mary, paraded down the line as prayers are sung for the "Mother" and "Intercessor"—an event that actually happened with the same reported effect.

The narrator is abetted by two of the main characters, Prince Andrei, an officer, and Pierre, a civilian, whose conversations also prep us for the battle to come. The latter, playing the ingénue, poses the questions readers likely have as well. What decides a battle? What will happen tomorrow? Andrei, the veteran still sour on Russia's shameful defeat at Napoleon's hands less than a decade before at Austerlitz near the Austrian capital, senses a profound change. The war in 1812 is unlike all previous ones. The French have invaded, laying waste to their country; they are marauders and killers, and that, he insists, is why the Russians will prevail. Never has their spirit been so aroused, and that collective force, their combined willpower and determination, is something no cunning plan, tactical trick, or weight of arms can overcome. Unorthodox as usual, Tolstoy almost baits us if we choose to believe Andrei: will the novel's rendition of Borodino be different from what history has told us?

Pierre and Andrei are also our battlefield guides, though again with an ironic twist. With the first, who is unarmed, we are drawn into the thick of fighting; with the second, fully armed, we stand back among the reserves. However, both positions—and this is the point that distinguishes the battle—are for Russians equally perilous. In short, Tolstoy reaffirms Borodino as a special day of death but, in his own way, wraps a new significance around that.

Pierre accidentally finds himself at the center of the line in the Great Redoubt as French shot falls among the Russian cannoneers and bullets whiz through the embrasures. As the dead and wounded accumulate, calm nevertheless pervades the surviving crew members. Joke and light banter abound while they service their guns, and though fear is present among them (since they are human beings), they show no concern for their own safety, only for Pierre's as the out-of-place outsider. Indeed, for every enemy shell that finds its mark, a "hidden fire" flares up in each, binding them together, and the contagion spreads to Pierre, who begins to feel like a part of this "family circle"—of which, at battle's end, he will be the sole survivor.

With Andrei we join the troops massed in reserve behind the entrenchments who were nevertheless under continuous bombardment. By early afternoon, his regiment has lost two hundred men while standing in place. Moved a bit forward, it loses another third of its strength, still without having fired a shot. These soldiers also feel fear, but here little is spoken and faces are pale. Only a little brown dog, appearing out of nowhere and then scampering away, tail between its legs after a near miss, brings a moment of laughter. For eight hours, Andrei's men endure this condition, lethal to many and psychologically tormenting to the survivors. We are allowed to leave the scene only when Andrei is hit in the chest by shrapnel and carried off.

What does Tolstoy show us? For one thing, if in earlier memorializations losses among common soldiers were celebrated in the abstract, now they have been individualized, such as when Pierre, searching for the remnants of his "family," comes across one "twitching" in his death throes. Andrei's wound, in turn, allows for a harrowing visit to the field hospital, with its piles of limbs and grotesque odors. Death, we learn, is not just immediate martyrdom on the battlefield but can stagger on for days as Andrei slowly slips away. Yet at the same time, Tolstoy's realism is neither cynical nor depressing. Quite the opposite—for scenes like these allow him to raise a new standard on how to understand the carnage of that day.

Was Borodino a victory or defeat for the Russian side? In real life, Kutuzov claimed the former in his battle report to Alexander I, but there remained the vexing point that, nevertheless, he did not succeed in stopping Napoleon, and Moscow fell to the French just days later. In this sense, using the standard of that time, it would seem that the battle was lost. However, Tolstoy, ever the patriot but always the contrarian, found his own answer in these very same labels. How one describes a battle need not derive from tactical outcomes measured in short distances or strategic ones measured in long-term gains. In certain circumstances, such as with this battle, the criteria should be different. A demonstration of force against an invading, seemingly invincible foe tells its own story, and how *that* story concluded at Borodino turns the table on conventional wisdom.

If the defending force is decimated yet remains in fighting formation, Tolstoy argues, then it sends a special message about itself, its cause, and the price it is willing to pay. He slowly leads his reader down this path of logic, fully confident that his is the only correct answer. "At the beginning of the battle they [the Russians] merely stood on the road to Moscow in order to block it," he observes, "and at its end they continued to stand in the same way just as they had at the beginning." Knowing that it is difficult not to accept this proposition if boiled down to these essentials, he then adds a conditioning corollary: "the Russians, while remaining in their positions, lost *one half* of their troops." No matter how many fell, no matter the punishment it suffered, the army did not break; when the sun set, it "stood just as threateningly at the end as at the beginning of the battle."

In short, the toll itself, when combined with this steadfastness, sets a new standard. Never had Napoleon's men experienced anything like this, Tolstoy continues. For the French, usually a "tenth of the effort" was sufficient to send their enemies running. The Russians at Borodino proved that maxim wrong; it may apply to others but not to them. Napoleon's army had just inflicted on them the greatest damage *ever* done to one of its opponents, and yet nothing happened. This realization sent a jolt of "terror" through the French ranks, as if to foreshadow that most would never leave Russian soil alive, and gave Tolstoy full rights to declare Borodino a "moral victory" for his countrymen. Ever since, that halo has remained.

One reader who fervently endorsed Tolstoy's conclusion was General Mikhail Dragomirov, two years the writer's junior, who was inspired by *War and Peace* to publish a response that ran over one hundred pages. To be sure, he was deeply taken aback by Tolstoy's criticism of leaders' inflated sense of self-importance on the battlefield—as a career officer how could he not be?—but sang the opposite about the novel's combat scenes. Not only were they extraordinary, to Dragomirov their accuracy pushed them beyond the borders of fiction, making the novel indispensable as a guidebook for both a civilian and military audience. What secured its edifying value, in his view, was that Tolstoy had dropped the Homeric clichés and characters, long dominant in previous retellings of 1812, favoring instead "ordinary people" thrust into a climactic role. On page after page in the novel, we meet these Russians, full of simple virtues and common vices, but joined by a single, elemental impulse that, in Dragomirov's opinion, makes them an exceptional breed of soldier: the willingness "to lay down their heads for their friends."[10]

While the use of John 15:13 was by then, in the late 1860s, already axiomatic, Dragomirov was no ordinary reader or soldier. He was destined to become, for his time, one of Russia's most revered warriors—a reputation he earned as a prolific and widely popular writer on war whose essays, textbooks, and histories enjoyed print runs in the thousands. He also excelled as a commander, particularly in the Russo-Turkish War of 1877–1878, and then as the country's leading military theoretician and instructor during his eleven-year tenure as director of the General Staff Academy. When Dragomirov retired in 1901, it was with one of Russia's highest military awards on his chest, the Order of St. Andrew, pinned on personally by Emperor Nicholas II, under whose great-grandfather he had begun service five decades before.

Dragomirov shared Tolstoy's belief that soldiers' morale or "spirit" plays the decisive role on the battlefield—a conclusion he came to independently of *War and Peace* based on his experience as an official observer during Europe's milder, mid-century conflicts, such as the Austro-Prussian War. There he saw other troops in action, which, along his own field service, helped him pinpoint what it was about the Russians that made them different in battle. Tolstoy's novel, particularly the Borodino scenes, lent dramatic weight to a conviction that later hardened into the jolting first line of Dragomirov's signature essay, "A Note on the Russian Soldier."

"Knowing how to suffer, knowing how to die—that is the basis of a soldier's prowess, of which the Russian soldier possesses a high degree." Dragomirov's introductory declaration is, in a perverse, almost masochistic way, no better summation of what has fascinated and exasperated opponents. For him, the quality of "knowing how" was not a mythic but a real proposition. It derived both from life before the military and from service in it. And together they ensured two things:

that the Russian soldier cannot be duplicated elsewhere and that the coercive, necessary hand of the officer should not be forgotten. (The general was a fierce disciplinarian.)

In Dragomirov's view, what primes the Russian peasant, what constitutes his "racial distinctiveness," are the deplorable conditions in which he enters the world, even after the abolition of serfdom in 1861. From birth, a "Russian lad" is "accustomed to suffer, to look death calmly in the eye." Thus military training only reinforces these initial conditioning factors and hones them to their proper end, that is, the mystical-like power of *stoikost*. Once awakened, this spirit keeps the ranks steady and the soldiers' nerves in check no matter how many might be cut down and no matter where the blow might come from. "For us," thundered one of his favorite axioms, "there is no flank and there can be no rear because the front is always where the enemy is."

Dragomirov had occasion to see his beliefs put to the test, including on himself. Though an American attaché described him as "having the appearance of a German professor," his combat profile was anything but the stereotype of a dour academic. He was the consummate leader, winning his soldiers' respect (despite a fetish for their deaths) by sharing in their lot. During the Russo-Turkish War, his division shined, whether forcing the Danube River against enemy fire or rescuing a contingent of fellow Russians desperately holding a mountain pass against a much larger Turkish force. At that engagement, Dragomirov's entourage came under direct fire. One bullet shattered the general's knee and another mortally wounded his chief of staff. "Yet everyone," the astounded American recounted, remained "as cool as if we were a party of tourists."[11]

If such battlefield demeanor shows that Dragomirov was not an armchair general, the ideas he favored, especially when lined with Christian homilies, take us to the roots of the war myth's obsession with death that others can find unsettling. If he begins "A Note on the Russian Soldier" with John 15:13, he closes with Matthew 10:22 which teaches that "the one who stands firm in the end will be saved." As to how such firmness best manifests itself, on the same page Dragomirov offered a single line. "The Russian dies simply, as if performing a rite."

This is not to say that Dragomirov celebrated long casualty lists, but it helps explain the eerie conclusions one can sometimes encounter. A fellow instructor at the General Staff Academy, for example, proudly compared casualty totals from various wars. Russian soldiers, it would seem, generally got the worst of it, suffering more in aggregate than their European counterparts. *That,* however, was a positive sign, Dragomirov's colleague suggested, because it pointed to the Russian soldier's superiority. More dead, ran his implied logic, meant less retreat, which, in turn, meant more *stoikost* on display on the battlefield.[12]

The late imperial period was also, it will be recalled, when Russia's myth of exceptionalism solidified. One of Dragomirov's successors as director of the academy was General Nikolai Sukhotin, introduced in Chapter 2 as the author of *War in the History of the Russian World.* What the latter championed at the level of nation—the "special nature of Russia's experience of war" being its propensity to sacrifice for others—Dragomirov and others did at the level of soldier. Both propositions reflect how ideas that sprouted in the Age of Romanticism matured into doctrinal pillars at the military's very own brain center. Both mobilized the same past to illustrate their points, but both also explicated those lessons in the present tense, thereby elevating Russianness to its performative axis of self-sacrifice: nation for world; soldier for brother and country.

Yet belief in such a pedigree, perhaps not surprisingly, soon bore bitter fruit. So special was the Russian soldier's temperament and inner strength that many of Dragomirov's kind believed it gave him the power to overcome the rapid rise in the lethality of modern weaponry. The general himself famously brushed off the machine gun as good only for wasting bullets; his preference instead was for the bayonet, following his idol from the eighteenth century, Generalissimus Alexander Suvorov. Undefeated against the Turks and France's revolutionary armies, Suvorov became a legend by favoring cold steel over firepower (and also for aphorisms advising his soldiers, "You yourself die, but save your comrade"). Not everyone at the command level shared Dragomirov's mind-set, but that legacy played itself out with fatal consequences when soldiers trained by him fought the Japanese in the first major war of the twentieth century.

The fighting lasted barely a year and a half, from 1904 to 1905, yet it was such a disaster for Russia that it ended in a revolution at home. Japanese prowess, backed by long-range artillery, automatic weapons, and superior communications and supply, shredded Russian armies fighting in East Asia, while its warships pummeled the Russian fleet. Back home, street fighting broke out in cities, sailors mutinied, and workers went on strike, and there were even plans to call Dragomirov out of retirement to help quell the insurgency that his policies had indirectly helped create. Yet it was not to be. He died by the war's end at home, unlike tens of thousands of countrymen, trained on his manuals, whose bodies were strewn across a distant Manchuria.

The war, addressed in greater detail in Chapter 5, was a harbinger of the industrial slaughter that would stain the twentieth century and with so much of it tearing through Russia itself. Tellingly, however, the unprecedented scale of tragedy to come did not dispel this cult of death. If anything, the staggering losses that befell Russians during this past century kicked it into overdrive, so that to this day its dominance remains as firm as ever.

An Almost Perfect Battle

The enduring power of this cult comes mostly, of course, from World War II, in which death's lead crosses into every genre of remembrance. This was true in Stalin's time, when the preferred official heroes were not vaunted commanders, such as Marshal Zhukov—lest their stars rise too close to the dictator's—but those who could be safely scripted into a martyr's role, the most famous being Zoya Kosmodemyanskaya, a teenage partisan tortured and publicly hanged by her German captors.

During the Thaw, death remained the obligatory template as reflected in four internationally acclaimed war movies from the late

1950s and early 1960s. In *Ballad of a Soldier,* we are informed at the outset that the protagonist does not survive in such a matter-of-fact way as if to underscore that this fate is the defining mark of his generation. In *My Name Is Ivan,* its inescapability is broadened by including the boy in the title, who comes to us already as an orphan, thanks to the German invaders. In *Destiny of a Man,* death takes the hero's wife, two daughters, and a son; and in *The Cranes Are Flying,* it claims the heroine's fiancé, killed at the front, and her mother and father, bombed in their homes—both reinforcing how the war cut like a scythe through the entire population, no matter how far from the front line.

In the 1970s, two of the most popular war movies, *And the Dawns Here Are Quiet* and *They Fought for the Motherland,* continued with annihilation and decimation as their common theme. In the first, an all-female unit of antiaircraft gunners is wiped out as it defeats German paratroopers; whereas in the second, set during the 1942 retreat toward Stalingrad, a regiment is cut down to a small band of soldiers. Another favorite from that decade, *One-Two, Soldiers Were Going,* dramatizes the maxim that only 3 percent of those who were of draft age when the Germans invaded survived the war. It flashes back and forth between grateful family members gathered in the present to honor their fathers and the battle in which all eighteen of the elders lose their lives in perfect symbolic symmetry by destroying eighteen German tanks on March 18, 1944.

Just before glasnost began to brighten the cultural landscape of the Soviet Union in the late 1980s, audiences were stunned by the graphic portrayal of SS troops burning villagers alive in a wooden barn in *Come and See,* a joint Belarussian-Russian production, which takes its title from the horsemen of the apocalypse and its subject from the real mass murder by immolation that befell over six hundred villages in Belarus alone. For the 1990s, as we have seen, the shocker was Viktor Astafev's *The Damned and the Dead,* which appeared alongside other autobiographically based works by frontline veterans that portray their generation as a lost one.

Whether death comes in dramatic, maudlin, or saccharine colors, the rule of thumb in reading Russian literature on World War II or watching its films is to expect it, usually in copious amounts. The sheer amount often proves a stumbling block for outsiders. If Western films on the war tend to be casualty averse—death typically operates as an element of suspense to keep audiences guessing as to who might be killed—then their Russian counterparts are casualty perverse. The twenty-first century, in which the procession of annihilation films has substantially increased, only proves how conventional the approach has become—so much so that it would be ripe for caricature if the subject were not the war. (The body count in gangster movies, for example, has generated its own parodic responses.)

The first in this latest generation, *Star,* appeared in 2002, and it demonstrates both the scenario's utility and why the film was sponsored in part by the state. Made with the director's express intent to instill youth with national pride and simultaneously provide them with role models, it is based on a similarly titled 1947 novella that features a band of scouts on a reconnaissance mission behind enemy lines. In both versions they succeed, but in the original we do not know their fate. The movie supplies the answer, with the scouts trapped in a barn and burned alive as a musical crescendo drowns out their final shots.

Moreover, the film version of *Star* packs a political punch stronger than its Stalin-era predecessor, difficult as that might be to believe. Evoking Pushkin's "To the Slanderers of Russia," yet without the express anger, the final scene features a long column of Red Army ghost soldiers marching right to left so as to reprise a Soviet cinematic staple by mimicking how liberation proceeded on a map from east to west en route to Berlin. As they silently pass before our eyes, a fellow ghost captain informs us that they represent the human price paid to free Eastern Europe from Nazi tyranny.

If Russian fiction revels in annihilation, the war itself has provided no shortage of real-life models, and one, virtually unknown in the

West, stands alone in Russia's war memory: the siege of Brest Fortress in 1941.

The fortress had been built the previous century as a frontier bastion of the Russian Empire to protect against invasion from the west. Located at the convergence of two rivers, one of which now separates Poland from Belarus and Ukraine, Brest dominated the crossroads where central and eastern Europe meet. That location also meant that, when the empire collapsed after the Bolshevik Revolution in 1917 and Poland reemerged as a sovereign country, Brest passed into the latter's hands. On September 1, 1939, the fortress still belonged to Poland. Weeks later, however, as per agreement in the carving up of the country, the victorious German invaders ceremoniously handed Brest over to the victorious Soviet invaders. It was now on Soviet soil, seemingly at peace again, until 1941, when across the river Bug, German forces, still nominally allies, began to gather.

When the attack came on June 22, the entire western border of the Soviet Union, stretching almost one thousand miles from the Baltic to the Black Sea, collapsed. In that calamity, the fate of so many and so much was forever wiped from existence, either ground into dust by panzers or obliterated by Stuka bombers. At only one point, as far as we know, was that outcome reversed: Brest Fortress, perched on the very edge of that border, held out for weeks against overwhelming German forces, handing them their first setback and giving Russia its most famous "moral victory" in the war.

While, by World War II standards, Brest as a fortress was outdated, its impressive walls, casemates, and network of tunnels allowed its garrison of approximately four thousand soldiers, some accompanied by families, to offer a tenacious defense. As a primary target—from its border location runs a direct rail line east to Minsk, the capital of Belarus, and then to Moscow—Brest was supposed to fall in hours, yet it didn't, becoming instead a site of fierce close combat, despite the garrison being cut off from all hope of rescue as the rest of the Red Army evaporated in retreat. Racked with hunger and thirst, Soviet soldiers fought to the death, rejecting numerous offers to surrender. Their last stand came in the underground tunnels, where, amid fetid corpses and the rats growing fat on them, some held on to the third week of July, and legend even suggests that one soldier, on a solitary mission of vengeance, continued the fight all the way to April of 1942.

If Stalin had had his way, Brest would have remained as little recognized in Russia as it is in the West today. Under his rule, the war's first months were usually ignored to avoid uncomfortable questions as to why he was caught off guard by his ally, Hitler, and why the Red Army, the pride of the Soviet Union, collapsed. It was always better to skip to December of 1941, when the Germans were defeated at the gates of Moscow and the first six months of the invasion could be rewritten as Stalin's ingenious plan to lure the enemy deep into Russian territory before springing a trap.

Credit for bringing Brest to national attention goes to Sergei Smirnov, a historian and journalist, whose work on the fortress began to appear in 1956 as the Thaw began. He faced two challenges in producing it. How to find out what happened if so many had perished there or later in prison camps? And how then to make sense of it all—how to turn Brest into a symbolic counterpart to the wholesale disaster that marked the beginning of the war?

Painstakingly, he was able to track down a few of the battle's veterans who had either escaped into the woods of Belarus and joined the partisans or, more incredible still, survived German prison camps. As word got out, others contacted him, and bit by bit he pieced the story together that culminated in his 1965 *Brest Fortress,* a veritable bible of *stoikost* in action as the garrison "took upon itself the enemy's first terrible blow." Outgunned, out-teched, and outnumbered, Red Army soldiers fought like superhumans, sometimes only with bricks and bare hands as they stumbled out of the barracks in the early hours of that Sunday morning, just as dawn began to break. By virtue of surprise, the Germans were first able to seize the center of the fortress complex, a church rededicated by Soviet atheism into an officers' club, but a bayonet charge by the defenders, some still in their underwear, drove the attackers back.

As German plans to take Brest in hours stretched into days, the garrison's tenacity grew. Women and children joined in, either attending to the wounded or, like fourteen-year-old Petya Klipa, maturing instantly into a soldier whose rifle with its fixed bayonet reached above his head. But the fiercer the resistance and the longer it continued, the greater the desperation as hunger and thirst turned into a weapon against them. Who would get the precious water, drawn by the helmet by those few who succeeded in crawling out at night to the rivers? First were the machine guns in order to cool down the barrels made red-hot from incessant firing; then it would go to the wounded, often leaving nothing for the soldiers who fought. Some of them, we are told, drank the blood from their own injuries to keep from collapsing or going mad.

From the accounts of the living, Smirnov crafts a paean to the dead that is the engine driving this four-hundred-page history. Its sequential profiles in courage often end, therefore, on a macabre note:

> Thus perished the garrison of a bunker, next to the fortress. They numbered twenty-three and were commanded by two junior lieutenants, P. Seleznev and N. Zimin, and a sergeant, I. Rekhin. For two entire days the small, reinforced concrete structure stood in the path of the enemy, blocking its attempts to cross the Bug. Only when the Germans brought up flamethrowers and directed their streams of fire into the bunker's embrasures was the course of the struggle decided. The garrison was burned alive.[13]

Defiance to the end also generated a roll call of kamikaze suicides as those wounded or feigning to surrender detonated grenades on themselves when Germans approached. Others, trapped underground and too injured to fight, killed themselves so that water and food would not be wasted on them.

The truth is, however, that Red Army soldiers were not otherworldly and their numbers dwindled as the Germans committed more bombers, tanks, and flamethrowers, and as exhaustion and deprivation took their toll through the long, hot weeks of July. Organized resistance seems to have stopped near the end of that month, but most important of all, the fortress was never surrendered.

Though Smirnov's work was not free of the censor's hand—Poles living near the fortress are described as "true friends of our country"—and though its contents in a few places defy reason, it became the most popular and consequential account of Brest by opening a new chapter in the war, introducing new heroes who had been absent from the (often falsified) Stalinist pantheon, and establishing the template for how the beginning of the war could be remembered: not as a disaster but as a bloody surprise that awakened in the people that special inner force harkening back all the way to the warriors of medieval Rus who martyred themselves in defense of the land.

Smirnov's *Brest Fortress* has retained that seminal status, being one of the few histories from the Soviet period that is serially reprinted, finding its proper place in any political context, since it reprises the core lesson of 1812: in Russia things are different. Just as Borodino taught the French, Brest taught the Germans that "here," in comparison with their successful invasion of earlier opponents, "it was not to be like that." The irony was not lost on Smirnov that the panzer group leader charged with capturing Brest was none other than Heinz Guderian, the very icon of blitzkrieg warfare. The summer before, with him spearheading the charge, France was overrun in little over five weeks; at Brest alone formal resistance lasted almost as long.

Rubbing salt into the wound even more was the fact that this was Guderian's second go at the fortress, since he had led the German forces who took it from the Poles in just days in 1939. In 1941, who, then, got the better of whom? From this rhetorical question, Smirnov can jump easily to the end-of-war laurels. Even if Brest was a defeat in tactical terms since the fortress ultimately fell, its heroic stand offers a "key to the entire war, to its later decisive turn, to our glorious victories in the years from 1943 to 1945, and to what outside of our country has often been called 'the Russian miracle.'"

Courage, a monument that rises nearly one hundred feet at the center of the Brest Fortress Memorial Complex. Beside it burns an eternal flame. Author's personal collection.

Smirnov weaves into this one battle all the threads of Russia's "good" World War II. The first pages introduce us to an innocent victim. On June 21, the rivers' shores are wreathed in lilac and jasmine, "filling the fortress with sweet scents," and on that fateful night it drifts off, like a babe, "into quiet, peaceful sleep." Like any boy in summertime, Petya Klipa's Sunday plans, before their cruel interruption, were simply to go fishing with a friend.

At Brest one already finds the desperate, do-or-die struggle that the war would become; so, too, how it would engulf the entire population, indiscriminately claiming and sometimes directly targeting women and children as its victims; already here is present the hunger that will kill hundreds of thousands in Leningrad, and the heroism that will save Stalingrad. In fact, on this very soil, one can trace the war's story arc: invasion, occupation, and liberation. For the fortress, that third chapter came in July 1944, and when Soviet troops then crossed the Bug in the other direction, they initiated the arc's fourth and final chapter, delivering other nations from the Nazi yoke. "In speaking the word 'Brest,'" observed Smirnov's compatriot, the writer Konstantin Simonov, "somewhere in our memory we also hear the word 'Berlin.'"[14]

What Smirnov delivers is not just Russia's war in microcosm, but also its archetypal battle, following in line with Avraamy Palitsyn's celebrated account of the siege of the Holy Trinity–St. Sergius Monastery during the Time of Troubles. If Russia's fate is to be surrounded by enemies, one might ask again, then what other kind of battle best captures that isolation? What else, pressing the point further, but an assault on a fortress also housing women and children literalizes a "people's war"? And if the defining characteristic of the Russian soldier is never to give up, no matter the odds, then the siege presents the ideal opportunity to follow that through.

Brest delivers on all these notes, which is why it shines in Russia's war memory. It has no claim on the superlatives of being the longest, largest, or most consequential siege—save one. In microcosm, its stature rests on being one of the greatest in what it symbolizes and for having produced the most famous statement epitomizing what it means to be a Russian solider:

am dying	farewell
but will not	Motherland
surrender	
7 / 20–41	

These words were carved onto one of the fortress's stones by a desperate defender, and they were discovered only in the 1950s. Now the stone lies in perpetuity in Moscow, inside the Central Armed Forces Museum. Cold and silent, it is still a living testament to the place where reality and mythic tradition became one.

*   *   *

In Smirnov's wake, others have helped Brest retain its elite status among battles. Boris Vasilev, a fellow writer and veteran, though like Smirnov not of the fortress, fleshed out the last man legend in his 1974 novel *His Name Was Not Listed.* It had to be fiction because no records exist to verify what would be, if true, the supreme account of *stoikost* in Russian history. According to the legend, for ten months a Red Army soldier survived in the tunnels and carried out a one-man war against the Germans, picking them off when the opportunity arose. By April of 1942, however, he was nearly blind from living in the darkness belowground and was brought to the surface by a Jew, sent down into the tunnels under threat of death to bring him out. Upon coming to the surface, the last defender collapsed and died, and the Jew later perished in the Holocaust—yet not before ostensibly passing this story on to another who survived and made it known after the war.

Vasilev's novel picks up from there. It begins just before June 22, when Nikolai Pluzhnikov, a naive lieutenant, is posted to the fortress. Patterns of innocence abound here as well, though not without jabs at the false impressions of security fostered on the population by Stalinist propaganda. The surprise attack is Nikolai's baptism of fire, after which he hardens into a seasoned soldier. The novel plunges us into the savagery of the fighting, inspires us with the defenders' heroism, but also surprises us with the kinds of things the Soviet canon tended to avoid. Within the Red Army, for example, lurk cowards and deserters, and Vasilev, no stooge for officialdom, jolts us with unexpected and atypical realism, such as when a blast from a German flamethrower fully engulfs an elderly woman trapped underground, after which we are treated to the image of rats gnawing on her charred bones. A parallel plot of Nikolai falling in love with a young Jewish woman falls into romantic kitsch but then escapes it when she is killed by the Germans in a visceral scene of her skull being repeatedly smashed by a rifle butt.

With Nikolai alone, Vasilev recasts his protagonist as a one-man killing machine, hunting unsuspecting members of the German garrison. As his eyesight begins to fail and his end approaches, his name and identity are downplayed in favor of the function he fulfills. Both the narrator and the protagonist feed the reader a steady diet of expressions such as "die, but don't give up"; "defeat death with death"; "you can't conquer a real man even if you kill him."

When Nikolai is finally brought before the German troops, he fulfills this charge. They demand his name and rank, to which he provides only one answer before falling dead: "I am a Russian soldier." Like Smirnov, Vasilev's novel has been serially reprinted for twenty-first-century readers, and Vladimir Putin has included *His Name Was Not Listed* in his top-ten list of books foreigners should read to understand the Russian side of the war (an assignment that can be completed, since it has been translated into English).[15]

Cinema has done its job as well. Since the Thaw, three movies have been made of Brest, not counting documentaries. Released in 2010, the latest, *Brest Fortress,* takes both the title of Smirnov's history and his real-life roster of heroes for its cast, thereby assuming a mantle of historical accuracy but with sufficient license for present-day messaging. Pre-attack profiles in innocence introduce us to the names and faces of those who must die, which makes us compliant witnesses to their martyrdom, whether by suicide to avoid capture or by jumping on a grenade to save a child, executed against a wall, or immolated by flamethrower tanks that crawl through the ruins like beasts of the apocalypse. Blood seeps into bricks, which in turn hemorrhage, effecting the cinematic equivalent of a trope favored by the bards of 1812. Not only is the land anthropomorphized, it gains life through the very death of its people.

The cast's one survivor is a Petya-like boy, caught fishing when the first bombs fall. His role is to be our guide through the fighting, since all others follow through on their "vow to die." In the final scene, seven decades later, Petya returns to the fortress with his own grandson, who wears the uniform of a military cadet of the Russian Federation, to stand before its eternal flame. The ghosts of the fallen come back to assume their preinvasion lives—dancing, playing, strolling arm in arm—as if to remind a Russian audience that, if they can do the same today, it is only because their elders laid down their lives. Without them, there would be no Russia, thereby obligating every subsequent generation, as a ritual of self-affirmation, to pay homage, just like newlyweds at the Tomb of the Unknown Soldier.

As this scene demonstrates, that ritual can be honored inside the actual walls of the fortress. It has been preserved in its ruinous state, as a unique totem of the war, garrisoned by two huge, Soviet-era monuments. The first, Courage, is a soldier's stone face, forever frozen in a never-surrender stare, that glowers down on all who enter; the second, Thirst, depicts a prostrate soldier, helmet in hand, thrusting his arm out in a final lunge to reach the river but, as it would be, falling short. At that time, Brest was also awarded the title "Hero Fortress," putting it in the same class as the twelve "Hero Cities" such as Moscow, Leningrad, Kiev, and Minsk—all sites of defiant resistance. Large marble blocks hold soil from each of the brethren cities and have turned Brest into a shrine for the entire war effort. Following the breakup of the USSR—the accord formally dissolving it was signed in a nearby forest—a more traditional frame of memory was added. The officer's club was restored and rededicated as the Victory Church, which, similar to Borodino, consecrates the land on which the fortress rests as well as its scarred bricks and collapsed tunnels that still hold the bones of many. In 2011 another statue was raised, smaller than the Soviet gargantuans but broader in scope, since it honors not only the soldiers who fell but the women and children who, alongside, did as well.

Visiting the fortress's remains reifies how its stamp on Russian history culminates, in a sense, with its own death. That it is now located in Belarus does not dispel that notion since, culturally speaking, Brest Fortress has always operated as Russian space. Born as a project of the Russian Empire, Russian was the garrison's language and the flag under which they served. Smirnov wrote of Brest as an "old Russian fortress," even though its defenders included other nationalities of the Soviet Union. Today at the Memorial Complex, as it is formally known, Russian is the language of remembrance, and in literature and cinema it is presented as a Russian saga—which is why all three presidents of the Russian Federation have made official state visits, following the practice of Soviet leaders.

However one encounters Brest—in a text, on-screen, or on-site along with the thousands who visit each year—its story resists the revisionist pull that casts a shadow on so much of World War II in Russia. No intimation of dying in vain or of wasted lives attends its legacy—something that cannot be said about Leningrad's, a siege of unparalleled proportion. While that city never surrendered and still stands unrivaled as a demonstration of collective *stoikost* for civilian, soldier, and sailor alike, even within that halo a question tugs on the chords of triumph. Did so many have to die? Did the siege have to come to this? What combination of arrogance, ignorance, and straightforward foolishness on the part of the Soviet command allowed the Germans to penetrate so far, or failed to evacuate the population in time, or failed to prepare properly in order to prevent the starvation that killed hundreds of thousands over nearly three years.

Why does the shadow of revisionism pass Brest when, after all, its loss was due to the greatest folly of all: Stalin's inability or unwillingness to heed the ominous signs and warnings of Germany's impending invasion? One factor, no doubt, is the double victimization of those who served and died there. Buried in official silence for over a decade, their ordeal was virtually erased in order to uphold a dictator's pretensions of infallibility.

Something, too, attends the fact that these soldiers have come to represent the war's first-day fallen, the first among millions who would lay down their lives on the path to victory. This distinction wraps their sacrifice in a special light—something that can be observed as well in how America honors the dead at Pearl Harbor. As a national point of pilgrimage for thousands, the naval base likewise provides visitors with the war's complete story arc, from its beginning with the memorial to the sunken *Arizona* to its end with the battleship *U.S.S. Missouri,* on which Japan formally surrendered, berthed alongside.

Battles defined by unusual circumstances, especially when marked by a great loss of life, have a way of gaining a permanent foothold in a nation's collective consciousness. France has its Camarón, when in 1863 a company of Foreign Legionnaires was wiped out in Mexico, which still lives on as the legion's most honored day. Next to Pearl Harbor, America remembers the Alamo in similar fashion. What was first a battle for Texas independence now stands as the symbol of American resilience. Its message, die but never give up, was given official imprimatur on its centennial in 1936 when President Franklin Roosevelt pronounced that the fallen there "became deathless in their dying."[16]

The template for immortalization extends back to the Classical Age, when at Thermopylae in 480 BC King Leonidas and three hundred Spartans fell fighting thousands of Persians. No greater testament to death as a soldier's dutiful end has been written than Simonides's epitaph inscribed on the memorial there:

> Go tell the Spartans, passerby,
> That here, obedient to their laws, we lie.

Brest follows this Western tradition, but it does so while also operating as a model of Russia itself, which is why I highlight it here instead of more famous and strategically significant battles from World War II. An isolated fortress under siege by a foreign invader, able to rely only on itself, never surrendering and thus unconquerable even in death—that is why the story of Brest ranks so high in the must-tell, must-remember category now and for generations to come.

The March to Golgotha

Yet even from the lofty perch of Brest, one cannot escape the harsh reality of the physical sacrifice on which Russia's myth of exceptionalism is built: the colossal body counts that mark so many of its battles and, almost as a matter of course, so many of its wars. If the ritualized

Kholm Gate, entrance to the citadel of Brest Fortress, deliberately unrestored following the German attack in 1941. Author's personal collection.

memory of episodes like Brest seeks to cushion these losses by investing them with purpose and distinction, each enactment can push one closer, consciously or not, to consider another exceptionalism, albeit of a grisly kind. If the potential for death by enemy hands is the common denominator that all war stories share, then two modifications are needed to properly russify it. Expectation should replace potential, and enemy causation should be deemed optional. The result is a default story of the Russian soldier where he must die.

The reality underwriting *this* story begins even before sighting the enemy. Whatever peasants did on the battlefield to earn themselves legendary status, many never made it that far. While serving in the Crimean War, Lev Tolstoy set aside part of his diary to record the "facts," as he titled them, of daily observances. For one day in 1855, it was the simple point that a certain rifle unit numbering 186 men set out from St. Petersburg on January 4 and arrived in Crimea on June 16. Only ninety-two were still in it.

Tolstoy jotted this down without commentary, as if a more than 50 percent prebattle attrition rate was less important than his gambling losses, over which he expended barrels of ink. In truth, he was not this callous; rather, such wastage was commonplace in the Russian army. One reason was the environment itself. Conscripts often had to march long distances—sometimes in chains—from village to camp and then to the border or beyond, often in punishing weather. Eastern Europe also hit hard any army dependent on foraging, since its low population densities meant that food supplies were often precariously low as compared with other areas of the continent.

Yet another reason—and one that raised Tolstoy's ire—was how common soldiers were treated with such contempt by officers who were relentlessly violent toward them. However romanticized Russian infantry are in legend and lore, it cannot be forgotten how pitiful their lot was. They were nothing more than serfs in uniforms or, for Tolstoy, "slaves."[17] If America could speak of its draftees as "G.I.'s," government-issued, then the proper term for Russian soldiers would be "G.O." or government-owned. Indeed, for a brief period under Peter the Great their status as property was conferred by branding conscripts with a cross. Though meant as a deterrent against desertion, it was also a stark reminder of how death and service were deemed inseparable.

On the battlefield, prevailing attitudes proved equally fatal. Throughout World War I, for example, thousands upon thousands of Russian soldiers were sent into battle without rifles or were deliberately shelled by their own when, in their trenches, they were understandably reluctant to go over the top. Worse practices came in World War II, abetted by communists' willingness before the war to chew through millions of lives in pursuit of its social experiments. One frontline veteran, Vladimir But, called this a "knacker mentality" in his quasi-autobiographical novel *The Grass of '43*, published in 1996, right after Viktor Astafev delivered a similar punch with *The Dead and the Damned.*

Set during the Soviet attempt to retake Crimea by amphibious assault, But's title, suggesting grass mown down by a scythe, already portends the bloody disaster that will follow. Officers do not lead but "drive" starving, ill-equipped, and untrained men like stock animals into fruitless yet suicidal frontal attacks. Those fortunate to survive discover in their own rear an equally deadly foe: blocking detachments made up of Soviet soldiers with superior weaponry prepared to shoot anyone who retreats. Caught between a Scylla and Charybdis, the conscripts' lives are worth no more than "shit," as one commander declares. Why, indeed, another general points out, should any of them even care about the number of soldiers lost? After all, "Russian women are fertile like cats; they can give birth to more."[18]

At a certain level, even the cult of *stoikost* can be called to account for the dark realities myth seeks to cover. If honored in the abstract like the values of courage and valor, then presumably no harm is done. However, if exalted to the point where it becomes a license to ignore facts on the ground, then it can take a lethal turn. Such would be the case with one of its most impassioned believers, General Dragomirov, who always favored the Russian soldier's assumed mystical powers over the rifle he carried and the armaments he faced. While Dragomirov does not bear full responsibility for the carnage of the Russo-Japanese War, his impact as a tactician and policy maker was enough to stir protest when it ended and when dissent could be voiced.

One who assailed the "unshakeable rule" of the general's principles was a distraught veteran and regimental commander, Evgeny Martynov. How could it be, he asked, when Japan and all other Western powers rushed to maximize the firepower offered by successive renovations in weapon design, that "Russia alone" would effectively have little of it? Who could follow a general (by now deceased) who dismissed those favoring magazine-fed rifles as "fire-worshippers" or cannon crews seeking gun shields as "shield-worshippers"? Dragomirov had frowned on anything that might inhibit the reigning ethos of self-sacrifice—even such rudiments as entrenching or keeping one's head down. Any unit obeying the edict "not to lie down," Martynov concluded with sobering humor, found out "very quickly that all had laid down but only for the reason of never getting up again."[19]

Death looms so large in the Russian experience of battle that speculation invariably leads from doctrines and conditions of service to an essentialized quality of the people themselves. As a rule of thumb, here too the divergence splits along an outside-inside axis. If one cannot ignore the body counts—"reports from all fronts," the German chief of staff, Franz Halder, underscored in his diary just a week into the German invasion of 1941, "confirm previous indications that the Russians are fighting to the last man"—then, for those so inclined to ruminate on national character, what does this suggest?[20] Is the ability to absorb normally devastating casualties without breaking further proof of some innate Russian barbarism, of a fundamentally non-European nature? Or does that toughness stem from something more spiritual in which death transforms itself into stoic martyrdom?

The most fervent opinions arguing the former come from German veterans of the Eastern Front. In his best-selling memoirs from the 1950s, *Panzer Battles,* General F. W. Mellenthin concluded that a fault line should be drawn here as well.

> A feature of the Russian soldier is his utter contempt for life or death, so incomprehensible to a Westerner. The Russian is completely unmoved when he steps over the dead bodies of hundreds of his comrades, with the same unconcern he buries his dead compatriots, and with no less indifference he faces his own death. For him life holds no special value; it is something easy to throw away.

Given that the German side of the war was officially as much about race as anything else, from this it is but a simple step, as other veterans observed, that the Russian is a "primitive man," possessed of an "animal-like instinct" and unable "to think independently."

This chain of thought inevitably goes further. No matter if the troops the Wehrmacht faced were also, inter alia, Ukrainian, Armenian, Kalmyk, or Azeri, the essential mark of being "Russian" was "cruelty bordering on bestiality." Inevitably as well, what put this "stamp on the Russian national character" leads back to "the infusion of Mongol blood."[21]

Notably, these impressions echo with outsiders who have not been Russia's enemies. The Russo-Japanese War was the first in which foreign journalists covered Russia's side in appreciable depth, and they too were struck by the Russian soldier's apparently emotionless disposition. In describing it, they also preferred the analogy of a herd mentality but with the twist of turning that into a positive battlefield trait. "The Russian private," observed one British war correspondent, "seemed to me to afford the finest fighting material conceivable. In the first place, he is indifferent to death; in the second place, he will fight as long as he is told to do so; thirdly, he will endure any amount of hardships and privations good naturedly and without complaining."[22] And thirty years before that, the American attaché who rode with General Dragomirov in the Russo-Turkish War in 1877 stood in equal awe before the soldiers he met.

> But these same qualities, which are so different from those of our own quick-witted volunteers, have their good side. The Russian soldier's patience is boundless; his endurance, his good humor under hardship, his capacity for fighting on an empty stomach and under difficulties, are beyond all praise, and will enable a general who appreciates these qualities to work wonders with them; and he is probably the steadiest of all soldiers under defeat and adversity. Deprived of their officers, a body of Russian soldiers may degenerate into a helpless, inert mass, and be slaughtered by means of their very cohesiveness, but they will never take a panic.[23]

The Russian side generally prefers religion, not race, in order to conceptualize this special quality. The neo-Christian epics from World

War II that embrace death, as described in Chapter 3, are really the tip of a cultural iceberg that drifts across centuries and across ideologies. This includes Soviet atheism, which Boris Vasilev's *His Name Was Not Listed* avidly illustrates. As his final days come, Nikolai, the novel's last-stand protagonist, is dressed more and more in Christlike robes. He lingers over the idea that death can be defeated with death, and when he is finally led out of the tunnels of Brest, he falls prostrate on the ground with his arms out, as if crucified. As if to ensure that the atheist reader does not miss the point, Vasilev writes that Nikolai now "was above glory, above life and above death" and, as if on cue, the Roman centurion said to have converted at the Crucifixion reappears here as a German lieutenant who spontaneously salutes Nikolai as he expires.

Vasilev, himself a member of the Communist Party when he wrote *His Name Was Not Listed,* pushes his point further with a sly numerological puzzle that no censor seems to have caught. When Nikolai learns, moments before dying, that the date is April 12, he smiles to himself and says, "off by seven days." In what sense he is "off" is never clarified and cannot be unless one puts down the novel and consults a real calendar from 1942. According to the Julian calendar that the Orthodox Church follows, Easter fell on March 23. However, according to the Gregorian calendar, which the Red Army and Nikolai, as an officer, would have followed, the date of Christ's rebirth was April 5.

Vasilev's twists may strike us as a game, and in a sense they are, as is often the case in censored societies. But the novel points to something quintessentially "Russian" if we are talking about its cultural gloss on war: a claim on victory irrespective of battlefield success and attainable by death alone. A search for where the roots of this tradition might lie also takes us back to the Middle Ages, though not in pursuit of a "Mongol infusion." Death, to be sure, is the guiding light, but this time it was murder.

Princes Boris and Gleb were the sons of Vladimir, Grand Prince of Kiev, known both for the political feat of ruling over a powerful, unified Rus that stretched across present-day Ukraine, Belarus, and western Russia, and for the religious one of converting his kingdom to Christianity in 988. His brood matched those achievements, as he had at least nine other sons, born to several wives dating from his pre-conversion polygamy and enormous concubine. (The number of recorded daughters was roughly the same.) However, that size did not bode well when it came to political spoils. Upon Vladimir's death in 1015, one son, Sviatopolk, sent assassins against his younger siblings, Boris and Gleb. They succeeded in their mission, but Sviatopolk himself then lost in battle to yet another brother, Yaroslav. Restoring unity to the realm, Yaroslav departed life by natural causes decades later.

There is nothing in this story to distinguish it from countless others across the medieval world; indeed, the way Boris and Gleb were dispatched by their half brother was almost banal for its time. Yet such is not the case of what was made of them posthumously. Already during Yaroslav's reign they were canonized as Russian Orthodoxy's first native-born saints. Why, according to the hagiographies written about them, did they deserve sanctification? Were they models of Christian piety? Perhaps, but they were not killed for their faith, the truest and traditional path to canonization. Instead, they earned sainthood by choosing to die when, as the sources present it, they were informed ahead of time of Sviatopolk's nefarious plans. Neither victim ran or resisted when the assassins descended, but instead met death willfully like "lambs." Lest the newly converted Orthodox community miss connecting that feat with Christ's, Boris, while awaiting his fate, reportedly delivers the following prayer: "O Lord Jesus Christ, Who in this image didst appear upon earth, having by Thy will chosen to be nailed to the cross, accepting Thy passion for the sake of our sins, make me worthy of accepting my passion."[24]

The canonization of Boris and Gleb marks an early yet transformative step in Russia's acceptance of Christianity. It essentially russified Christ's mission by bringing the example of his triumph onto its soil through the bodies of two of its own. (The chronicle version speaks of "the land blessed" by their blood.) Even more importantly, however, they turned that mission into an explicitly military one. If the Prince

Saints Boris and Gleb. Russian icon from the fourteenth century. Russian State Museum, St. Petersburg, Russia / Bridgeman Images.

of Peace died for human sin, the brothers died to preserve Russia it-self. For after canonization, they returned on icons in full military gear as heavenly warriors with their purpose now reversed to active resistance.

According to the chronicles, contemporaries had visions of Saints Boris and Gleb before decisive victories, such as Alexander Nevsky's defeat of the Swedes or Dmitry Donskoy's rout of the Mongols. In so doing, much as Mary functions at the highest level as both the Mother of God and Protector of Russia, they also bridge two normally exclu-sive realms, divine grace and divine violence. But they do it as Rus-sians for Russia and achieved that unprecedented status solely by their willingness to sacrifice themselves. And in their veneration one can already see the premodern convergence of three trajectories that would later form the bedrock of Russia's war myth: military force op-erating under the banner of innocence; defense of the land reinforced as a sacred duty; and the inescapability of death as its outcome.

Caution, to be sure, should always be on hand when linking the modern-day with medieval antecedents, but Boris and Gleb help rein-force that the reason why death operates at the myth's center is both historical and cultural. If the repeated traumas caused by war are a defining feature of Russia's historical experience, so too is its devotion to Christianity and the Orthodox emphasis on the suffering Christ. When combined, they can make for head-turning pronouncements, such as the one that opens the handsomely illustrated, deluxe 2008 volume, *Icons of Holy Warriors,* sponsored by the Office of the Patriarch.

> The warrior's path is one of the most glorious enterprises from the point of view of Christian teachings. And glory here is not understood as fame, outstanding victories, or rank and medals, but as the opportunity to achieve *the* feat of a Christian's life since "there is no greater love than that to lay down one's life for one's friends." Therefore military service is the most Christian of

professions for it provides the opportunity to demonstrate the highest love to one's neighbor.[25]

However much the roots of this sentiment echo the eleventh century, it has proven indispensable, as will be seen, in delivering a past in which Russians can take pride—especially when that past includes wars whose outcomes fall short of the bar set by 1812 or 1945.

5

Defeat Undone

No conflict has vexed Russia's self-image more than the Soviet-Afghan War. The quandary only begins with the fact that it ended in 1989 in a defeat that helped bring down the Soviet Union. Equally problematic is that it took place outside of the imagined space of the motherland and, worse still, violated inherited tradition. Soviet Russia was the unqualified aggressor, invading a neighbor torn by a civil war, and the conduct of its troops was often abominable. "You soon realize," a veteran explained, "that what you find really objectionable is shooting someone point blank. Killing en masse, in a group, is exciting, even—and I've seen this myself—fun."[1]

Such sadistic undercurrents were supposed to define Russia's opponents; now the near-genocidal practices of Soviet invaders pointed to the darkest of precedents. "I couldn't see any difference between myself and a Nazi," another admitted. "It's the same thing: rolled-up sleeves, submachine guns, cries, villages."[2] If all wars abound with atrocity, this was one of a singular kind for Soviet Russia and helped earn it, before the fighting ended, the unshakeable tag as an "empire of evil."

Equally agonizing is how the frightful mess began. Exactly why Soviet leaders—a mere handful in a secret meeting—chose to invade Afghanistan in 1979 is still unclear. Assumed reasons run from the desire to shore up a socialist ally in that country's civil war to concern over the ripple effect of Islamic revolution in neighboring Iran. What is not a mystery is that they lied about it. Kremlin documents published after the breakup of the Soviet Union include the actual blueprint of how the war was to be scripted for public consumption and shines with gems of mendacity. The country itself, reads one diktat, "does not have any connection to the changes in leadership in Afghanistan"— except that Soviet commandoes killed its president in a coup that spearheaded the invasion. Another falsehood, thought up by someone oblivious to the irony, insisted that the sole purpose of sending the Red Army was to protect the Afghan people in their "struggle against foreign aggression."[3]

An arsenal of lies accompanied the troops into battle as well. In the war's first years, there was little fighting, at least according to the Soviet press; instead, troops stationed there were helping their Afghan "friends" by building schools and hospitals. Only midway through it, when Mikhail Gorbachev became the leader of the Soviet Union in 1985 and then instituted the policy of glasnost, did the veil begin to lift. A new generation of journalists, slowly breaking free from the state's monopoly on expression, started to raise questions, and veterans' voices, such as those cited above, gained public attention.

Privately in the Kremlin, the same doubts were being expressed by Gorbachev himself, who declared in a secret meeting that the war was like a cancerous wound. After their opponent, the Mujahideen, acquired shoulder-fired missiles capable of knocking down Soviet jets and helicopter gunships, the conflict was deemed unwinnable and plans for withdrawal were made. That process was completed in early 1989, and by the year's end the legislative body, the Congress of People's Deputies, ruled that the decision to invade had violated the constitution. However, none of the gang of four involved in it—Party Secretary Leonid Brezhnev and the heads of the Foreign Ministry, Defense Ministry, and KGB—was prosecuted since they were already dead, leaving as their collective legacy over a million Afghans killed and, by official count, nearly fifteen thousand Soviet soldiers.

At that time, as the Soviet Union itself began to implode at the beginning of the 1990s, chilling revelations became the war's primary face, not just in journalism but in fiction and film as well. A veteran's novel, like Oleg Ermakov's *Sign of the Beast,* fed the image of an army broken by self-inflicted blows as much as from the Mujahideen; whereas the movie *Afghan Fracture* painted it as an immoral predator—so much so that at the end the protagonist, an officer, lets himself be killed by an Afghan boy as if to atone for the sins committed by all Soviets there. Nevertheless, journalists still led the pack, and none more so than Svetlana Alexievich, whose 1990 oral history *Zinky Boys* helped win her the Nobel Prize for Literature in 2015.

With a minimalist's touch, she lets the soldiers speak for themselves. They appear both as the war's villains—one gloats over having shot up an Afghan wedding party and dispatching the "happy couple"—and as its victims. "The lead vehicle in our column broke down going through a village," another reported. "The driver got out and lifted the hood, and a boy, about ten years old, rushed out and stabbed him in the heart. . . . We turned that boy into a sieve."[4] Alexievich's work showcases a war in which, absent a concrete mission, atrocity became policy on both sides, forming an endless cycle of terror. The Mujahideen excelled at beheading, castrating, blinding, and flaying prisoners alive, the Soviet military at flattening villages and sowing countless mines, many disguised as toys and other knickknacks so as to attract children's attention.

Appalling, too, were the conditions of service, which remind us of the worst the Red Army soldiers experienced in World War II. Abused by superiors, subjected to abject medical conditions, humiliated by brutal internal hazing, wasted by typhus, forced to steal clothes from the dead, driven desperate from hunger while being issued canned rations dating from the 1950s stamped "eat within 18 months"—this is what the common soldier faced off the battlefield. The only relief was drug use, which crippled the army and exacerbated the very circumstances that caused its decline in the first place.

Zinky Boys goes further by detailing how the war's destructive impact hit home as well. The accounts by anguished family members push its physical and psychological toll even higher. Post-traumatic stress disorder became rampant; anger at the government went unrelieved, first for sending soldiers there and then, to compound the betrayal, neglecting them when they came back.

Betrayal extended even to those killed and their families. Death itself, in the words of one, was subject to a "conspiracy of silence" propagated by the state. A body would be placed in a zinc-lined coffin so as to slow its decay and thereby generating the ghoulish nickname given to Soviet soldiers and resurfacing again as Alexievich's title. Shipped back to the Soviet Union secretly, sometimes at night, the coffin would arrive at an airport without any ceremony. From there it would be delivered directly to the family's home—often with no forewarning. After relaying one mother's account of meeting her son in such fashion while she was coming down the stairs in the morning, Alexievich gives us a string of others desperately trying to understand the frigid heartlessness of this policy.

> "It wasn't like that for me. They [the soldiers who brought it] just said: 'The coffin's outside. Where shall we put it?' My husband and I were getting ready to go to work, the eggs were frying, the kettle was boiling. . . ."
>
> "Mine was called up, had his hair shaved off, and five months later they brought him back in a coffin."
>
> "Mine too. . . ."
>
> "Mine—nine months."
>
> " 'Is there anything in there?' I asked the soldier accompanying the coffin. 'I saw him being laid in the coffin. He is there.' I stared at him and he lowered his eyes. 'Something's in there. . . .' "
>
> "Did it smell? Ours did."
>
> "So did ours. We even had little white worms dropping on to the floor."[5]

Coffins could not be opened, depriving families of the all-important ritual of washing the body and visually parting with the deceased. Thus many could still believe that, no, it could not be their son. (In one way, though, perhaps this was for the better. If not enough of a soldier's body was recoverable, then dirt was added to give the coffin proper heft and offer the impression of a loved one peacefully intact.) As a final insult, dead soldiers were not buried with military honors and were not grouped together in cemeteries so as to hide their true number. (Many, in fact, believe the official figure to be woefully low, estimating that it should be around fifty thousand—closer to the mark of the Vietnam War for Americans.) And on the headstone itself, only dates of birth and death were indicated, thereby erasing the cause and place of death.

A War Turned Upside Down

Often seen by contemporaries as Russia's Vietnam, the legacy of the Soviet-Afghan War would seem destined for the same black hole in national remembrance. The scripts for each read more or less alike: a superpower invades a Third World country already embroiled in civil war; drunk on the arrogance of its assumed infallibility, yet hobbled by its profound ignorance of the region, the invader's only advantage is overwhelming firepower in a conflict not winnable by conventional military means. Wholesale slaughter ensues; My Lai moments abound. The result is quagmire, a broken army and a broken nation back home. Vietnam and Afghanistan would become the graveyards of superpower exceptionalism, their worst defeats in living memory.

Neither Russia nor America can fully escape this shadow, yet in the former, at least, popular culture has laid a path that, if one diligently follows its twists and turns, can make the unthinkable acceptable and even stand history on its head.

Upon its release in 2005, the blockbuster *Ninth Company* became a landmark among Russian war movies. Hailed by some as a masterpiece, for others it signaled a "renaissance of Russian cinema" following the previous decade's plunge in production quantity and quality. Meteoric ticket sales made *Ninth Company,* for its time, the highest-grossing domestic movie in Russia and, bolstered by numerous awards, it also charmed the political elite during a private screening for President Vladimir Putin and the minister of defense with the cast and director in attendance.[6]

In Russia no other war film made since has eclipsed its impact. That achievement is all the more astounding, given that *Ninth Company* was the director's feature-film debut. Before making it, Fyodor Bondarchuk had dabbled in music video clips and television production—nothing that would foretell such success. What made him stand out in the cinematic world, however, was his family name. He is the son of Sergei Bondarchuk, whose own pedigree in war movies was secured by directing and starring in the 1966–1967 adaptation of *War and Peace,* which won the Academy Award for Best Foreign Film, and in the 1975 World War II classic *They Fought for the Motherland.*

The story Fyodor Bondarchuk tells to gain his own laurels is straightforward. Five inductees volunteer to serve in Afghanistan. Each represents a different persona and background: a reflective artist, a street-smart tough guy, a family man and new father, a timid sentimentalist, and a seen-it-all, done-it-all type who grew up in an orphan house. Distances between them dissolve during harsh training, with each scene structured around a bonding moment, whether marked by pain, laughter, alcohol, or sex. This pattern continues when they are deployed as replacements to a squad of older veterans led by Fyodor Bondarchuk himself, playing the father figure. The five bond with the larger unit as the action toggles back and forth between combat and rest, until the unit is sent to protect a convoy and is wiped out on a hilltop. Out of them all, only the orphan survives. The claim is made that the story is based on real events.

Ninth Company baits us with hints of an antiwar tenor, as if echoing its predecessor, *Afghan Fracture.* It is, after all, Afghanistan, and at an orientation in a dark, foreboding hangar just before the five depart, they (and we) are informed that ever since Alexander the Great, all who have invaded have suffered defeat. Pointing in that direction as well are nods to defective equipment, insufficient supplies, hunger, command incompetence (the unit is forgotten on the hilltop), and the sheer waste of fighting there. Not only does the convoy never materialize, but the war itself is ending, the dazed sole survivor learns from his helicopter rescuers.

Even more explicitly, *Ninth Company* reproduces a host of motifs from iconic antiwar Vietnam movies such as *Apocalypse Now, Platoon,* and *Full Metal Jacket.* Bondarchuk has acknowledged his debt to them, and thus we have in Russian garb the sadistic drill sergeant, the fiery village destruction scene, the child killer being killed, and the plot's division into training here and deployment there. However, these parts in no way equal the sum, for Bondarchuk pulls off the unimaginable: making a feel-good movie about a manifestly horrific war.

In some theaters, Russian audiences cheered when the credits rolled, and such a wild response surprised many Western reviewers who could see in *Ninth Company* little more than a knockoff action piece—"a middlebrow slog," as per the British press, or, from an American academic, "as unrealistic as anything from the Stalin era."[7] The gulf between domestic and foreign reception (allowing for dissenters in both camps) almost suggests that two different movies were being viewed. And, in a sense, such was the case if we are talking about audience expectations. To critics, *Ninth Company* trivialized a conflict ultimately defined by its criminal and genocidal aspects; no one, in short, would ever dream of making such a movie about the American experience in Vietnam.

In contrast, its supporters saw a movie cast with popular young actors buttressed by cameos from established stars. Set to a hypnotic yet appealing elegiac score, *Ninth Company* dazzles with landscape shots and features the kind of combat camera work made famous by Steven Spielberg in *Saving Private Ryan.* It also offers another variation of the now universal "band of brothers" theme (just as the director's father had done before in *They Fought for the Motherland*). And by not demonizing the Afghans—indeed, their culture is referenced with respect—*Ninth Company* is a welcome respite from the racist and condescending tones often generated in movies depicting imperialist ventures into the Third World.

But beneath all this lies the core of *Ninth Company:* it is myth by the numbers, cued especially to those hard-wired on Russian narratives of World War II. The final scene reprises one of its most famous tropes, fighting and dying "on a nameless height," and the surrounded-besieged-outnumbered defenders are, of course, its most enduring characters. The aura of death hovers over the entire movie, even in training camp, and a distinct Russian-ness is underscored by the minimal inclusion of Soviet symbols and rhetoric. More than anything, however, that spirit is trumpeted in the final lines when the survivor declares that no matter what happened in the war, "we"—that is, he and his dead comrades—"were victorious."

Bondarchuk also defuses gestures to Vietnam War movies. Poor equipment becomes a point of humor, and the sadistic drill sergeant turns out to have a warm heart. The actual killing of an Afghan boy, no matter how jolting, is justified, since he has just shot the first of the five, the new father Stas, in the back. The same village, where the Mujahideen have hidden, is obliterated by rockets, but we only see buildings, not people, explode in brilliant, beautiful fireballs. The camera then centers on Stas in the foreground, as he expires in the hands of his weeping friends, Pietà-like, while music sweeps in to drown out the exploding rockets.

Bondarchuk even dares to single out one of the more barbarous practices of the war: the indiscriminate use of mines targeted at Afghan civilians and combatants alike. Featured here is the PFM-1 mine or "Green Parrot," a particularly nasty, small plastic explosive, tossed from planes and helicopters like confetti, that armed itself upon hitting the ground. Similar to the blue Dragontooth mine favored by the U.S. military in Vietnam, it was designed not to kill but to blow off a limb, and the toll it wrought, particularly among children, helped spur the formation of the International Campaign to Ban Landmines in 1992. As squad leader, Bondarchuk's character saves the artist from stepping on one, prompting him to declare: "we sow them and we're the ones who get blown up." This, perhaps, is *Ninth Company* at its most controversial, but, like the village destruction scene, lays bare the nature of the game: overturn gestures to war atrocities by making Russian soldiers the victims.

These maneuvers, along with characters' story lines and doses of well-timed humor, save *Ninth Company* from the usual fate of by-the-number mythic productions: one-dimensional predictability. Yet they also pull it far away from the real-life event on which it is ostensibly based. That source would be Operation Magistral, when in the fall of 1987 the Soviet army launched its last major offensive against the Mujahideen. Its immediate objective was to clear a mountain road between two cities, Gardez and Khost, since the latter had been cut off and could only be supplied by air. However, the real objective was more symbolic. Gorbachev would announce at the same time a timetable for the phased withdrawal of all Soviet forces from Afghanistan. In this way, Magistral would offer a face-saving, albeit thin, cushion. Unable to admit defeat, Gorbachev would at least have a final victory in the field before declaring the war over.

Tactically, the operation was only a minor success; the road was clear for only a few weeks. For propaganda purposes, however, this was sufficient to trumpet once and for all the official narrative by which the Soviets had first entered the war. Operation Magistral was a humanitarian mission to help the population of Khost, particularly women, children, and old men, who allegedly greeted Soviet soldiers as saviors. Comfortable with this result, Gorbachev officially proclaimed that the Soviet withdrawal would commence in May of that year. It ended in February 1989, when, walking last, the commanding general, Boris Gromov, crossed the "Friendship Bridge" from Afghanistan to Uzbekistan, then part of the Soviet Union.

No mission would be complete, however, without some form of self-sacrifice. For press purposes, this came midway through Magistral, when Ninth Company, 345th Guards Parachute Regiment, beat off a dozen attacks over two days while defending Height 3234 in

January 1988. Heavily outnumbered but refusing to surrender, did they not prove, Soviet newspapers could ask, that this generation of soldiers was worthy of their forefathers from World War II? Their pledge "to fight to the last bullet" was nothing less than the spirit of Stalingrad come to life once more.

What does the Battle of Height 3234 actually share with Bondarchuk's screen version? Very little, except that both occur on a mountaintop. Not even the seasons coincide, since Bondarchuk preferred a snowless set. Yet the most staggering difference is the respective death tolls. In real life, of the thirty-nine paratroopers there, six paid the ultimate price. As one more testament to the attraction of annihilation scenarios in Russian culture, that number—already high by military standards—was for Bondarchuk woefully insufficient.

Where the two do converge is in the messages made of them: duty and sacrifice. In the Central Armed Forces Museum, for instance, the hall devoted to Afghanistan showcases a roll call of heroes whose signature exploit was to give up their own life, usually to save their comrades, while performing their "international duty." There Height 3234 occupies a prominent place, and within those walls there is essentially no other story line available to remember the war. This, in a word, is the same criterion by which Bondarchuk's sole survivor proclaims triumph: they gave their lives but did not give up the hill.

In fact, this measure is the only way that the Afghan War itself—arguably Russia's worst if measured by lack of discernable purpose and the degree of brutality deliberately inflicted on civilians—has found redemption in Russia. It allowed General Gromov in his memoirs to give a taut, unapologetic summary of the entire conflict: "At the end of 1979 Soviet troops entered the country without resistance, completed their assignments and returned in an organized fashion to their homeland."[8]

In making *Ninth Company,* Bondarchuk had something of that totality in mind. Not only is it dedicated to those who died in the war, but the generation of soldiers born in the 1960s is Bondarchuk's own.

(He did not serve in Afghanistan due to his father's fame.) But he also moves his Battle of Height 3234 a year forward to 1989, and that switch in years, as we realize in the last scene, boldly puts the movie forward, as if to pass sentence on the entire conflict. Just when the sole survivor learns that the war is ending, he delivers the final lines that they, nevertheless, "were victorious."

Some Russians, including veterans, have been taken aback by the movie's feel-good gloss, and its core message of duty fulfilled floats on a cloud of vacuity, since it defines no concrete action beyond the following of orders, no matter how mistaken or deadly they might be. Yet that very same property is what allows the movie to graft itself onto the story of World War II, and it has received praise from the real-life commander of the 345th Guards Regiment both as a collective tribute to all who served in the war and as an educational tool for youth to instill patriotism. Likewise, upon his viewing of *Ninth Company,* President Putin offered an exemplary summary of the war's newfound meaning. "This is a tragic story from the life of our country and our people," he concluded. "But the people who fought there for their ideals did a good job."[9]

By creating a bridge from the military's take on the war to the national stage, *Ninth Company* has paved the way for the reimagining of the Afghan War to continue in other cinematic and television venues, and Bondarchuk's own star has risen sharply among the cultural elite. Indeed, the next war movie he directed even broke his own record for highest gross ticket sales. His 2013 *Stalingrad* highlights another band of brothers amid Russia's largest battle and arguably greatest victory. The only distinction plot-wise is that this time they all die.

The one thing that has eluded Fyodor Bondarchuk is his father's Oscar laurels. Russia offered *Ninth Company* as its nominee for Best Foreign Film, but the Academy refused to consider it. Nevertheless, at home it has been rewarded with perhaps the greatest prize of all, militarily speaking: an official seat in commemorating World War II. For *Ninth Company,* just like the elder Bondarchuk's *They Fought for the*

Detail from the monument honoring Soviet soldiers who fought in Afghanistan, 1979–1989. It was erected in 2004 in Victory Park on the grounds of the Central Museum of the Great Patriotic War, 1941–1945, Moscow. Author's personal collection.

Motherland, has been shown on state television on May 9—a fitting gift, indeed, for the younger Bondarchuk, since that is also his birthday.

This path out of the Afghan War's shadow is a familiar one. The desire to turn loss into more palatable fare is, in fact, when myth rises to the occasion. Victory can write itself; defeat needs a boost to deflect attention away from the reality on the ground. For this purpose, if one accepts Bondarchuk's *Ninth Company* as intended, the vein of received tradition and archetype never runs dry, no matter the war. The result is a ritualized discourse on war that essentially admits no defeat. This playbook is a well-thumbed one; Bondarchuk inherited his from his father.

The defeat the elder Bondarchuk turns on its head in *They Fought for the Motherland* is a challenging one from World War II: the 1942 rout of Soviet forces in Ukraine and southern Russia that brought the German invasion to its greatest extent, reaching the Caucasus and threatening the country's lifeline on the Volga at Stalingrad. Disaster ultimately befell the Germans when their offensive punch foundered in the city and then was obliterated in a massive enveloping assault that many mark as the turning point of the war in Europe. Yet explaining how things came to this point has always been a delicate matter, since by this time, the second year of the German invasion, the excuse of being the victims of a surprise attack, as in 1941, has vanished.

Stalinist historians, empowered by gross infidelity to the truth, presented the 1942 rout as a feint, designed by Stalin himself to lure the Germans to their doom deep inside Russian territory. His plan, so went the common refrain at least when the dictator was alive, repeated one of the boldest and most brilliant operations in military history: Hannibal's annihilation of a larger Roman army by feigned retreat and then double envelopment at Cannae in 216 BC during the Second Punic War.

Yet Stalinist lies are something of an exception, a conscious step to make up a false history. The mythic lens generally avoids that, preferring instead to treat events selectively, even delicately, in order to spin them so that they burnish a nation's pride. This is how *They Fought for the Motherland* removes the sting of 1942. It shows the retreat for what it was—chaotic, massive, and unexplainable—but mollifies these negatives by treating viewers to a never-ceasing series of feats of *stoikost* as a regiment of rifle-toting soldiers faces German tanks.

Cataclysm on a large scale is thereby displaced by so many triumphs on a smaller one. A pact is made with the audience that even though the soldiers are in continuous retreat, it will see them win every engagement with the enemy, including a stunner even by Soviet standards: a successful bayonet charge against panzers. No wonder then, by movie's end, with the regiment nearly wiped out, its commander crowns their anabasis a victory because they, the survivors, never broke and never surrendered. In sum, they only did what the movie's title asked.

Myth excels at these deflecting sleights of hand, and there is nothing distinctly Russian about them. Its Western allies have resorted to the same to cover two of their disasters from the same war: Pearl Harbor and Dunkirk.

The Japanese surprise attack in 1941 left in its wake not only a crippled American fleet but a country humiliated and seething with anger. Avenging Pearl Harbor became the war's defining slogan, evoked everywhere from songs and posters to bubblegum wrappers and dinnerware. Yet as Japanese successes continued in the first months of the war, not all that fury was directed at the enemy; the U.S. government received its share as well. How could the nation have been caught so unprepared, many wondered? What other incompetent commanders or mistaken policies threatened the nation's security?

No longer, of course, is Pearl Harbor remembered this way. The question leveled at President Franklin Roosevelt by a senator—"how did we get caught with our pants down?"—has passed into the hands of a narrow group of historians and conspiracy theorists. The searing sense of anger and humiliation has long evaporated as well. In their place, in fact, the opposite has arisen: Pearl Harbor as a site of solemn veneration but also of celebration, where Americans were called forth to fight the righteous fight. Whether experienced on-screen or by an actual visit to the base, Pearl Harbor soars as an inspiring moment of American history when everyday soldiers and sailors became superheroes in their nation's defense.

The blueprint for transforming the battle was established by Walter Lord's popular history, *Day of Infamy,* an instant best seller in 1957, and still the most reprinted and read work of nonfiction on the battle. His success comes from reframing disaster through America's favorite story line: its rugged, can-do mentality born on the frontier. With Pearl Harbor recast as an outpost in the Pacific wilderness, Americans wake up to an attack that turns them into mavericks and gunslingers. They "bang away" on shotguns and fire pistols at the attacking planes like "in a Wild West movie."

When a wave of Japanese aircraft descends, the true character of America has been unleashed; nothing will hold back these next-generation Davy Crocketts:

> By 9:30 the dive bombers were back, but now everybody seemed to have some kind of gun. Ensign Hubert Reese and his friend Joe Hill sat in their clump of weeds, popping away with rifles. Others had mounted machine guns on water pipes, on tail wheel assemblies, on anything. Big, friendly Aviation Machinist's Mate Ralph Watson, cradled a .30 caliber weapon in his arms, kept it going long after he was hit. . . . Everyone had the same idea at once—it seemed like telepathy.[10]

Scenes like this—delivered again and again in subsequent cinematic adaptations—restore confidence to readers and viewers that no matter what may come, America's indomitable resilience will always shine through. The "telepathy" coursing through each is the American spirit itself. Alive and well, it never will fail these soldiers and sailors even though they themselves might die. To borrow from Tolstoy, Pearl Harbor, like with other defeats such as the Alamo, is now only and always a "moral victory" for America.

In similar fashion, Britain recoups the fiasco of its 1940 campaign in France by focusing on the Dunkirk evacuation. Instead of serving as final proof that they had been smashed by Hitler's blitzkrieg, it can call the extraction of its beaten army a "miracle" and a clear demonstration of that irrepressible and quintessentially British pluck. That the people sallied forth from the coast of England in their own boats to help save the army and, in so doing, the nation itself is a moment of unparalleled pride. It has given birth to the so-called Dunkirk spirit—rekindled shortly thereafter during the Blitz—that can be called on whenever times are tough. "Against all odds," reads a typically hagiographic account, the everyday folk who risked their lives in that perilous operation "wrote a page of British history that should be inscribed in letters of gold."[11] Such reverence has continued on-site as well by the ritual reenactment of the journey across the English Channel by the actual vessels used in 1940.

What these examples share, besides happy endings, is a mirroring effect. Viewers, readers, and visitors see their nation's unique character in full action. This is why stories born of defeat are, in their own way, more revealing than those sired by victory. To achieve the looking-glass result, myth inserts itself as the primary subject and in the process exposes its DNA, the raw material of its claims on a pedigree status. Not for nothing are the sagas of Pearl Harbor and Dunkirk, like the stories of Russian retreats or last stands such as Brest Fortress, often set on an infinite loop through popular history, fiction, and film so that generation after generation can rehearse and reaffirm the core beliefs that make them special. Presented in this way, defeat can serve as comfort food for the national soul.

Where Russia parts company is in applying this principle to reclaim entire wars. In this regard Fyodor Bondarchuk's playbook for *Ninth Company* is not just his father's, but a staple of his culture, extending back to the imperial age, when Russia suffered three blows of such magnitude that they, just as with the Afghan war, led to social upheaval, revolution, and even dynastic collapse. One we have already encountered, the Russo-Japanese War at the turn of the twentieth century. It was preceded by the Crimean War (1853–1856) and followed by World War I (1914–1918). All three defeats at the hands of rival powers exposed Russia's backwardness and the weaknesses of its archaic system, and each raised the bar of national humiliation. Yet in their wake, one can also follow how their commemoration can curve in a different direction. It can gravitate to a siege, a ship, or an idea and invest it with sufficient symbolic power to contest the very outcome of the war.

Hero City

For Lev Tolstoy it could be recalled decades later as a "pitiful mistake," for Friedrich Engels a "colossal comedy of errors." For those who study it, the Crimean War tends to dwell between these two poles, rarely rising above the rank of stumble and blunder. How it began augured as much.[12]

At first the war was but another outbreak in the seemingly never-ending Russian-Turkish conflict. Four of them had been fought in the eighteenth century; two more already in the nineteenth. This time the spark came from the dispute between the Orthodox and Catholic churches over which one should represent Christian interests in the Holy Land, which was controlled by the Ottoman Turks. When the latter sided with the Catholics led by France, Tsar Nicholas I took personal offense, exacerbated by his growing belief in (some would say obsession with) his special role as protector of all Orthodox Christians, especially those under Ottoman rule.

In what has become a maxim for modern European history, discord in its southeastern corner could never remain a regional affair. For Britain, any Russian expansion of power there threatened its imperial lifeline, which extended through the Mediterranean Sea and the Middle East en route to India. Napoleon III, who had restored France as an empire in 1852, also looked there as a place to flex some muscle, both to regain the luster once enjoyed by his uncle, Napoleon Bonaparte, and to undergird his somewhat shaky reign. Austria, beset with its own Balkan entanglements, looked with alarm at Russia's protectionist stance, since Orthodox Christians resided within its borders as well. And anything that concerned these great powers immediately drew in the interests of Prussia, sandwiched between all four.

What helped set aflame these geostrategic fields of conflict and launch the first major European war since 1815 was another factor coursing through western Europe: the acute fear and loathing of Russia, its people, its ruler, and its religion. Anchored first and foremost in England and then France, the sentiment penetrated the highest offices of state, the popular press, and even the pulpit, be it Catholic or Anglican. What could be worse for the spread of God's faith, one might hear, than the false word of Orthodox heresy? It locked its followers in the shackles of superstition and obscurantism, just as Russia's institution of serfdom imprisoned so many peasants. Russia menaced the "civilized world," one reverend declared to his parishioners, like a "modern Attila."[13]

Conservatives were joined by liberals who, alternatively, decried Russia instead as the "gendarme of Europe" that strove to keep all the countries and peoples on the continent frozen in place so as to extinguish the spread of reform, democracy, and self-determination. Already in the 1830s its blood-soaked truncheon had crushed Polish dreams of liberty, and following the revolutions of 1848, it struck once more when Nicholas sent Russian troops to suppress Hungarians rebelling against Austrian rule.

Nowhere across that vast eastern land—politically, socially, religiously—could there be any glimmer of hope or any chance of it assimilating with the rest of Europe. The Russian Empire was an archaic, autocratic colossus that deserved nothing less, Lord Palmerston, the British Home Secretary, announced in a Cabinet memorandum shortly before war was declared, than to be carved apart. The knife would strike deepest along the Russian Empire's western and southwestern borders, slicing off Finland, the Baltic States, Poland, territories near the Danube River, Crimea, and in the Caucasus. Some, like a restored Poland, would become sovereign nations, whereas others would be handed over to neighbors, such as the Baltic States to Prussia. Palmerston's dream, if realized, would essentially have pushed Russia off the map of European consciousness once and for all.

Tsar Nicholas was equally to blame. Unable to grasp that Europe no longer saw Russia as the liberator of 1812, he pushed his country into a war that unleashed all its nightmares. To pressure the Turks, in 1853 he mobilized troops on the Danube, the artery that ran from the Black Sea through southeastern Europe to the Austrian capital, Vienna. The Turks declared war, but Russia scored the first decisive victory when ships under Admiral Pavel Nakhimov destroyed a Turkish naval squadron in its Black Sea port of Sinope. Success of this kind, arguably Russia's most lopsided naval victory, raised alarms in the West that it might press on and take Istanbul, the Ottoman capital, and let its fleet spill into the eastern Mediterranean. In the spring of 1854, both Britain and France entered the war on the Turks' side, setting the stage for a clash of Napoleonic proportions.

The war was global; it had Baltic and European theaters, and fighting occurred in the Pacific. However, the main battleground was at the Crimean port of Sevastopol, the home base for Russia's Black Sea fleet. For over three hundred days, a combined French, British, and Turkish army invested the city, giving Europe its first taste of the bloody stalemate of trench warfare, six decades before the outbreak of World War I. Great killers during the siege included the modern rifled bullet, capable of traveling hundreds of yards farther and with more accuracy than muskets shot at Borodino or Waterloo, and heavy artillery far more massive than anything encountered there as well.

Yet the most lethal agents belonged to neither side. Tens of thousands perished from hunger, malnutrition, disease, and exposure when a brutal winter struck, catching the British, in particular, still in their summer uniforms huddled in field tents that hurricane-strength winds easily swept away. So bad, so unprecedented was their suffering, so scandalously unprepared was the army, that it brought down the government, forcing the resignation of the prime minister in February 1855.

It was even worse for the Russians. While Sevastopol was not totally encircled—the southern half bore the brunt of the defense while the northern, separated by an internal harbor, served as an outside link—it remained critically and chronically short of basic supplies. Allied cannon repeatedly pummeled the compressed southern side, leaving it in ruins and its civilian population devastated. The accumulation of putrefying bodies, severe deprivation, and, after the winter horror subsided, of increasing Allied pressure sapped the Russian defenders. In August 1855, unable to hold out any longer, they abandoned the southern half, leaving it aflame, and escaped across a single pontoon bridge to the north. Months of diplomatic wrangling ensued with Austria and Prussia threatening to join the Allied side. Alone and disgraced, unable to defend a relatively tiny corner of its empire against an enemy numbering far less than Napoleon's invading army forty years before, Russia gave in.

The allies' conditions spared Russia Palmerston's dismembering wrath. Far more consequential was what defeat meant at home. The Crimean War also cost Russia its government or, in Tolstoy's words, a "stupid despotic order." Midway through, Tsar Nicholas, who defined his position almost exclusively in military terms, whether as defender of the Slavs, of the Orthodox, or of the continent's political order, died. Some would say it was from shattered self-esteem for having failed to match the feat of his brother, Alexander I, the champion of 1812.

The war also stripped the facade from Russia's continental might. While it possessed the world's largest army, it was fatally hamstrung by its attachment to past laurels. In the most modern of conflicts to date— in addition to the rifled bullet, Crimea debuted the strategic importance of steam-powered ships, railroads, the telegraph, and ironclads— nearly all such advantages lay with the allies. Except for a new uniform, designed by Nicholas himself, the Russian field army differed little from its 1812 forbearer.[14]

Nowhere else were these deficiencies more evident than at the core: the reliance on serf conscripts. The illiterate chattel famed for fearlessness against enemies of old now found themselves outgunned by armies of the industrial age. Here the war's domino effect continued, toppling archaisms all the way down to the institution itself of serfdom. Nicholas's son and successor, Alexander II, earned himself the title of "liberator," though not for any wartime accomplishment. Instead he abolished the serf system in 1861 out of political, social, and military expediency.

How would Russia come to remember this calamity? Certain defeats fade with the passage of time, washed aside by the search through history for more enriching points of reflection. The Crimean War, however, was not of the requisite minor scale or significance to warrant such willed amnesia. What came to its rescue instead was the spirit of 1812—even if the outcomes were reversed.

Where did Russia find itself in 1854 if not isolated once more, defending itself against a coalition of the West? Even Tolstoy, on the same page where he lambasted the war as a mistake, saw it as one in which "we fought almost all of Europe." To be sure, the "European" powers consisted only of four, as the Kingdom of Sardinia later joined the allies, yet the totality of opposition to Russia also included Austria, once again playing the role of ingrate. Just five years before, Nicholas had sent troops to defend it from its rebellious Hungarian subjects; now Austria had nearly joined the coalition against him.

Yet the Crimean situation stung even more. At least in 1812 Britain was still at war with France. In 1854 the two joined together against Russia and, worst of all, had allied with a Muslim nation to attack a fellow Christian one. All the fault lines that ran through Russian history—religious, national, cultural, geographical—no longer seemed paranoid projections or speculation. They were real, for what else united the world outside? What else brought the Christian West into the arms of the Muslim East than undeniable and intractable Russophobia?

Before the enemy landed in Crimea, contemporaries had already let loose a history-laden barrage of invective. For the poet Fyodor Tiutchev, who was close to the tsar's circle, the conflict was just a "resumption" of the year 1812, reaffirming that "Russia cannot and should not rely on anyone else but itself." Others underscored the contrast of national character. When Alexander I entered Paris in March 1814, only eighteenth months after Moscow was turned into ashes, he only showed mercy, since his goal was peace, not vengeance. How was that magnanimity repaid forty years later? With "the kiss of Judas," the poet Vera Golovina declared. Most striking were the voices of actual veterans of 1812, no more so than Fyodor Glinka of Borodino fame, who, in his late sixties, announced that if "then upon our steel chest / Napoleon himself broke," now the consequences were arguably greater:

> And what will the chronicles say to the world
> Of your unholy game?
> The Briton in hand with Mohammed,
> And the Frenchman turned Turk—O' what shame![15]

The action at Sevastopol brought out more parallels with the past. With their sailed warships hopelessly outclassed by allied steamers, the Russians made a striking move at the beginning of the siege: sinking its own fleet across the mouth of the harbor to deny the enemy entry. Sailors wept as their ships went down, some by the fire of their own guns. Morale was restored, however, when Admiral Vladimir Kornilov reminded them of a previous sacrifice. "Moscow burned, but Rus did not perish."

Soon after he assumed command of Sevastopol's defenses, Kornilov would ask the same of his soldiers and sailors. According to Tolstoy, who as a young artillery officer volunteered for service there, Kornilov's presence on the front lines was magnetic. In a letter to his brother, he described the admiral shouting before the troops: "If it comes to death, lads, will you die?" "We will die, your honor, hurrah!" was the collective reply. This was not done "for show," Tolstoy observed. "It was clear on everyone's face that this was for real—as already 22,000 have fulfilled that promise."[16]

Fate would also hold Kornilov himself to those words. In the second month of the siege during a fierce bombardment, he strode up and down the defenses, refusing to take shelter. That defiance proved fatal when a shell exploded nearby, shrapnel tearing through the lower half of his body. Replacing him was Admiral Nakhimov, victor at Sinope, who set a similar example of personal bravery by serving up front among the soldiers and sailors. For this he earned their love and lost his life, felled when a bullet struck him in the head. Respect for the example he set was such that it crossed the trenches, and allied guns went silent during his burial, as Nakhimov was laid to rest alongside Kornilov.

More heroes emerged at Sevastopol, including such rarities as Surgeon Nikolai Pirogov, an expert in amputation and, thankfully as well, in the use of anesthesia. He also invented a triage system for prioritizing casualties that gave hospitals under his direction a survival rate higher than those of the allies. Others earning distinction

included General Eduard Totleben, in charge of the city's fortifications and whose star would rise again two decades later during the
Russo-Turkish War, as well as a peasant-turned-sailor, Petr Koshka,
who became a legend during his own life. His specialty: nighttime
raids conducted alone behind enemy lines from which he would
return with food, weapons, and a hefty dose of enemy ire. His most
celebrated escapade was to recover a comrade's corpse half-buried
upright by the French to use for target practice. For this he was awarded
the St. George's Cross and lived on as the near-perfect embodiment
of the dutiful veteran. His end came nearly thirty years later, when he
saved two girls who had fallen through the ice on a pond and in so
doing caught a cold that allegedly proved fatal.

That Sevastopol was the story of a city under siege also meant that
while women and children suffered equally from deprivation and the
bombardment, they too could enter the ranks of heroes, whether
digging entrenchments, bringing supplies to the defenders, tending
to the wounded, or, for the bravest of children, collecting spent cannonballs in no-man's-land. In sum, all the ingredients were in place
to turn Sevastopol into one of Russia's proudest moments. The only
thing needed was the right person to give it voice—and that would
be Tolstoy himself, but not the older, disgruntled one who would
judge the war a "pitiful mistake"; rather the younger one who
served there. From his eyewitness perch he published a story that in
real time would canonize the siege like no other before.

With the disarming title "Sevastopol in December," Tolstoy's short
piece initially flirts with a shocking you-are-there, quasi-journalistic
stance. He confronts the reader with the sights (carcasses of horses
littering the streets, ditches full of human waste), the sounds (ear-
piercing cannonades), and the smells (gangrenous rot in a hospital)
typically absent from war stories of that time. Yet as he strips away the
expected romantic bromides, the accumulation of dirty details leads
to a different crescendo. By showing readers a side of the soldiers' experience not met in literature before, Tolstoy builds a new pedestal on

which to place the siege. No one soldier is depicted as a hero in traditional terms, but their collective feat—and the conditions in which they do it—make the Russian people themselves, the story proclaims, "the hero" of the "epic of Sevastopol."

Foreshadowing the irresistible pull of the Borodino scenes in *War and Peace* (to be written a decade later), the story fires on the same pistons, though in a fraction of the space. Calm amid a rain of cannonballs, soldiers and sailors go about their business, indifferent to death. Here too their courage is of the silent kind, fueled not by a desire for medals or promotions but rather "something that lies deep in the soul of each: love for the motherland."

The younger Tolstoy was not a puppet for propaganda. Similar sentiments pepper his diary, and "Sevastopol in December" was composed, literally, in the heat of battle. He completed the story while posted to the Fourth Bastion, which jutted out from the line and for Russians was the most lethal place to be in April 1855. There Tolstoy confided to himself how "great" it was to be in the thick of it all and how the "constant delight of danger," along with the companionship of his fellow troops, made it so that "I wouldn't want to leave here."

Tolstoy's paean to the mystical confection of patriotism and defense of the motherland was such a success that a special copy passed straight up into the hands of the new tsar, Alexander II, who immediately ordered it translated into French in order to gain greater circulation in Russia, since that still was the language of the educated elite. This news, needless to say, flattered Tolstoy and, ironically, helped feed his conviction to leave military service and devote himself full-time to literature.

In truth, Tolstoy's feverish emotions were not the only thing he felt in Crimea. They alternate in his diaries with contempt for fellow officers (he was the equivalent of a second lieutenant, the lowest commissioned rank), disgust at the army's backwardness, and anger at being seen as *"chair à canon,"* or cannon fodder—a comment he made when still at the Fourth Bastion. These sentiments also found literary expression in another story, "Sevastopol in May," which appeared just weeks after its predecessor. This time the result was quite different: a story so mutilated by the censor that Tolstoy's editor left the writer's name off it when it was published. Upon learning of this, Tolstoy assumed the secret police had their eyes on him, yet that would not deter him. "My goal," the entry for that day reads, "is literary glory. The good which I can do with my writings."[17]

Of the two Tolstoys at Sevastopol, the first is the one invoked when remembering the siege. Indeed, despite its agonizing outcome, Russian culture never put down the triumphant torch that animated those first months. For decades upon decades, while Tolstoy's negative opinion hardened and then turned caustic against everything having to do with patriotism, military service, and the Russian government itself, eulogies in song and poetry continued in the same rapturous vein. Such was the lasting effect of Sevastopol's positive legacy that in the twentieth century, when myth could be put on-screen, it was the subject of choice for Russia's first feature film.

The 1911 *Defense of Sevastopol* compresses the 349-day siege into catechismic episodes, each calibrated to check off a point that turns defeat upside down: the noble sacrifice of the fleet to block the harbor; the equally moving deaths of Admirals Kornilov and Nakhimov; women helping build fortifications; boys and girls gathering spent cannonballs for reuse; Koshka rescuing the body of the Russian soldier from the clutches of the French; the wounded receiving special care; the enemy commanders—British, French, and Turkish—taking seats around a table to plot Russia's demise.

Defense of Sevastopol also foreshadows the formula to be employed in World War II films such as *They Fought for the Motherland,* wherein all combat scenes end with Russians driving away the enemy with their bayonets. The result is a cinematic embrace of the people who, when not fighting, dance and then dance some more—not ballroom-style, of course, but the earthy, folk kind as if to underscore an inherent innocence threatened by foreign invaders.

Only one incongruity violates the spirit of 1854, and it reflects the political changes taking place as World War I threatened when the film came out. Now Russia, Britain, and France found themselves as allies facing a united Germany, and this realignment of former enemies sets up a surprise ending to *Defense of Sevastopol.* It jumps to the present day of 1911 and shows actual—and quite aged—French and British veterans of Crimea who are then joined by their medal-bedecked Russian counterparts, including women.

As a clear sign that this version of Sevastopol still was the correct one, the film easily passed into Soviet hands with the simple excision of scenes celebrating the monarchy and, to a lesser degree, religion. In fact, it survives only in this expurgated version. A more exalted addition to the Soviet canon of remembrance was the 1941 three-volume novel and recipient of the Stalin Prize, Sergei Sergeev-Tsensky's *The Feat of Sevastopol,* which cemented its leitmotif: even if the city fell, the invaders learned from its tenacious defense that war with Russia is never the same as with others.

As if history was on Russia's side, this truism was tested that very same year when in late 1941 Sevastopol again came under siege by Western invaders. The actors were different—Germans, supported by the Romanian army and an Italian naval squadron—but the plot remained the same. As Hitler's plans to conquer Russia seemed within grasp during the first year of invasion, Sevastopol, like Brest just months earlier, told a different story—one that would become a rallying point while the siege was still ongoing.

The World War II version of the Sevastopol saga also lasted from fall to summer. It pitted an outnumbered garrison against Axis forces commanded by one of their best generals, Erich von Manstein, who earned distinction as the architect of Germany's victory over France in 1940. Yet if that campaign was a matter of mere weeks, here it was different. Several times he attacked the city—the last Soviet holdout in all of Crimea—but the soldiers and sailors manning the dense network of fortifications threw back each one. "Sevastopol is no ordinary city," declared Ilya Ehrenburg, the famed novelist who served as a journalist in the war. Instead, after one such repulse he anointed it

"the glory of Russia." True to that spirit, some of the defenders refused to capitulate, preferring to blow themselves up inside their
bunkers and casemates—an act that for Manstein only proved their
"contempt for human life," which was all too characteristic "of this
Asiatic power."[18]

Savage resistance continued into the spring of 1942, causing the
German army to call on "Dora," the largest cannon warfare has ever
seen. Weighing over a thousand tons and requiring a crew of 2,500 to
put it into position, it boasted a gun barrel thirty-one and a half inches
in diameter—more than twice that of those on its contemporary, the
battleship *Bismarck*. Along with other fearsome siege weapons such as
"Karl," a twenty-four-inch behemoth used at Brest, Dora and its siblings blew craters one hundred feet deep and one hundred feet wide
in the concrete fortifications.

Surrounded, with no hope of reinforcement and with ammunition
dwindling, the garrison could hold out for only so long. But its showcase of courage and *stoikost* in the face of this massive bombardment
allowed Ehrenburg to announce that "no matter how this unequal
battle for the ruins of the city ends, it will remain a victory for Soviet
arms." That end did come in July 1942, when Sevastopol's last defenses were breached and overrun. For Russians, however, Ehrenburg's verdict, like Tolstoy's before, has remained inviolate.

Its soil twice-watered with Russian blood, Sevastopol offers the
kind of historical continuity impossible to resist. To this city, modern
Europe has sent its mightiest warriors, both times affirming that an-
tagonism toward Russia has its distinct way of uniting the continent's
great powers. Both times the city suffered the same fate but was never
besmirched by the stain of surrender. It now lives on crowned with a
wealth of honorifics as a "hero city," "holy city," "invincible city," or, as
per the 1911 film, a "resurrected" one.

Such titles yield another type of continuity that is equally compelling: the story of Sevastopol's ordeal never suffers with time. In 2004,
on the one hundred fiftieth anniversary of the Crimean War siege,

materials from its fiftieth, in 1904, were dutifully reprinted without any modifications whatsoever. There was no need, since the central message remained: "in terms of heroism" the city's "defense was unparalleled." More to the point, the siege could substitute for the entire war. "The strength of all Europe," reads a reissued commemorative from the earlier anniversary, "was concentrated on this small, far away corner of our nation and here a battle was concluded that served for Russia's growth and renovation. It was a battle which to this day the entire world marvels at."[19]

Given that the "corner" is once again part of Russia—addressed in more detail in Chapter 7—it is likely that the rhetoric of the fiftieth will resound for many more anniversaries to come.

Hero Ship

The year 1904 was not a propitious time to remember—let alone celebrate—the Crimean War. Historical continuity can cut both ways, for that year marked when Russia's imperialist ambitions in East Asia collided with Japan's, pushing in the opposite direction. The result, once more, was calamitous as Russia's military foundered, its veil of power torn off again by decisive advances in technology. On land, its army was hobbled by the obsolescent teachings of those like the bayonet-obsessed General Dragomirov, which condemned thousands to their deaths in the face of machine guns and rapid-fire artillery. By March of 1905, the army in Manchuria, where most of the fighting took place, had nearly disintegrated.

At sea, the situation was even worse, starting from the first day of the war, which began with a Japanese surprise attack that damaged Russia's Pacific Fleet. To amend that defeat, Russia could only call on its Baltic Fleet, halfway around the globe, and dutifully sent it forth. All the world followed its odyssey down the Atlantic, around the tip of Africa, across the Indian Ocean, and into the Pacific—only for it to be promptly annihilated in the waters between Korea and Japan in

May 1905. Nearly all of the Baltic Fleet's thirty-nine ships that set out seven months before were lost, including ones bearing such illustrious names such as *Borodino, Dmitry Donskoy, Admiral Ushakov* (in honor of the future patron saint of nuclear bombers), and *Admiral Nakhimov* (after the commander killed at Sevastopol). The Battle of Tsushima handed the Japanese their greatest naval victory ever and effectively drove Russia out of the war.

Less than two years in length, the Russo-Japanese War ended with Japan the dominant power in East Asia, and Russia reeling from revolution as long-simmering unrest erupted back home in mutiny, massive strikes, and street fighting. This time the domestic backlash caused by defeat almost proved fatal to the government, as Tsar Nicholas II was forced to surrender some of his absolute powers and agreed to the establishment of a rudimentary parliament in order to preserve his throne and contain the violent disorder. This proved, however, to be only a temporary brake on the road to decline and ruin. Twelve years later would come the Bolshevik Revolution that cost him and the royal family their lives and tore the empire apart.

Antiwar sentiments resonated in literature even before the peace settlement was signed in the early fall of 1905. A short story, "The Red Laugh," by Leonid Andreev, scored highest, anticipating the revisionism of Viktor Astafev's autobiographical fiction of World War II. In distinction, though, Andreev was not a veteran but a popular, progressive writer who framed the conflict as surrealistic horror. Appearing one year into the war, the story avidly captures the carnage characteristic of twentieth-century warfare, with hapless conscripts driven into battle "like oxen to the slaughterhouse." The structure itself of the story is equally disturbing, as if it too is the victim of violence. Presented as the fragmentary notes of an officer whose legs have been blown off by friendly fire, it then turns to his brother who seemingly continues the narration. By story's end both are dead from a creeping madness, born from the senseless killing at the front that manifests itself at home both in hallucinations of murdering women and children and in actual fighting in the streets.

"The Red Laugh" became a must-read for society and helped cement the popular image of the war as a distant sinkhole where Russians went to die. Nothing about it seemed to offer any leverage for mythic appropriation, which is partly why, unlike the Crimean War, it never enjoyed that initial patriotic boost before descending into quagmire. Projecting the "motherland" so far east was difficult, especially since one of the primary areas of battle, around Russia's base at Port Arthur, was on lease from China. And even if that involved a siege, the outcome was not how tradition would have it. Most un-Russian-like, the commander surrendered Port Arthur after five months. For this he was condemned to death—a just end, perhaps, from a traditional Russian point of view. (The sentence was later commuted.)

Moreover, none of the usual fault lines came into play during the Russo-Japanese War. If anything, something of the opposite was true. Against Japan, Russia was the face of the West, of the so-called civilized world, which made defeat that much more humiliating. Indeed, this was the first modern war in which an Asian country was victorious over a European one.

Stripped of all this potential, myth could only go in one direction—to its firewall, as it were. Official channels, at the same time that Andreev's story circulated, turned to the cult of death, but now its subject was neither a soldier nor sailor. Instead, it centered on a ship that, in its afterlife, was destined to become the most famous in Russian history.

Not all the warships of Russia's Pacific Fleet were at Port Arthur when the Japanese struck the first day of the war in January 1904. The cruiser *Variag* and the gunboat *Koreets* were docked at Chemulpo (present-day Inchon on the Korean peninsula) along with vessels from the British, French, Italian, and American navies. A Japanese squadron suddenly appeared, blocking the harbor and announced that a state of hostilities with Russia now existed. *Variag* and *Koreets,* came the demand, must either quit the harbor or face attack where they lay, with a warning given to the neutral warships to stand back. An hour before the ultimatum passed, the two Russian ships, hopelessly outnumbered and outgunned, sallied forth to give battle. Onlookers cheered them, and bands on the other European ships saluted by playing their respective national anthems.

What began as theater ended on a different note. Two hours later they returned. *Variag* was a wreck, having taken most of the Japanese fire. All its main guns were out of action, and the open upper deck, where half its crew had been stationed, was drenched, a surviving officer described, in "blood and more blood; everywhere there lay burnt hands and legs, bodies torn apart and raw flesh." *Koreets* was slightly damaged but there would be no further battle. Refusing to surrender, the Russian commander ordered *Koreets* blown up while *Variag* was scuttled, sinking to the bottom of the harbor.

That act, in effect a ship suicide, turned *Variag* into an everlasting legend. The mythic threads that could be teased out of this one episode almost guaranteed as much: the ship as victim of unprovoked aggression; its decks as the surrogate soil of the motherland; underdog status, yet accepting battle; honor secured by refusing to surrender. In fact, the ship's name alone projected tremendous symbolic power and explains why it and not *Koreets* became the center of an official cult. The latter means "Korean," which obviously would not do, but *variag* is Russian for "Viking" and bears the heritage of the Viking overlords, known as Varangians, who ruled Rus and from whom its medieval princes were descended. Two of them, of course, were Boris and Gleb, the martyrs who became saints, and in the cult of *Variag* one hears their direct echo: death chosen willfully, resulting in spiritual victory.

The cult was launched while the surviving sailors, safe on neutral ships, were still on their way home. Its first installment, oddly enough, came from a poet in Munich who published "Der Varjag" just weeks after the battle. Though suspicion has been raised that the poem was mock-heroic, satirizing the glorification of death in war, in Russia it was received as the opposite. Indeed, its first verse reads as if the product of a Russian mythmaker:

> On deck, comrades, all on deck!
> On to the final parade!
> Proud *Variag* never surrenders,
> No need for mercy have we!

Translated into Russian just as the crew arrived home, *"Variag"* was set to music and to this day remains the most popular song in the Russian navy and has long operated as its de facto anthem.[20]

How the sailors were first received—fittingly at Sevastopol—was a set piece in political choreography. The commander of the Black Sea Fleet congratulated them for "the feat of proving that Russians know how to die." Their victory in death recalled what the city's defenders had done a half century earlier and thus made the sailors "sons worthy of those heroes whose blood bathed these hills." Historical analogies were driven further, feeding off of Yellow Peril alarmism prevalent in Russia at the time. The Russo-Japanese War, read one proclamation, was not the first time "the Lord has brought our motherland face-to-face with the Mongols," and therefore the dead sailors and *Variag* itself should also be remembered alongside the slain at Kulikovo Field in 1380. If their blood sacrifice five centuries earlier resulted in victory, then from *Variag*'s undersea grave the same "rays" of triumph shined (or so ran the fatally erroneous presumption).

From there the crew proceeded north by train, hailed in each city with more bands and processions until they literally reached the top in April of 1904: a reception at the Winter Palace in St. Petersburg where Nicholas II delivered a personal toast:

> With love and deep emotion all of Russia and I have read about the feat you demonstrated at Chemulpo. From my heart I thank you for upholding the honor of St Andrew's flag [the navy's official colors] and the dignity of Great Holy Rus. I drink to the future victories of our glorious fleet. To your health, lads!

All the sailors received commemorative medals, silver watches, royal dinner plate and spoons with silver handles, while the ship's captain was promoted to serve as the tsar's adjutant.[21]

While the Russian Empire expired just over a decade later, the cult did not, underscoring more than ever how myth can serve ideological opposites. To be sure, Soviet historians dismissed the war itself as a "hopeless" conflict between competing imperialists, but the example of *Variag* stood out as proof positive of the "remarkable *stoikost,* self-sacrifice and loyalty demonstrated by Russian warriors on land and sea."[22]

Analogies soon became apparent. In his landmark history of Brest, Sergei Smirnov described the fortress as "the *Variag*" of World War II, and during that conflict Soviet sailors reportedly sang its famous song while going into battle. In 1946 a movie was made of the ship's final day, and *Variag* later surfaced on postage stamps, as toy model construction kits, and has lived on in the navy as the name of numerous successor ships.

Nothing else, though, shows the cult's fortitude more than when it came time to honor its fiftieth anniversary in 1954. Only seventeen of the surviving sailors could be found to be granted new, Soviet-minted medallions. Even then they reached the top once more, posing for official photographs under the portraits of Lenin and (the recently deceased) Stalin. Never before in Russian history had something as odd as this happened: only the crew of *Variag* had occupied the seat of honor with the emperor and then again with those sworn enemies who had him killed.

Variag, ever more so than Andreev's "The Red Laugh," remains the official point of departure in remembering the Russo-Japanese War. One of the latest occasions came in 2009, when South Korea returned items recovered earlier from the ship. The ceremonies surrounding it brought in the heads both of the church, Patriarch Kirill, and of the state, President Dmitry Medvedev. Chief among the ship's relics was the tattered bow flag bearing St. Andrew's cross, which presumably had been forgotten in the rush to scuttle. Receiving it at Kronstadt, the Baltic naval base guarding St. Petersburg, the patriarch christened it a

Postage stamp from 1972 featuring the cruiser *Variag,* scuttled in 1904 after suffering severe damage from Japanese warships. © Solentsov Alexander / Cliparto.

"sacred symbol of the Russian fleet" because it showed how "the ability to give one's life for the motherland or for others" is recognized by God "as the greatest of sacrifices." To those who follow that path, "He opens the doors of his kingdom."

As Kirill spoke, God seemingly did just this as a reported cross-like image graced the sky over those attending. A photograph of it adorns a volume commemorating the flag's return, which features both Nicholas's original toast and President Medvedev's endorsement, extolling *Variag*'s enduring contribution to Russia's patriotic spirit.

From St. Petersburg the flag went south to Moscow, reversing the direction of the sailors' original procession, and it was hung in the Hall of Victory in the Central Armed Forces Museum next to the actual Hammer and Sickle raised over the Reichstag in Berlin in 1945. A seamless arc of memory between the two wars was thus made complete: from imperial, to Soviet, and then to post-Soviet; from secular to sacred; from a regional conflict to a global one; and from abject loss to absolute triumph.[23]

A Heroic Idea

Until recently, commemoration of World War I has lingered behind that of the Crimean, Russo-Japanese, and Soviet-Afghan wars. At times it has even been called the "forgotten" one, which is grimly ironic, since it claimed more Russian lives than the other three defeats combined. The reason is numbingly simple: the war is overshadowed by the cataclysmic revolution that followed and helped set the twentieth-century world on course for an even greater conflict. Still, in quick summary, it unfolds in a familiar way.

While on the Western Front Germany's advance bogged down in the trenches stretching from the Swiss border to the English Channel, on the Eastern Front the theater of war was quite mobile—generally at Russia's expense, as German infantry pierced its border and advanced hundreds of miles into its imperial heartland. Once more, as in Manchuria a decade before, Russia's colossal army foundered because of leadership failure, poor strategy, outmoded tactics, and severe shortages in armaments and equipment.

This time, however, such circumstances proved fatal. In the winter of 1917, as morale plummeted and mutinies broke out, hunger and other deprivations brought women into the streets in the capital of St. Petersburg (then known as Petrograd). Demonstrations grew violent as soldiers deserted to join the protesters, and Tsar Nicholas II was forced to abdicate. This "February Revolution" left the empire adrift as a temporary government proved incapable of running the war and retaining central control. The Bolsheviks, led by Vladimir Lenin, seized power that same year in the "October Revolution," after which Russia collapsed into civil war and vast swathes of the empire, including Poland, the Baltic States, and Finland, split off.

Bolshevik victory in the civil war led to the birth of the Soviet Union, and in its official history, World War I was downgraded to the "Imperialist War" and not worthy of substantive commentary except as a prelude to revolution. Today, however, historians of a patriotic bent have provided guidelines as to how it too can be reclaimed in the manner of the other three. While the war itself can still be seen as a catastrophe for Russia, the same should not be said of its military.

Not all of its commanders were subpar, with the primary example being General Aleksei Brusilov. His 1916 offensive against the Austro-Hungarian army temporarily reversed the momentum on the Eastern Front and nearly succeeded in knocking Germany's ally out of the war. Heroes also abound among the common soldiers and can be honored in the same fold as those at Brest or Sevastopol. In the first year of the war, one of the few places where the German advance foundered was at Osowiec Fortress in Poland, then part of the Russian Empire, and strategically located along central rail lines between impassable swamps. From the fall of 1914 until the late summer of 1915, its garrison withstood repeated assaults and fearsome pounding by "Big Bertha," Germany's premier siege weapon for that war. What finally broke the Russians' resistance, however, was a new weapon: poison gas. Released from hundreds of canisters, it enveloped the Russian position, and the Germans marched forward, confident of an easy victory. Yet out of that lethal cloud, a band of soldiers, faces swathed in rags dripping blood as they coughed up their lungs, erupted on them, putting the startled Germans to flight. While Osowiec was later abandoned, those Russians, none of whom presumably survived long after, have been immortalized as "the attack of the dead."

The grand arc of the war can also be made to fit a recognizable mold. No matter its outcome, reads a recent history, Russia continually upheld its "duty" to its allies on the Western Front, without which the latter never would have won. Yet of Western gratitude there was none, only betrayal. Britain, France, and America fought not just "to beat Germany but to weaken Russia as much as possible" by deliberately denying it the necessary support and supplies to survive. In

View of the side of the Central Museum of the Great Patriotic War of 1941–1945, located at the center of the Memorial Complex in Victory Park, Moscow. Author's personal collection.

short, once again Russian blood was shed so that other empires could live.[24]

Centennial celebrations of the war's outbreak in 2014 have pushed it further toward the light of victory by also hitching it to World War II. In Moscow, the grounds of the Central Museum of the Great Patriotic War of 1941–1945 now showcase a monument dedicated to Russian soldiers of World War I. This move was long overdue, since the park surrounding the massive museum serves as the pinnacle of official war memory across the whole of Russian history. Besides commemorating the two world wars, the grounds also include the Church of St. George the Victor, which takes visitors back to Rus with its icons of warrior saints such as Dmitry Donskoy and also sacralizes the entire space. Moving forward to a more recent period, the park furthermore includes a monument to those who "fulfilled their international duty" in Afghanistan. The entire complex itself sits atop the very hill where Napoleon waited in vain for the keys of the city to be delivered to him, and from there it overlooks a museum dedicated to Borodino.

At the unveiling of the monument to World War I on August 1, 2014, President Putin sharpened the political edge of its remembrance. Only two weeks before, the downing of a Malaysian passenger airliner had caused a spike in international outcry over pro-Russian separatists in Ukraine, and he used the opportunity to make clear what the earlier war can teach us. In this version, Russia was the peacemaker, doing all it could to keep other European countries from joining what began as a conflict between Serbia and Austro-Hungary. After all, the desire for peace is "a defining feature of the character of our nation and our people." Yet no one listened and Russia was compelled to take up arms in order to defend the former, "a brotherly Slavic people," against Western aggression.[25] If we substitute pro-Russian Ukrainians for Serbians, then the Guns of August, which have already claimed thousands, point eerily into the future.

As the process of deflecting defeat continues unabated since the Crimean War, it would be easy to dismiss this just as a symbolic whitewashing of the past. Yet it is an essential tool in order to align all of Russia's modern wars along a single axis by invoking the same conceits again and again. It is also a powerful tool, even if its aims are transparent, because it provides a narrative hook to pull virtually any conflict into the inner sanctum of veneration fronted by the twin pillars of victory over Napoleon and Hitler. The result is an unbroken record of glory, *stoikost,* and virtuous martyrdom wherever one casts an eye on Russian history—with one exception, and it holds the most enduring lesson, especially today, as to how Russia is to survive in a hostile world.

6

Deadliest Sin

Another kind of war casts its shadow on Russia, yet its stain cannot be covered up by the sheen of self-sacrifice. Nothing violates the ethos of John 15:13 more than—instead of dying for one's brother or friend—raising one's sword against him. And there is no greater peril to the country itself than internecine conflict, which comprises its own, self-generated existential threat. As the Time of Troubles in the seventeenth century made clear, fratricide cracks Russia open to outside predators, which back then, it will be recalled, led the Poles to invade and occupy the Kremlin.

In fact, fear of civil war runs deeper than of any foreign enemy, which is why after Russia recovered and expelled the Poles from Moscow in 1612, a special word rose to capture the blood-soaked anarchy to which it had succumbed: *smuta* [smoot'-uh]. It was not a neologism but a concept redirected. When referring to water, for example, it conjures up a murky surface, perhaps with something foreboding below. If applied to the country, it becomes the most terrifying word in its history. In the iconic summary of Iury Gotye, one of the leading historians of the seventeenth century, *smuta* signals nothing less than when Russia lies "on the verge of extinction."[1]

The National Malady

Though living in the twentieth century, Gotye knew firsthand of what he wrote. In 1917, when he was in his mid-forties, Russia plunged once more into the abyss, following the collapse of the Romanov dynasty during World War I. The provisional government that replaced Nicholas II after his abdication in February held the reins of state but not of real power. That was exercised more and more by radical opposition groups able to harness the rage and discontent found on the street, in the countryside, and on the front line. By summer, the army was disintegrating as mutinies erupted and waves of desertion turned into a flood. Though the war was, for all intents and purposes, already lost for Russia, the provisional government would not give up on it. As recorded in his diary, Gotye's hope for his country's future plummeted as well. Its "heart and soul have been torn out"; its people "committing suicide." "Will there be," reads his silent cry, "a Minin and a Pozharsky" as in 1612 to save his country?[2]

Order did return to Russia, but not the kind Gotye could countenance. As a pro-monarchist (but critical of Nicholas) and conservatively patriotic with a typical streak of anti-Semitism, he was aghast when the Bolsheviks seized power three months later. Yet before they could impose their own version of autocracy, Russia and all its imperial domains were rocked by a civil war lasting three years and taking millions of lives while sending millions more into permanent exile abroad.

The conventional division of the civil war between the Bolshevik "Reds" and anticommunist "Whites" gives us only partial traction to understand the violence that ravaged Russia and ended with the empire's extinction. If the Reds and the Whites faced off primarily in the central regions of the former empire, numerous independence drives by national minorities on the periphery erupted as well. Some succeeded, such as those in the Baltic States, Finland, and Poland, which became sovereign states. Others did not, such as in Ukraine, where Bolsheviks fought to reclaim a province of incomparable industrial and agricultural value. Inside these overlapping conflicts, instability and vacuums of power gave free range for a host of others to arise, like anarchists (whose forces could number in the thousands), Cossack warlords, and heavily armed bandit gangs.

Fighting was often multifactional—in Ukraine alone it was a four-sided conflict between Reds, Whites, anarchists, and independence-seeking nationalists—and undisciplined armies sometimes turned on themselves or, as was more often the case, on terrified civilians nearby. Each came with its own calling card of atrocity. The Reds left in their wake mass shootings, hangings, and drownings of claimed enemies, while the Whites and nationalists plied a similar trade of terror, culminating in some of history's worst pogroms against Jews. Any who shunned politics or simply wanted to be left alone—a sentiment no doubt shared by many peasants—could not escape conscription, confiscation, or retribution at the hands of sadists lurking in all the warring factions.

As one might expect, civil war triggered foreign interventions that penetrated the empire's borders mainly through its ports on the Arctic and Pacific Oceans and the Black Sea. The roll call of countries that sent troops was impressive: the United States, Britain, Canada, France, Italy, Japan, and Serbia. Less so were their numbers or impact. They did not march on Moscow or lay siege to a city. There was no central plan, mandate, substantive coordination, or single motivation for intervention. Western allies initially had hoped to prop up the Russian front in order to keep German troops from being transferred to fight in France. But when World War I ended, the rationale shifted to that of protecting supplies shipped to their onetime ally and to make some statement about containing Bolshevism. What that would be was never clear, and what was done was feeble. For all the Red Scare fever, the fresh memory of the trenches left these other nations numb to the prospect of another war.

If the Reds lost their war with Poland, they won theirs with the Whites. It was an impressive comeback effort. In 1919, three White armies from the east, south, and west bore down nearly simultaneously on the center of Bolshevik-controlled land running from Moscow to St. Petersburg (then called Petrograd). What saved the Reds was their ruthless discipline, better motivated soldiers, and their enemies' foibles. ("White" embraced a political spectrum stretching from monarchism to socialism, which made internal cohesion and cooperation near impossible.) By 1921 the Bolsheviks had crushed their opponents, foreign intervention had ceased, and they were well on their way to reclaiming many of the former empire's territories.

The best literature to emerge from the war were the short stories by Isaac Babel, a Russian Jew who rode with the Red Army against the Poles, serving as a war correspondent. In the fewest of pages, they capture the conflict's immensity and its vicious, often indiscriminate lethality. Characters ranging from savage Cossacks and devout Bolsheviks to illiterate soldiers and victimized civilians, particularly Jews, embody its colliding political, social, and ethnic forces. Babel entices us to enter their world through innocent beginnings; by story's end, however, the trap is sprung with a harrowing revelation, delivered in that same quiet voice. A Red Army soldier's letter home, for instance, peels back from concern over his horse's welfare to inform "Dearest Mama" how their father, fighting for the Whites, tortured to death his sibling brother, only to suffer the same fate from yet another brother, when "Papasha" fell into their hands.

The emotional punch, delivered as a soft underhand, can tempt us to sympathize even with the killers. For they are engulfed in a war stoked by indecipherable ideologies and confused passions that nevertheless arm them with the conviction that justice is served by their violent acts. A Cossack in a train car protects a nursing mother from assault by his comrades, only to discover that in her bundle there is no child, only precious salt. Enraged by her deception, he despairs over Russia's suffering—"the peasant fields without an ear of corn," the "raped girls," "the comrades who go to the front as many and return as few"—and struggles over what to do. Finally, his fellow Cossacks step in, advising him to "get her" with his rifle. "And so I took my trusty rifle from the wall," he informs us, "and wiped that stain from the face of the laborers' land and the republic."[3]

Babel's stories endure not only because of his creative talent but also because of his insistence—contrary to the gallery of one-dimensional heroes honored by the Bolsheviks—on their political ambivalence. One doesn't read the story cycle, known collectively as *Red Cavalry,* and necessarily come out in favor of that side. It was a bold step, given that the Bolshevik Revolution that would give birth to the Soviet Union left little room for ideological neutrality or patience for such nuances. Babel's ingenuity and innovation ultimately did him in, and he was shot by Stalin's police in 1940 during the Great Terror which claimed, among others, many of the country's artistic and intellectual elite.

If such a fate makes Babel the last casualty of the Russian Civil War, how many preceded him during the actual conflict? As in the Time of Troubles, the toll was far worse off the battlefield, where typhus and cholera reigned. Particularly hard hit were those uprooted by the violence, which caused massive migrations of refugees across the empire's vast lands. Famine also struck again and again, pitting cities against the countryside, as the Bolsheviks sent out armed requisition teams to strip peasants of their meager resources in order to feed a starving proletariat.

In all, an estimated ten to eleven million perished, though by no means were the victims only Russians, as death and destruction swept across the breadth of the former empire. This figure represents approximately 7 percent of those who lived within its borders. It also pushes the conflict toward the scale of World War II losses, especially when one folds the civil war and World War I together as overlapping conflicts lasting from 1914 to 1921, which would add another 3.5 million dead to the toll.

Iury Gotye's wife became one of that number as the couple struggled to survive, scrambling for food and firewood to avoid freezing in Moscow, a "dead and murdered city," in his words. Deprivation, eroding conditions, and the shock of war and revolution "cracked" her nervous system, Gotye wrote shortly before her death, leaving her an "invalid" who succumbed to a diabetic coma in 1919. Another victim was her uncle, summarily shot by the Bolshevik secret police that same year.

Gotye survived, one of a few to remain at his position as a history professor and archivist, despite his political views. Part of that was luck (his diary was smuggled out of the country in 1922), and part because his specialty was, ideologically speaking, relatively "safe": the seventeenth century. No one was better positioned to relate the earlier *smuta* to the present one, and the same year that tragedy struck his family he wrote a monograph on the Time of Troubles, the conclusion of which was quite unsettling. *Smuta* was not a one- or two-time occurrence; it was a specifically Russian condition that constituted "the country's historical disease."

Why this condition might be cast as pathological long predates 1918 or the Time of Troubles itself. The first symptoms of the disease can be traced back to the Middle Ages, when similar cries rise from the pages of the chronicles, spilling over into sermons and homilies. They resonate in the period's literary masterpiece, *The Lay of Igor's Host,* and, for those so inclined, are even embedded in the foundational story of Rus. According to legend, it took place in the ninth century, when the eastern Slavs, forerunners both of Russians and Ukrainians, were distressed over internal feuding. Their solution was to invite their neighbors to the north, the Vikings, to rule over them and bring order to their land. Thus came Riurik, who founded the putative state and the royal dynasty that would last until the Time of Troubles.

The infusion of Scandinavian blood proved a temporary cure. Just a few generations after Riurik, the princes of Rus were immersed in relentless power struggles as the royal line grew into several branches that collided with one another. Some fights were of the small-scale kind between princes' retinues, others pitched battles involving several principalities. Sometimes a city was taken; sometimes it would be sacked. Occasionally peace might prevail, but it was almost always a precarious and short-lived one, until the Moscow princes became supreme in the fifteenth century—a position they gained in large part by stamping out rivals.

Elsewhere in medieval Europe, the picture was pretty much the same. Yet what made the situation in Rus more acute was that the dynastic system itself promoted internecine warring. Terms of succession could run in two directions, laterally, from elder brother to younger, or vertically, from father to son. Moreover, principalities themselves were not necessarily hereditary possessions and could be reshuffled, redrawn, and redistributed countless times, depending on their current value and prestige. Determining who deserved what in this maddening game of musical chairs could therefore pit uncles against nephews, brothers against cousins, and a myriad of other configurations when in-laws and the children of second marriages were factored in.

Men of letters at that time, who were exclusively clergy members, could be forgiven their obsession in recording and decrying the ruthless constancy with which the elite of Rus went to war with themselves. The curse could strike at any time, among any relations, as seen in the testament to his sons given by Yaroslav the Wise, Grand Prince of Kiev during its golden age in the middle of the eleventh century.

> Love each other because you are brethren from one father and mother. If you love one another, then God will be with you and will submit the enemy under your hands and you will live peacefully. In case, however, you live hatefully in feuds and dissension, then you will destroy yourselves and you will destroy the land of your fathers and grandfathers ... remain peaceful, brother obeying brother.[4]

The safeguard he instituted was simple: upon his death the eldest would become Grand Prince of Kiev (which at that time was the seat of greatest prestige), and the other two would receive lesser principalities. Upon the eldest's death, the next in the fraternal line would rotate to the Kievan throne, and the youngest would take the second spot.

Why Yaroslav might not trust his sons to keep the peace can be recalled from the stark fact that he himself came to power in the most famous of sibling conflicts. It was he who avenged the killing of his brothers, the soon-to-be-canonized Boris and Gleb, by defeating yet another, Sviatopolk the Accursed. Even after that victory Yaroslav could not rest, for still another sibling rose against him and succeeded in splitting Rus in half until that brother's (natural) death. And while Yaroslav's sons heeded their father's wishes upon his death, their cousins and nephews did not and killed his eldest son in the process. As if to make a mockery of any attempt to fix the system, Yaroslav's grandchildren resumed the cycle of consanguine killing. Peace, when it came to Rus, was never more than a staging post before the next outbreak of violence.

Essentially no hero from that time is free from this sin. Vladimir, who converted Rus to Christianity and was the father of Yaroslav, Boris, Gleb, and Sviatopolk, fought his own eldest brother after the latter had killed yet another brother. Alexander Nevsky put down his younger brother's mutiny against their Mongol overlords, and Nevsky's own sons hacked their way through the family tree. And however much Dmitry Donskoy serves as an icon of national unity by leading the Russians to victory at Kulikovo Field, less remembered is what happened after. When it was his grandson's turn to become prince of Moscow, a vicious war erupted with the grandson's uncle—Donskoy's second son—that spilled into the next generation and featured the tit-for-tat blinding of cousins on both sides.

Medieval injunctions against internecine fighting make it both the original and deadliest sin of Russian statecraft, but those who issued them added another, more ominous note to their warnings. Nothing attracts the enemy's eye to Russia more than domestic disorder and disunity, as proven by the Mongols in the thirteenth century. To be sure, if we step out of the medieval reference frame, the causality does not hold; invasion from the east was coming regardless of princes' murderous habits. To contemporaries, however, the connection was always true. Inciting princes to fight each other was a favorite game of the devil, and those who succumbed brought down God's wrath, inevitably expressed through foreign attack. And that punishment fell not just on the guilty princes at the top, but on all his chosen people.

The Return of Civil War

However distant, these dark chapters of Russia's past now have a steady claim on a twenty-first-century audience. The reason is simple and is inseparable from the key narrative behind President Vladimir Putin's rise and mainstream popularity despite his turn to authoritarianism. In 1991, the catastrophic implosion of the Soviet Union extinguished the latest ruling dynasty—of the communist kind—leaving chaos, decline, and loss in its wake. For the decade following, a single word—"crisis"—could describe virtually any concern: political stability, socioeconomic infrastructure, financial solvency, standards of living, demographic health, and international prestige. "Nearly everything that could be destroyed," declared the metropolitan of St. Petersburg during the turmoil, "has been." Another Time of Troubles gripped the country.[5]

Internal fractures again brought foreign invasion, though of a different kind. Western prophets of wildcat capitalism and shock therapy descended like vultures, just as foreign goods and franchises inundated the formerly closed society. The impact flipped its value system so that consumerism, not Marxism, became the new religion. Oligarchs arose like the warlords and marauders of before, rampaging freely through the country, seizing large swathes of its economy, and preying on a helpless populace. The leader who emerged, President Boris Yeltsin, not only shared the first name of his ill-fated predecessor of 1605, Godunov, but unfortunately liked to jest that he was "Tsar Boris."

His hands were also stained with the blood of his countrymen after a violent clash with hard-liners in 1993, and much more Russian blood was spilled in the first war with Chechnya, which ended in 1996 in defeat. More and more, the government fell victim to the intrigues and corruption of the henchmen surrounding Yeltsin, who manipulated him much as the nobles who had plied their own self-interests through the dizzying bounty of claimants and imposters during the Time of Troubles. Yet just as in 1612 Russia rose from its knees, and this story's hero is none other than Putin himself. When he famously declared that the collapse of the Soviet Union was the century's "greatest geopolitical catastrophe" that launched an "epidemic of disintegration," he was also placing himself at the center of Russia's eventual resurrection. What he inherited upon becoming president in 2000 was, in his words, a country teetering on the brink of "civil war," which is why events of the Middle Ages, 1612, and 1918 have been repackaged in order to bear present-tense meaning for a resurgent Russia.[6] Each of the packagings differs, but, if examined in reverse order, they converge on a single point: what are the causes and the cure for its special disease?

The civil war between the Reds and the Whites is the trickiest to handle because of historical realities and the challenge of today's political landscape. Regarding the first, interventions by other nations remained on the periphery of the empire and were quite small in strength. There were no major battles or marches on Moscow to fire the imagination, thereby depriving Russia of its default invasion card. As for the second, it runs straight into the knot that has bedeviled Russia since 1991: what is to be the legacy of the Soviet period?

No event has been more polarizing for modern Russia than the Bolshevik Revolution and the rise of the Soviet Union, both of which hinged on the outcome of the civil war. After the Reds won, two ways of understanding Russia's subsequent experience of the twentieth century went to war as well, each nursing irreconcilable narratives. One was of birth and creation; the other of death and destruction. Did the revolution launch Russia on a trajectory of unprecedented greatness, culminating in its industrial drive, its victory over Nazi Germany, its legendary achievements in science and technology, and in its place atop the world as one of two superpowers? Or did it send Russia into its deepest hell, marked by the Gulag, the Terror, absolute dictatorship, and millions of corpses?

Each side could summon an impressive cast of characters to enforce their point. Into the Soviet canon came ironclad heroes such as Vasily Chapaev, a dashing commander who died a martyr's death fighting the fearsome Admiral Kolchak, "Supreme Ruler and Commander-in-Chief" of the White forces. For the latter, in turn, the typical hero was the noble officer victimized by rapacious Bolsheviks—a story line to be repeated with gruesome regularity when it came to the intelligentsia, the peasantry, and countless others as well.

The two absolutes reigned for decades, but now the divide is no longer tenable. Post-Soviet Russia has pushed for reconciliation, embracing this troubled period as a tragedy for the nation no matter where allegiances once lay. As a result, neither side is demonized, and a series of striking moves has signaled the transition to a new reality. In 2000, Tsar Nicholas II, murdered with his family by the Bolsheviks in 1918, was canonized along the same criteria of Boris and Gleb as "passion bearers." A few years later, the ashes of Anton Denikin, a leading general of the Whites who titled his history of the civil war *Sketches of the Russian Smuta,* were taken from the United States and interred in the Donskoy Monastery in Moscow by the express order of President Putin. (The same could not happen to Kolchak, who was captured and shot by the Bolsheviks. His body was stuffed under the ice in a river and never recovered.) Even the Russian Orthodox Church itself has moved on from that troubled past. In the 1920s, it was split in two with one-half governing exiles and émigrés and the other serving believers inside the Soviet Union. In 2007, the church was reunited under the authority of the Moscow Patriarchy.

How, then, does one commemorate such a terrible conflict if the ideological moorings that caused it have eroded into obsolescence and no longer can serve as a mobilizing force? The answer would seem counterintuitive, but increasingly is the one encountered: decouple the war from politics as much as possible so as to make the Russian people as a whole the war's protagonist. Two emblematic portrayals are *Fall of the Empire,* a star-studded, award-winning 2004 miniseries, and *Admiral,* a 2008 feature film that has reappeared on television in a much longer format as a miniseries as well. Both productions highlight characters that before would have been galvanizing for either side. In *Fall of the Empire,* good-guy secret agents thwart foreign plots against Russia before the revolution and continue serving the Whites in the same capacity, while *Admiral* brings to screen for the first time none other than Kolchak and his failed campaign to overthrow the Bolsheviks.

Despite its title, *Fall of the Empire* offers no Gibbonesque explanation of why the Russian Empire collapsed. There is, surprisingly, out of ten episodes not one on the actual revolution; it happens off-screen, as it were. Bolsheviks themselves, while in no way pleasant figures, are also not monsters. Their seizure of power only gives a green light to the anarchy and violence in the streets committed by those who would be criticized anywhere for such behavior. They are expressly not condemned because of their ideology, and, in fact, no reason is given as to why Bolsheviks (or other brands of revolutionaries) are who they are. By abstaining from what would be a logical inclusion, *Fall of the Empire* removes the chance for a clash of ideologies or confrontation of ideas. Gone as well is any debate over social justice and the grievances that gave rise to revolution in the first place. (Bolsheviks were by no means alone in opposing imperial Russia; they just represented the most violent and uncompromising of those who did so.)

The series' effect is not a whitewash of history; ample atrocities are committed and ample blood is shed. But what these dramatic absences mean is that if tears are shed, they are not for a movement or a cause, but for the condition into which Russia has fallen. The director, Vladimir Khotinenko, makes this clear by ending the movie in 1918—precisely when civil war would break out in full. Such an abrupt end is necessary, because to finish it on film would compel one to choose sides. Unable to do this, *Fall of the Empire* slides literally into the murkiness of *smuta,* which is the very title of its final episode. Not for nothing is the series' overall title more menacing in Russian than in its translated release. The word for "fall" points not to the Roman Empire but instead means "perish" and is the precise term used by Iury Gotye to warn of Russia's "extinction" in his own history of the Time of Troubles.

The movie *Admiral* takes a similar pose. Revolutionaries can be brutal and cold-blooded, and we certainly do not condone the violence they inflict. Yet we also never hear from their leaders or about the reason itself for revolution. Kolchak himself is somewhat cleaned up and introduced to us in a memorable battle scene, where he is in command of a Russian ship in World War I fighting the Germans. Courageous against all odds and one of the few survivors on deck, he succeeds in personally disabling a stronger enemy ship by targeting its bridge, thereby establishing his credentials: love for country, above all else, including the willingness to sacrifice one's own life for it.

That sense of duty—quite safe by any political standard today—is what compels him to fight the Bolsheviks, and the sentiment conveyed dovetails with *Fall of the Empire.* In a scene where the dead are collected after Kolchak's final defeat, one gravedigger asks another if the Reds and Whites should be buried together. The answer he receives is yes, since they are all of one people. There can be no winner, if the case is one of fratricide.

A similar nonjudgmental approach pervades official venues as well. In the Central Armed Forces Museum run by the Defense Ministry, what was once a shrine to Bolshevik glory has given room to include the opposite, such as portraiture sympathetic to the Whites (and painted after 1991). The three-volume text sponsored by the Ministry, *The Military History of Our Country,* also refuses to choose sides. Except for a curt note on Bolsheviks' problematic relationship with democracy and Whites' self-defeating support for landowners, political commentary is strikingly absent, and the tone drops precipitously to a dry enumeration of the organization and operation of Red and White armies.

The boldest it ventures is a colorless exposition of "this army did that" and to underscore what foreign interventionists stole during their brief incursions.

Less noticed in all the post-ideological maneuvering today is the precedent it had during the war itself as established, for instance, by the renowned poet Marina Tsvetaeva. She was an ardent supporter of the Whites, and her husband even fought in their ranks. Yet the violence she witnessed had crossed a threshold, compelling her to provide an eloquent summary of the war's tragic reach.

> All around they lie
> No difference between.
> Just a soldier can be seen,
> Where is ours? Where is theirs?
> The one once White—turned red:
> Blood has stained him so.
> The one once Red—turned white:
> Death has laid him low.

Tsvetaeva's lines, written while the war's outcome was still unknown, capture the savage depths of Russia's accursed disease. The labels "White" and "Red" may decide who kills whom, but ultimately *all* Russians are victims of the fighting. A similar lament, invoking the reversal of John 15:13 that defines civil war, came from Tikhon, the church patriarch whom the Bolsheviks would soon imprison: "Stop dividing our land into warring camps, for we are brothers and all share the same mother: the native Russian soil."[7]

The metaphor of a family tearing itself apart was struck again in the two most famous novels to describe the fighting and which helped both writers win a Nobel Prize: Mikhail Sholokhov's *And Quiet Flows the Don,* appearing in 1928, and reprised as a fourteen-part miniseries in 2015; and Boris Pasternak's *Dr. Zhivago,* which made its world debut in 1957 (but was published in Soviet Russia only in 1988) and has returned again as a miniseries in 2006. As nurtured by filmmakers, historians, and politicians in this century, this sentiment attains something of a new absolute in the push for reconciliation and remorse. "Never again in our history," the current head of the church has declared, "should there be a repeat of what happened a hundred years ago."[8] Violence within the Russian family cannot be redeemed by recourse to some greater ideological mission, since it craves no particular political banner save one: that which serves as its best protection.

One would expect similar problems to arise in reclaiming the Time of Troubles itself, what with its dizzying array of usurpers, false tsars, imprisoned patriarchs, and nearly impregnable political intrigues. Here, however, the sheer scale of foreign interventions makes it the easiest to depict, with the Poles earning a permanent spot among the cast of villains. This is how it always has been ever since the Romanovs raised statues honoring Minin and Pozharsky in Red Square in the nineteenth century and later canonized Patriarch Hermogen, who wrote the secret missives that launched the liberation campaign. Stalin followed the same path but with an even more brazen punch. In 1939, the Soviet film industry released *Minin and Pozharsky,* featuring the Poles as evil aggressors, just weeks after the Red Army invaded Poland. To no surprise, its two directors and two leading actors won the Stalin Prize.

Today, while nothing can displace World War II as the crown jewel in Russia's self-imaging, the Time of Troubles serves as its greatest comeback story. (Even Hitler never occupied Moscow.) Indeed, the two conflicts can operate as complements to each other, as given in the 2007 blockbuster *1612: A Chronicle of the Time of Troubles.* While the movie makes a minimal claim on historical accuracy, preferring instead swashbuckling action buttressed by magical realism, the scenes of Poles torching Russian villages are strikingly reminiscent of those in *Come and See,* the 1985 depiction of genocidal Nazis that climaxes with the burning of a barn full of a village's inhabitants.

The director of *1612,* Vladimir Khotinenko, who also made the miniseries *Fall of the Empire,* had no qualms admitting that his take on history was tailored to current political demands. "[In *1612*] I'm talking about the period after perestroika. We lived in a Time of Troubles. Its duration even coincided with the one in the seventeenth century."[9] The movie's release date, November 4, was also carefully chosen to mark the debut of a new holiday, Day of Unity, which falls on the day when the Poles were driven from Moscow. (Such a heavy-handed approach, however, backfired and, commercially speaking, it was a flop.)

In 2012, for the four hundredth anniversary, the anti-Polish platform grew into a catch-all, anti-Western one in Vladimir Medinsky's novel *The Wall,* published just before his appointment as minister of culture. The title itself mobilizes a number of connections—some symbolic, others literal. It evokes Mary in her role as mother-protector, but also the fault lines ostensibly separating Russia from the West. True faith lies on the Russian side, as do moral propriety, compassion for others, human decency, pure love, and traditional family values. On the other side, we find debauchery, bordellos, and a world of corruption and lies. In Medinsky's re-creation of the seventeenth century, Russia's superiority over the West even extends to habits of hygiene and literacy rates among peasants.

All of these walls merge with a physical one comprising the fortress of Smolensk, a major city then on Russia's border, sitting astride the road between Warsaw and Moscow. (The Kingdom of Poland was at this time in union with the Grand Duchy of Lithuania, and their combined territories included present-day Belarus and much of Ukraine.) Like the Holy Trinity–St. Sergius Monastery, Smolensk was under siege for nearly two years, but at Smolensk the Polish-led army breached the fortress walls. Exhausted and starving, the last survivors retreated to the city's cathedral, where the main powder supply was also housed. It blew up, killing all inside. The explosion may have been an accident, but that view runs weak in Russia. Two centuries ago in his groundbreaking *A History of the Russian State,* Nikolai Karamzin was beside himself with pride when he described it: "Russians ignited the powder and flew into the air with their children, with their possessions—and with glory!" In Medinsky's rendition, the hero himself sets the fuse in proper self-sacrificial mode, which yields the proper outcome. After the explosion, angels bear all the defendants' souls to heaven, and we learn that, though the city fell, "the Russians were victorious."[10]

The Wall is a by-the-numbers rendition of myth that mirrors Kremlin postulates. Russian forces are inherently nonaggressive; the only move they would ever make—with hindsight it now rings ominously—would be to reunite with the "Russians" in Ukraine and Belarus, two countries that did not exist then as independent states. Conversely, the Western army is precisely that: a combined Polish, German, and Hungarian core supported by mercenaries representing the rest of Europe. A precursor to the Nazis, it is also quite ruthless, killing Russians for their faith (even during church services) and planning to enslave the rest under a "New Order." The division between good and bad also breaks along the value system expounded by the Kremlin. In the novel, the West is apparently awash with predatory homosexuals, and the hero's first act when abroad in Germany is to kill in self-defense a "sodomite" who attacks him.

One trusts that a work like *The Wall* will never make it to screen; on paper it already is a xenophobic cartoon. (Medinsky is also the author of a wildly popular series debunking the negative stereotypes the West has of Russia and Russians.) Where the novel does succeed, if that is the word, is in showing how malleable the Time of Troubles has become as a period piece, able to accept and hew to any ideological or cultural shift, while still enforcing the bedrock rule bequeathed by Karamzin and here drummed endlessly into its readers. A great Russia stands on two rocks: a strong tsar and a state made equally strong by those willing to serve it.

When it comes to the Middle Ages, the same edifying impulse holds true and invariably leads back to one individual, Alexander Nevsky. From his hagiography written a few decades after his death in 1263, to his canonization as a saint in the sixteenth century, to his status today

Battle of Lake Peipus. Scene from Sergei Eisenstein's 1938 film *Alexander Nevsky*. The Teutonic knights are identifiable by the crosses on their shields and white-robed horses. Sputnik / Bridgeman Images.

as Russia's premier war leader and statesman, the superlatives that surround him have accumulated to the point where he represents Russia's supreme hero. Across its history, no one's star shines higher, no one's legacy offers such a wealth of teachings, and no one else serves as a fail-safe model of how to cure Russia of its disease.

Nevsky's significance rests on four feats: the defeat of the Swedes at the Neva River in 1240; the defeat of the Teutonic knights at Lake Peipus in 1242; the promotion of positive relations with Mongol overlords; and the rebuff of papal overtures to convert to Catholicism. The first two reprise the existential threat motif, no matter if historians (almost exclusively in the West) question the size and intention of the attacking forces. His champions have no such doubt, as reflected in a new hagiography, updated for the twenty-first century. Nevsky, it asserts, was the "last hope" for Russians, and his alleged thoughts before battle were providential: "Either we will perish together with Orthodoxy or all Rus will live with it forever."[11]

The third feat recognizes that when Nevsky was beating back the West, he and his people were also vassals of the Mongols. While the willingness to work for them and enforce their policies—such as suppressing his brother's rebellious impulses—might earn for someone else the title of collaborator, that position instead can be flipped into a salvational one. By upholding a policy of temporary nonresistance, he ensured that Russia would survive until the moment was right to cast off the Yoke, even if centuries after his death. He "lived and acted," one popular history explains, "just as the fate of the nation required." With the fourth, his refusal to submit to the pope, Nevsky's role as national savior is complete. He "saved Orthodoxy as the bearer of Russian culture and the Russian idea," wrote Boris Vasilev, author of *His Name Was Not Listed,* "and thus ensured for centuries the opportunity for the Russian people to develop on their own special national basis."[12]

So rendered, Nevsky serves as the exemplary leader, Christian, and Russian. In Karamzin's history, he appears simply as "the Hero," blessed with "superior intelligence, courage, and the looks and strong muscles of Samson." In his new hagiography, such strength is simultaneously tempered and magnified by religious modesty. His favorite activity in childhood (of which in truth we know virtually nothing) was "reading holy books" and "prayer." As an adult, he emulated Jesus, being the "true friend of all the needy and poor, the father to widows and orphans, and provider for the destitute."[13] Even Eisenstein's eponymous film, produced at the height of Stalinist culture, makes gestures in that direction by introducing Nevsky dressed all in white, fishing with nets, before outside circumstances will force him to turn from Prince of Peace to invincible Warrior Prince.

No one, in short, is more qualified to lead Russia onto safe and secure grounds. The key to Nevsky's success in anything he touched, Vasilev wrote in 1993 amid the shards of the latest *smuta,* was that he was motivated by the "farsighted policy of uniting the separate identities of the proto-Russian into a single-state mentality." That unifying spirit has, needless to say, turned him into an icon for the twenty-first century. His coronation, literally, as Russia's best came in 2008 when Nevsky won a nationwide contest, "The Name of Russia," sponsored in part by the Academy of Sciences, and beat out the likes of Peter the Great (and Stalin, for that matter). While we might normally dismiss that title as mere gimmickry, since the results were broadcast on national television, the contest gained a certain gravitas through the appeal of Metropolitan Kirill of St. Petersburg to support the prince. Nevsky, in the metropolitan's opinion, is a "post-perestroika" hero, "whom we need in order to resurrect ourselves as a great power." Leaving no doubt as to Nevsky's unique status, this is when he declared, as noted in Chapter 1, that "without him there would be no Russia, there would be no Russians."[14]

Two years later, as Patriarch of Russia, Kirill again drew upon the prince's legacy on the seven hundred ninetieth anniversary of his birth. In a full-color, magisterial volume devoted to Nevsky, Kirill gave official blessing to his role as the pivotal figure of Russian history and as the model for successful statecraft today. This recognition was seconded by the head of the government, President Dmitry Medvedev, who in his own address praised Nevsky for "strengthening the

Russian state and the formation of a sense of national identity among its citizens." Other contributors to the volume gave precise illustration of how he did this: he always put the national interest before the personal or parochial and thus was "able to lead the country out of crisis."[15]

No doubt Nevsky's reign will long endure. Able to match any ideological orientation, able to appear in any time period, able to shine in the hands of the Orthodox and the atheist, he is the perfect protagonist for Russian history. Because the known facts of his life are so few, his contributions will likely never be challenged outside of small academic circles, which is why his legacy has never been subject to revisionism. In mainstream usage, there is no debate about him, rather a contest of encomium. To this degree, Nevsky's battles are superior even to those of World War II. With few facts available, there are no troubling spots in the historical record to cover up or falsify. There is no living memory to insult and no neighbors to offend. (At least in this case grudges don't extend back to the thirteenth century.)

A final factor behind Nevsky's place atop Russia's pantheon of heroes is how he reproduces the building blocks of Russia's war myth. Not only does he defuse its two primary anxieties, foreign threat and internal disunity, but his story broadcasts its essential corollaries. Just cause, innocent defender, Western treachery, the need for vigilance, the triumph of faith—it's all there, down to the organic tie between the people and the soil when in Eisenstein's film, as noted, the peasants rise from hovels in the ground to face the Germans, accompanied by a chorus singing of the "People's War."

Since Nevsky's record against the West is spotless—after all, he is the hammer that smashed NATO's predecessors—one can anticipate further appearances and invocations as Russia's terrestrial and heavenly guardian. Already he is the patron saint of the FSB, successor to the KGB. Perhaps the only thing he didn't do was die on the battlefield—but even that potential mark against him can be recouped as a plus, according to his updated hagiography. His labors became a "crown of thorns" to which Nevsky ultimately succumbed, but after death he

Alexander Nevsky. Painting by Vasily Shebuev (1777–1855). State Art Museum, Nithny Novgorod, Russia / Bridgeman Images.

earned what was once claimed of Lenin: the prince still "is alive and present in our lives."[16]

Keys to Survival

The rich yield of names and events drawn from the well of internecine conflict in Russia nearly matches that of World War II in its edifying potential. Yet if the latter is more outward focused—evil Nazis and those who appease them—then these scenarios are more inward focused and thus relatively unknown outside of Russia's borders. Nevertheless, no matter the century from which they are pulled, they operate in tandem with each other, demarcating the alpha and omega of Russia's political health. Nevsky reigns at one end as the gold standard: leadership in its proper place; an ordered society that is resilient and impervious to outside influence; a state and populace united and sharing the same interests. Any step away from this ideal, whether due to foreign or domestic cause, threatens to infect the body public with a virus that, if it approaches lethal strength, grows into *smuta*. The symbiotic relationship between the two poles is self-reinforcing and, if accepted on its own terms, essentially irrefutable: the only known cure for *smuta* and the only shield against its reoccurrence is centralized power, secure and unchallenged from within.

This is the doctrine behind which President Putin claims political legitimacy and projects authority. He may not call himself a latter-day Nevsky or Pozharsky, but the role he has assigned himself in Russian history is more or less the same. Crushing the oligarchs, attaining unrivaled political power, making Russia a force to be respected once more—these are his signature achievements. And though not all are due to his hand—the rise in oil prices, for example, helped rescue the state from fiscal insolvency in the first decade of his administration—the laurels claimed are exclusively his. Putin is Russia's savior, which, more than anything, fuels his domestic support, no matter how he might appear to the outside.

Although the West prefers to reference Russia through its Soviet past, the 1990s is sometimes a better frame to understand Russian politics and presidential power. No one wants to return to that decade's debacles and humiliating retreats, and that knowledge greatly simplifies the question of what kind of leader and political system Russia ostensibly "needs." It also arms the governing elite with exceptionally strong language to speak about their country and their presumed role in it. Favored refrains concerning "chaos" and "disorder" tap into some of the deepest fears of Russia's collective consciousness while, at the same time, reflexively justifying the power the elite have amassed. Without moves like these, Russia's very survival would fall into question—or so mythic history would teach us.

Clarification on this matter can come not only from the Kremlin but also from other centers of authority, such as the Academy of

Sciences, the country's most powerful academic institution. In 2008 its roundtable of historians offered a point-by-point breakdown of the "disorder and instability" that inevitably follows any "weakening of central authority." Warning signs that the country is slipping into *smuta*-like murkiness include such things as the rise of "different political groups." They breed "conflict," with results "that are deplorable and disastrous for the country and for the people." The crisp cause and effect puts any political opposition or, theoretically, mere disagreement under the shadow of suspicion. Pressing the analogy further have been others who rail against "*smuta*-sowers" today—recognizable as anyone who questions authority or harbors "anti-Russian" attitudes.[17]

The Russian Orthodox Church has also contributed to this line of reasoning, demonstrating how closely its interests are tied with political ones. The same year the roundtable met, a television sensation rocked Russia. What caused it was, of all things, a documentary, entitled *Death of an Empire: The Lesson of Byzantium,* produced and narrated by Archimandrite Tikhon, a wildly influential, best-selling author who is also rumored to be President Putin's personal confessor. The premise of the documentary, which won the Golden Eagle for best in that category, is simple: show viewers how the Third Rome can avoid the fate of the Second, with the Time of Troubles as the perfect tie-in.

Just like Russia in the 1990s, in the fifteenth century the Byzantine Empire was mired in the same kind of rot. "Oligarchs" drove stability into the ground by supporting "frequent changes in political direction." They also "privatized" the empire, letting its untold wealth drain out to the West. No emperor was strong enough to overcome this "internal enemy," which meant that when the external one came in the form of the Ottoman Turks, the empire's destruction was foregone.

If the Byzantine elite carried blame by undermining political and financial stability, then so did society as a whole for failing to uphold core cultural values. Even before the Turks appeared, decay had set in due to fatal choices it made. Enamored with Western lifestyles, society pulled away from the principles of its once-solid Orthodox faith. Such kowtowing, however, only bred contempt in the West, causing the latter to "pass sentence" that the Byzantine world "must be destroyed." While the actual hand of destruction came from the East, the West guided it because "hatred" for Byzantium festered "at the deepest level of its genetic makeup." That geo-biological fact means that "to this day" the "heirs" to the Byzantine throne, that is Russia, face the same.

Yet Russia, one presumes from this documentary, will be fine as long as it stays *smuta*-free with a strong central government and maintains its solid spiritual base. That impression reveals the silver lining in continually invoking the curse of *smuta*: if handled properly, each revisiting of the subject yields more ammunition to justify attitudes and policies in the present. Indeed, a telling omission in current commemorations of the past is any substantive attention to full-scale insurrections against the throne. Around 1670, for instance, the Volga region exploded in revolt because of the systematic subjugation of the population into serfs. Led by Stenka Razin, it united rebellious peasants and others seeking to escape the state's rapidly expanding iron fist, and its core featured Cossacks, virtual icons of freedom who lived in loose, self-governing communities. A century later, the same area burst into conflict once more, as the same disaffected groups rose up under Yemelian Pugachev, who hailed from the same region as Razin and claimed to be Peter III, the murdered husband of Catherine the Great.

Both Razin and Pugachev ended up commanding armies in the field that threatened the state's control over its southern and eastern territories. (Pugachev even set up an alternative court as a kind of tsar for the people.) Both became legends in their own lives, worshipped by supporters as messianic figures, fighting to deliver them from oppression. Both terrified nobles and landowners as the specter of wanton violence grew into a nightmarish reality, with peasants turning on their masters, killing them and their families, and rampaging across the land.

Both Razin and Pugachev also ended up on the chopping block in Moscow when their populist armies eventually succumbed to the better-armed and more disciplined forces of the state. They neverthe-less lived on for a long time as heroes in folktales and song, but are considerably less well remembered today. What positive lesson might authorities draw from their example? Thus these two, though they led the largest and most destructive popular revolts in Russian history, are ignored, indicatively, where they most deserve attention: in the multiple volumes of *The Military History of Our Country,* which first helped craft the parameters of Russia's military heritage for twenty-first-century readers.

That silence is itself telling in another way as well. If, according to myth, no foreign power can vanquish Russia, then only one thing can bring it down, and those seeds of destruction will first sprout on its own land. Internal discontent and division constitute Russia's Achilles' heel, which is precisely how Vladimir Putin concluded his first inaugural speech upon becoming president in 2000. It was his "sacred duty," he vowed, "to unify the people of Russia."[18]

7

War Neverending

If President Putin's message at his first inauguration was clear, so too was the one sent by his honor guard, soldiers in uniforms recalling the Napoleonic Wars. That reach into the past was bolstered by another. The ceremony was scheduled on May 7, just two days before the country performed its annual ritual commemorating VE Day. By foregrounding this story line from the very outset of his administration and repeating it at all subsequent inaugurations, the Russian head of state has ensured that war, more than anything else, binds Russians together in sharing a distinct heritage.

National identity so defined assumes that history, at least for Russians, repeats itself, extending back for centuries through a pattern of confrontation in which the actors' names may change but not the primary action. It flattens differences, turning sui generis conflicts into a single, paradigmatic one that pits Russians against an implacable foe, where they are always the victims but never the vanquished. Victory always obtains; Russia always comes back.

This proposition reenergizes a mobilizing tool whose halcyon days hearken back to World War II. One of its most cogent expressions was, as seen in Chapter 1, Metropolitan Sergii's national address delivered the day the Germans attacked in June 1941. His roll call of previous invaders made "this army of fascists" nothing more than "the pitiful descendants of the enemies of Orthodox Christianity." This alone armed him with optimism, since these previous trials demonstrated that Russians' willingness to sacrifice for the "motherland" not only ensured future victory, but is what defines them as a people.

That sentiment penetrated into private, secular realms as well. In the winter of 1943, the day he finished reading *Batyi,* a popular novel on the Mongol invasion by Vasily Yan published just before the war, Colonel Petr Tiukhov turned to his diary and wrote:

> How much suffering and how many sacrifices did our country endure, just as if it was truly dying? Yet against all odds it rose again and that alone has instilled in us a love for it and our heroic ancestors. Knowing the past always gives you faith in the future. So why did our country suffer then and why does it suffer now at the hands of foreign enemies? Because it is beautiful. Individual Russians may perish but the immortal Russian people and Russia itself never will.

Though seven centuries separate the war described in the novel from Tiukhov's, in his imagination they were contiguous, as if constituting unbroken links in a chain of invasions. Quietly and on his own, Tiukhov broached the heart of the Russian war myth. Just as with Sergii, the ideational and experiential planes of exceptionalism align perfectly: Russia is attacked because of its special character, a pulchritude, he implies, that graces everything touching the land and the people. The logic, if accepted, also holds true in reverse: what makes Russia special and what makes one love it more is the very fact that it is attacked.[1]

Call of Duty

This badge of national distinction has been in continuous service ever since Vladimir Putin's ascendancy. Just months before his promotion by Boris Yeltsin to acting president on New Year's Eve 1999, Russia went to Chechnya to make up for a war that had previously been lost and, in a way, was even more humiliating than the defeat in Afghanistan in the 1980s.

In 1994, when Yeltsin was still president, the Chechens sought independence from within the wreckage of the Soviet Union. At first, such a dream might have seemed quixotic. After all, Chechnya was quite small and was located within the territorial boundaries of the Russian Federation itself. It had no official army or government and was not recognized as sovereign by any outside country.

Surprisingly, however, while Russia—the primary heir to the Soviet military machine—held all the advantages, it failed to quell the Chechen insurgency. The Russian army could launch rockets, drop bombs, and send in tanks, but it could not break the back of Chechen resistance. So excessive were its efforts with so little return—beyond the wholesale destruction of the region—that the conflict saddled Russia once more with the reputation of being a savage aggressor that, perversely, was something of a paper tiger in the field. There was no better sign in the 1990s of Russia's dysfunction and weakness than the ability of a few thousand hardy Chechens to withstand the forces of a former superpower.

Desperate to extract itself from this quagmire, Russia cobbled together a peace agreement in 1996 that left Chechnya in a semiautonomous condition but without formal status as a sovereign state. As fitting testament to this conclusion, the First Chechen War defied the usual pull of mythic appropriation. None of the three most recognized films devoted to it, for instance, dared even play the default card of turning defeat into heroic martyrdom. Whether painted elegiac in *Prisoner of the Mountain,* darkly comic in *Checkpoint,* or blood-churning in *Purgatory,* the one common denominator of these Yeltsin-era productions was that Russian lives were being lost for no discernible reason.

The cease-fire turned out to be temporary, as did the sting of humiliation. The second time was to be different, and real-life events helped to flip that sentiment. Radical Islam began to infuse Chechen insurgents, which attracted the support of outsiders such as the Taliban and made it easier for Russia to classify operations there as antiterrorist. Pushing the envelope even more, by the summer of 1999 insurgents sought to expand control by invading neighboring Dagestan, also predominantly Muslim and part of the Russian Federation. At the same time, most dramatically in Moscow itself, explosions were set off in a number of apartment buildings.

While in certain quarters suspicion for the bombings fell on Russian security forces, the convergence of factors nevertheless erased for many lingering doubts as to just cause and gave the green light to Putin, then prime minister before he became president, to launch a second war against Chechnya. Little was spared both in terms of the breakaway region's populace or infrastructure. Widespread atrocities reported by the likes of the journalist Anna Politkovskaya led to international outcry. The capital city of Grozny was flattened, its ruins eerily reminiscent of photos of destroyed Soviet cities sixty years before. In her dispatches, Politkovskaya described off-battlefield behavior as no less than "medieval," marked by hostage taking, the torture and mutilation of prisoners, scalping, the indiscriminate killing of civilians, and the systemic rape of women and men. With both sides to blame for this descent into barbarism, she pronounced the entire area "a small corner of hell."[2]

In mainstream culture, however, the Politkovskaya side of the conflict was pushed into a corner, and she herself was murdered in 2006. What turned public opinion was the series of large-scale terrorist attacks by Chechens on Russian soil, such as the taking over of a Moscow theater in 2002 and a school in 2004. Even if in both cases botched rescue attempts caused the needless death of hundreds of hostages, never again could Russia look at Chechnya the same way. These events and the Russian government's success in establishing a Chechen as a proxy ruler, virtually unfettered in his ability to brutalize opponents and the local population, turned the story of the conflict into that of paramilitary and police forces battling domestic terrorists. The fighting scaled down dramatically, such to the point that in 2007 the minister of defense declared the war over with a curt "the problem is solved."[3] In a strict military sense, perhaps it is, yet the mutual hatred and potential to explode again are destined to last.

From the official perspective, one battle has come to symbolize the Second Chechen War, as if tailor-made for that promotion. In February of 2000, a company of paratroopers on a hill found themselves unexpectedly in the path of a far greater insurgent force led by a Saudi Arabian jihadist. Sixth Company of the 104th Guards Airborne Regiment numbered ninety strong; by battle's end, after their defensive positions were overrun, only six were alive.

The Battle of Height 776 was the most costly engagement for the military during the war, and it came shortly before elections would decide if Putin would stay on as a real president, no longer a provisional "acting" one. These two circumstances initially led to a cover-up so as to avoid painful questions that might damage the narrative, only just begun, behind his reputation as Russia's strongman savior.

Then something happened. At a certain level in the administration came the blunt realization that Height 776 could tell a different story, indeed, an irresistible one where a fiasco could be recast as a singularly Russian feat of arms. The two primary ingredients for a mythic coronation were already there: collective self-sacrifice in defense of the borders and noble last stand against an enemy waging an openly religious war.

Reversing tack just days before the election, Putin and Patriarch Aleksii led a joint ceremony honoring the company and awarding the highest military order, Hero of Russia, to twenty-two of its members—while only one was alive to receive it. Just as a new president was coming into his own (for he would win the election resoundingly), the death of these paratroopers could be linked to a new Russia that was emerging from the previous decade's debacles. "Precisely this battle showed," the Defense Ministry declared in a hastily released commemorative volume, "that the Russian Army is alive, that Russia itself is alive, as long as there are those prepared to sacrifice themselves for the sake of victory, for the sake of life in our much-suffering Russian land."[4]

Monument to the soldiers of Sixth Company, which was virtually wiped out on Height 776 in Chechnya in February 2000. Located in front of the Central Armed Forces Museum, Moscow. Author's personal collection.

From that moment on, the Battle of Height 776 mushroomed into *the* event of the Chechen conflict, even displacing the story of the first war as well. After his electoral victory, President Putin made a state visit to Pskov, the city where the regiment was based, to lay flowers at a new monument dedicated to the fallen, and on the battle's first anniversary he took a helicopter to the actual site and laid flowers there. Later, when it came turn for the Central Armed Forces Museum to tell the story, the exhibit hall devoted to Chechnya was turned into a virtual shrine to that battle alone, with special attention drawn to the company commander who died alongside his men after calling down artillery fire on their position, and remains so to this day.

Numerous songs and poems have also sprung up, and in 2004 a musical was made, *Warrior Spirit,* that for its debut brought family members onstage bearing portraits of the deceased. (It also received special mention from the patriarch for compelling audiences "to think about the meaning of life, about its true values, and about the times in which we live when so much depends on the moral choices each of us makes.") From the stage it came to television in the form of two miniseries, *The Honor Is Mine* and *Thunder at the Gates,* and then to the screen in the 2006 feature film *Breakthrough.* (The initial desire to title one of these productions *Sixth Company* was derailed by Fyodor Bondarchuk's epic of Afghanistan, *Ninth Company,* which was smashing box office records at this time.)

Crafted in this fashion, the legacy of Height 776 allows for the continual replay of mythic imperatives. Just cause and the transparent division into good versus evil, for example, are secured in *Thunder at the Gates,* which begins with a fictionalized attack by Chechens, their leader dressed as Grandfather Frost (the Russian Santa Claus), on holiday revelers in a peaceful Russian town. That such threats are existential can be heard in President Putin's own rhetoric. "Precisely these kinds of heroic actions," he declared at the Pskov memorial, "not only save the Motherland, they also block all of those who seek the destruction of Russia."[5] Who "those" might be, according to *Breakthrough,* can extend beyond Islamic jihadists to a larger international cast including African and Irish mercenaries, Baltic snipers, and the occasional rogue British agent.

The nature of the battle itself provided optimal grounds, as stated in the Defense Ministry's official account, to showcase how Russian soldiers' "genes" are hardwired to "fight to the last." The outcome even prompted it to rewrite John 15:13, replacing "love" with "victory" to give Jesus's injunction a more martial edge so that on these pages it reads, "As it is written in the scriptures, there is no greater victory than he who gives his life for his friends."[6] In more dramatic fashion, *Breakthrough* ends with the last soldiers rising for a bayonet charge accompanied by an image of heaven with clouds parting so as to welcome its newest entrants. *Thunder at the Gates,* in turn, makes this hill the soldiers' Golgotha, the final scene depicting a cross being erected there after the battle.

The significance of the Battle of Height 776 would not be complete without its induction into the circle of World War II renown. *Thunder at the Gates* makes that move when a soldier discovers a rusted rifle from the earlier conflict buried in the soil, thereby transporting the war against Nazis into the present and vice versa. Same battlefield, same mission, same result: victory by way of a staggering loss of life. To cement the contiguity, it also shifts the action, though "based on real events," from February to May so that the cross is erected amid VE Day celebrations. In real life, Putin made a similar maneuver two days after his third inauguration as president when he received family members of the deceased in the Kremlin on May 9, 2012.

The formula for recasting fiasco as a heroic feat was called on again during Putin's first year as president in order to cushion his administration from yet another military disaster, this time the worst of its post-Soviet existence. Just days after his trip to Pskov in August 2000 to honor Sixth Company, one of Russia's largest and most powerful attack submarines, *Kursk,* sank with all hands on board. The cause was a torpedo that accidentally exploded in its tube during a naval exercise, and it brought Putin's popularity down to its lowest levels because of his callous response. First, he did nothing, refusing to break from his

summer vacation in the resort of Sochi, even though some sailors had
survived the explosion but were entombed in their vessel below the surface. Then came disinformation: speculation was floated of a possible
collision with a NATO submarine. Finally, there was a cool dismissal
of rescue efforts offered by some of those same nations until it was
too late.

As the 118 sailors slowly and agonizingly died, a country looked on
with astonishment and disgust at their new president, and the media,
still enjoying a measurable freedom of expression, assailed him. Putin
lashed back, but redemption, at least culturally speaking, didn't really
come until 2004, when Vladimir Khotinenko, of *Fall of the Empire*
and *1612* fame, brought it to the screen as *72 Meters,* the title referring
to the depth at which his fictionalized submarine founders with its
all-star cast on board.

Two twists—both predictable in their own way—helped turn the
story into an inspiring one and earn Khotinenko the Golden Eagle,
one of Russia's highest awards in cinema, for Best Feature Film. First,
once the submerged sailors' fate is clear, attention shifts onto how
they will die. There is only one functioning rescue suit for which they
can draw lots. Instead, they all opt to die, awarding life to a civilian
researcher, the only non-serviceman among them, who succeeds in
reaching the surface. The second is to shift the cause for the accident
to an acceptable past. The submarine strikes a mine left over from
World War II, lingering on as if a reminder to a new generation that it
can never escape that conflict's shadow and its calling card of obligatory sacrifice for those in uniform. Though Khotinenko disavowed
that his movie was inspired by *Kursk* (which expired at 108 meters),
others clearly have not, since it has been shown on state television
precisely on July 30, Russia's official holiday for honoring its navy.[7]

That the deaths of the soldiers in Sixth Company and the sailors on
Kursk are considered fitting tributes to Russia's entrance, militarily
speaking, into a new century is communicated unequivocally by bronze
memorials to each erected in the sacrosanct space in front of the Central Armed Forces Museum. There they join two Soviet-era memorials,

Monument to the sailors who died on the submarine *Kursk,* which accidentally sank
in August 2000. Located in the front of the Central Armed Forces Museum, Moscow.
The inscription, in part, honors their loss while they were "fulfilling a military training
mission." Author's personal collection.

a T-34 tank commemorating World War II and a ballistic missile
marking superpower might. They are, so far, the only monuments
raised there since the breakup of the Soviet Union, but the message all
four convey—an amalgam of just cause, liberation, deterrence, vigilance, defense, and sacrifice—has by no means abated.

When Russia went to war with Georgia in 2008, the conflict lasted
only five days, yet accounts of it resonate with similarly polished rhetoric. Its story line can be followed not only in official pronouncements but also in a spate of popular histories and even in fiction, such
as the made-for-television movie *Olympius Inferno,* which appeared
just months after the conflict ended. Together, they invariably portray Georgians who attacked the breakaway regions of Abkhazia and

South Ossetia as sadists guilty of war crimes. Standing behind them are the United States and other NATO powers using Georgia as a proxy to further their own expansionist interests. This version, in effect, reads like a replay in miniature of World War II with the hot-headed, fanatical Georgian president Mikheil Saakashvili playing a latter-day Hitler. Presented this way, the Russians appear as peace-seeking humanitarians whose intervention rescued the Abkhazians and Ossetians from possible genocide, a word used with almost casual frequency for this conflict, despite its scale and brevity.

History has once more called upon Russia to do its duty, and this time the victims are seen as true brothers, the pro-Russian separatists fighting in eastern Ukraine. As of yet, Russia itself has not taken up arms; it mission has remained strictly humanitarian by providing food, medicine, and other supplies to the breakaway territories across its border.

This show of restraint is even more remarkable given the stakes involved. In early 2014, Viktor Yanukovich, the pro-Russian Ukrainian president, was ousted in an illegal putsch orchestrated by the CIA, which brought to power an anti-Russian government that picked up where previous ones had left off—persecuting, oppressing, and dis-enfranchising those who speak Russian or identify with a Russian heritage. The ensuing violence has already claimed thousands, as the separatists are now locked in a fight for their own survival, attacked by Ukrainians, with only Russia standing behind them.

That, at least, is the official version heard there. Few on the outside would see it as little more than an Orwellian inversion of the truth. Russia bears responsibility for fomenting violence; its troops are actively deployed and fighting on Ukrainian soil; it provided the antiaircraft system that destroyed the Malaysian passenger jet in the summer of 2014; it provided support to the pro-Russian government when the latter began killing popular protesters in the streets of Kiev; and it provided shelter to the very same murderers and heinously corrupt leaders who ordered the crackdown. Russia's bloody fingerprints are all over this war, beginning with its first act of aggression, the annexation of Crimea.

Virtually none of this, however, penetrates the wall thrown up by Russia's state-controlled media. Its messaging keeps the "national conversation" pointing in one direction that manages to pack everything in: swastikas, the Time of Troubles, Third Rome isolationism. Sustained by choreographed disinformation campaigns, manufactured events, and multiple layers of obfuscation, this story line is also buttressed by a historical narrative centered on a grand sense of déjà vu that is playing itself out precisely where all of Russia's fault lines converge.

President Putin's speech to the Russian parliament in March of 2014 defending the annexation of Crimea was a model of this method in action, both synchronically and diachronically. Crimea, as he laid out, beckons all the way back to Rus, when, as legend has it, Grand Prince Vladimir embraced Christianity on its soil in 988, thereby making it the birthplace of Russia's spiritual soul. The Mongol invaders tore it away after the Orthodox Byzantines and then it passed to the Crimean Tatars; only under Catherine the Great, five hundred years later at the end of the eighteenth century, was it recovered by Russia. That effort cost many Russians their lives, and their blood watered the land as did that of thousands more defending Crimea against foreign attacks in the nineteenth and twentieth centuries.

The speech makes ample use as well of the lessons of *smuta*. Crimea was essentially stolen from Russia when it reeled after the breakup of the Soviet Union. The 1990s is when the arbitrary transfer in 1954 of Crimea to Ukraine, then a Soviet republic, should have been redressed, but Russia was too weak. At long last, Russia has recovered from its Time of Troubles—in the speech, it remains unstated but understood that this was due to Putin's leadership—but Ukraine never has. "Usurpers" and "pretenders" prey on it from inside, while on the outside NATO and the West encroach as part of their centuries-long effort to contain Russia, "to drive it into a corner." Yet as anyone knows, Putin warned, "if you press down on a spring hard enough, it will snap back with force."

In so many words, this is what Russia did. It had to intervene in order to "defend the rights and very life" of innocent Crimeans. There was, to be sure, no invasion; rather a defensive operation involving Russian troops legally stationed there and whose numbers were increased according to treaty. Threading through his speech is the core narrative that explains the popular overall response in Russia to annexation. Not only does it right a wrong by regaining territory unjustly taken from Russia—akin to a kidnapped child returning to its family. It also demonstrates on an international level that Russia has shed the curse of the 1990s; no longer can it be ignored or treated as a second-rate power. Russia, Putin declared, is an "independent, active participant in international affairs, and it has, just like other countries, its own national interests which need to be taken into account and respected."[8]

Hitler takes over from there. The Ukrainian side is also riddled with "fascists" and "Nazis," and just as Crimea was liberated from German occupiers in 1944, exactly seventy years later it was delivered once more from the same hands. Three factors bring these terms into play. First, during World War II some Ukrainian nationalists did, at times, work with Germany in the mistaken belief that with its support they could attain an independent Ukraine. Second, a few neo-Nazis did participate in the popular protests that toppled President Yanukovich. Third, "fascist" and, to a lesser extent, "Nazi," have grown into catch-all labels that can be applied to essentially anyone or anything construed as anti-Russian. They are the necessary terms to preserve a Manichaean vision of Russia's place in the world in the strictest, most uncompromising colors. The Second World War is not, therefore, the standard against which to measure other conflicts, as might be the case in other cultures. It is the bible by which to define them, locking all of them, including defeats like the Afghan War, in its box of irresistible tropes and analogies.

Their present-tense power opens the door to admit all of Russia's perceived enemies today into that camp. As we learn from the twelfth and final volume of *The Great Patriotic War*, fascism didn't die in a bunker in 1945. It has risen once more, and its followers need not wear brown shirts, goose step, or offer stiff-armed salutes. Any country with pretensions to creating a "unipolar authoritarian world order" is a de facto heir to Hitler's dreams. Yet only one country fits that bill—the one whose code words for invasion are "development of democracies" and "protecting human rights"; the one whose military bases straddle the world, in particular, surrounding Russia; and the one who, ultimately, is behind the war in Ukraine: the United States.[9]

Coding this conflict as a replay of World War II with America as the next generation of Nazis begs the question of how sincerely those who speak this language really believe it. Nevertheless, the further one travels to the right down the spectrum of Russian nationalism, the more fervent it becomes. Recent American actions help fuel the fire. The invasion of Iraq in 2003 and, especially galling to Russians given shared Slavic and Orthodox roots, the bombing of Serbia in 1999 are its signature criminal aggressions. And its insistence on militarily dominating the post–Cold War world as the global policeman is but a mask for universal designs.

No matter the degree of sincerity behind it, this paradigm has once more become the default way of understanding Russia's role in history, indeed, its raison d'être. Accordingly, Russia exists to stand up to those who seek to dominate the world—an article of faith that gained new life even before the wars in Georgia and Ukraine. In 2007, when Russia was at peace, Putin turned his May Ninth address into a warning about America's unilateralist aggressive nature. Even if Nazi Germany had long ceased to exist, "such threats," he concluded, "are not decreasing today. They merely transform themselves by changing colors, and in these new threats, like during the time of the Third Reich, we see the same disregard for human life and the same pretensions to global hegemony."[10]

The fact that this official narrative was already in play years ago means that the war in Ukraine—as if the Kremlin could have foreseen the future—has been back-slotted into a preexisting frame as continuing proof of the West's nefarious designs. Call the analogy with Nazis what one may—cynical, obscene, crackpot, or, for that matter, meritorious—it continues to bear a bounty of fruit for domestic consumption. Any action, for example, that America takes in support of Ukraine, whether political, economic, or military, confirms its verity. Anytime America assists Georgia or one of the Baltic States; anywhere it projects its military or ramps up NATO's presence—even in areas not of direct interest to Russia—the paradigm scores another success.

This myth rings even truer for those who believe Russia itself is already under full assault—a proposition the final volume of *The Great Patriotic War,* issued in 2015 with its title page sporting the president's approving signature, toys with openly. While the enemy has not, as of yet, crossed the border in arms, it targets all things Russian, especially its "traditional values," by seeking to impose "an alien way of life" upon it—which, though not stated directly here, is understood first and foremost as homosexuality. Elsewhere, some have gone so far as to profess that Russia is caught in a "Thousand-Year War" with the West that commenced when it embraced Christianity. Further down that path a few even feel that the struggle has entered its End of Time phase, when the battle is for their faith, land, culture, and, ultimately, their very existence. If in World War II Hitler threatened to exterminate Russia, then a genocide directed against its people looms once more. The only difference is that this time they are alone.

If genocide is the preferred term for fearmongers on the fringe of Russian nationalism, the Kremlin and state-run television—the primary source from which Russians get their news—nevertheless draw the world in Manichaean colors as well. Outside of Russia, darkness and disorder reign because the United States, drunk on arrogance as the sole superpower, has become a beast preying on those left vulnerable in the absence of the Soviet Union's protective cloak. Wherever conflict has erupted after the Cold War—from the Balkans in the 1990s to Syria at the present time—America's sinister hand can be found, whether open and obvious, as with the invasion of Iraq, or covert and conspiratorial, as with the overthrow of successive

Russia in 2015

pro-Russian governments in Ukraine during the Orange Revolution of 2004 or following the Maidan protests in Kiev ten years later.

In this world Russia stands alone, basking in the sun of its own exceptionalism, one inextricably linked to May Ninth. Every year at that time, the "Victory!" mantra springs up on posters in stores; it adorns billboards lining highways, and it flashes on television screens in between programs as if self-advertising the nation to itself. Yet increasingly it lives on after the VE Day celebrations and parades, gaining momentum as the slogan of a new Russia. Its spirit is carried forth not just by that single word, but by its partner, black and orange ribbons mimicking the Order of St. George, that now also stands for triumph during the war. Streaming from car antennas and rearview mirrors or pinned to one's chest and backpack, it signals allegiance to the idea of Russia as curated by the state.

The growing ubiquity of verbal and visual icons channeling triumph in World War II—and we can include here T-shirts, coffee mugs, stickers, and even an airline company called Victory—pushes the message to the extent that it eclipses its original referent. Often standing alone, this word—over what, over whom is left unanswered—rises defiantly just like Russia itself. In it one hears the echo of the country's ascent from the ruins of the Soviet Union, of its return as a power of consequence on a global scale, and of its success in standing up to the West, crowned by its seizure of Crimea and the jolt sent through its neighbors and all the way to Washington. The sentiment operates on a mystical plane, both provident and nostalgic, since it also invokes Nevsky's shield and Pozharsky's sword along with the fields of Borodino and the walls of Brest Fortress. If Russia's civic religion has a god, then Victory is its name.

History's Life Cycles

No matter how hyperbolic or extreme these sentiments, we can still see in them vestiges of the methodological mind-set that arose in the nineteenth century. To this extent, what we hear from the Kremlin is a reconfiguration and amplification of earlier traditions issuing from a shared core: an essentializing view of Russia's wars, as if they all emanate from a single transcendent one. Be it of a thousand years or not, it runs continuously, turning intervals of peace into temporary breaks or lulls until the next great foe arrives. It travels seamlessly through Russian history with a rotating cast of villains and conspirators, most often from the West but not necessarily so. Since the foe may not even wear a military uniform but come disguised as a cultural, linguistic, or economic threat, all points on the compass are suspect.

This perception, often derided by outsiders as a hyperbolic and delusional persecution complex, actually performs as a strength inside Russia since it provides the single most effective defense against the charge that the nation is innately more belligerent than others. Responsibility and blame for its militarism lie precisely on those outside its borders, for they have made war an inescapable part of Russia's existence. In short, if all nations mine their past to affirm a sense of commonality through shared parables, lessons, and storytelling, then Russia is no different; it's just been handed a different playbook.

At this level, the war myth, more than any other narrative available to Russia, can provide a stabilizing plane for a collective identity. If its history is full of tortuous vicissitudes—from the chaos and conflict of a divided Rus to dominating half the planet as a superpower; from being the bastion of Orthodoxy to the sword of atheism—then pressing those seismic shifts through this sieve aligns all of its twists and turns along a single axis. No matter what fate might bring, this story line can handle it, because when elevated to that transcendent realm, Russian history becomes consistent with itself by orbiting around the same themes, formulas, and scenarios. It creates its own internal logic that can find sustenance virtually anywhere and anytime.

A sure sign of the myth's stabilizing strength is that it is not dependent on Russia's actual condition as a country. When its power grows, myth makes that ascent feel right by serving up a large platter of just cause. When it recedes, myth provides the tools to explain why, yet with the comforting reassurance that any downturn is temporary. This flexibility marks Russia's exceptionalism as different, for instance, from England's, which also wrapped its rise to global prominence in the sentiments of a providential mission. "The dispensations of the Lord have been as if he had said," reads an official proclamation from the seventeenth century, "*England*, thou art my first-born, my delight among nations."[11] Assertions like these, however, tended to last only as long as the empire did—which is certainly not the case with Russia.

If anything, Russia's belief in its own exceptionalism reminds one of America's—in terms of adaptability, one hastens to add, not content. At some time or another, all of the latter's major wars have also been drawn up as examples of its special destiny. The revolution against Britain gave birth to it as a democracy; a civil war was the necessary blood sacrifice to purge America of the sin of slavery and preserve it as a unique experiment; and entry into World War I was required "to make the world safe for democracy," as President Woodrow Wilson famously announced. World War II launched the American crusade to save the world from global tyranny, which the Cold War extended into another chapter. Even Vietnam could be made to fit inside this category when, at the outset, it was drummed up as an essential step in stopping the spread of communism. Following suit, the War on Terror, the invasion of Iraq, and intervention in Afghanistan were billed at various times as part of a continuing and indispensable global mission.

Whether as a city on a hill or, for Russia, as a cross on a hill, nations such as these don't do lowercase history; something majestic always lies around the next corner. Where Russia is different, however, is the "feel" that myth lends to its passage through time. While any nation can chart its path as a linear one—king following king, peace following war—Russia has a second option, a cyclical one, that provides yet another layer of stability for its collective self-consciousness. If invasion, suicidal civil wars, and periodic implosions are constants of its existence, then is not the opposite also true: reciprocal bursts of rebirth and recovery?

Viewing the grand movement of Russian history in this way helps smooth out disjointed, jagged, and abrupt shifts in fate, as if they are all part of a common pattern. Sometimes a stretch is needed to fit history to that mold, but many have sought to do just that. In fact, an anticipatory hint of this tradition can be found in the sixteenth century at the conclusion of what, with hindsight, might be deemed the first cycle.

Ivan the Terrible's conquest of Kazan in 1552, we recall, spurred his realm onto the road of fantastic expansion. It brought the Volga under Russian control which then rapidly spread east into Siberia and south to the Caspian Sea. As reflected in *The History of Kazan,* written shortly after the siege, the true significance of that victory, the anonymous writer asserts, can only be understood in its preceding historical (and cosmic) context.

The rulers of Kazan were descendants of the Mongols which is where, in effect, his history begins. When those invaders first came, he writes, "our great Russian land was made an orphan and a pauper, and its honor and glory were taken from it." He then coyly adds, "but not forever." After Ivan's grandfather threw off the Yoke in 1480, Russia once more became "a united kingdom, a united state and a united power." The author's choice of metaphor brings nature's most basic cycle onto his side. "Just as winter passes into quiet spring," the Russian land "regained its former eminence, its piety, and its riches." But even with that the ordeal was not over. Now it was Ivan's turn to finish the task by wiping out the final vestiges of that infidel army, to lead Russia from spring into summer, and in so doing to take his Christian realm to new heights.[12]

Ivan did just that but, continuing on this train of thought, after his death Russia would plunge straight back down into the wintry depths of the Time of Troubles. Yet thanks to Patriarch Hermogen, Prince Pozharsky, and others, we know that it would rise again and grow to its greatest size ever. Halfway through that ascent, when Catherine the Great was conquering Crimea and carving up Poland at the end of the eighteenth century, Russia's first and largest epic poem in Homeric style appeared as if on order to mark that way station. Mikhail Kheraskov took up Ivan's conquest of Kazan as the fitting background for his nine-thousand-line *Rossiad,* yet but before launching readers on that odyssey, he dutifully instructed them in prose how, to date, the cycle proceeded.

As Russia continued to grow, passing through the romantic nationalism of the nineteenth century, an even more inspired way of viewing these cycles emerged. Was there not something of a Christian rhythm to its path through history? If rebirth always follows (near) death, then in the words of Mikhail Menshikov, a publicist of prodigious output at century's end, does not Russia bear "passions" just like Christ? As the true seat of Christianity, how could it not follow a Christlike pattern; what could be a more fitting link between land and faith?[13]

In a perverse kind of way, one can extend this chain further from the year of Menshikov's death, 1918. From the blood and ruins of civil war, Russia was born into a new life under the Hammer and Sickle and came to dominate even more of the globe. As we know, that life expired in 1991, leading the distraught poet Nikolai Triapkin to pose the question again: "O, Rus of mine / Is that not you there on the cross?"[14]

Dying in 1999, Triapkin would not see its resurrection from the ashes of the Soviet Union, yet one who has is Alexander Prokhanov, a former journalist who earned fame as a champion of the Soviet Union's foreign incursions, including Afghanistan. During the turmoil of the 1990s, he figured as one of the most vocal proponents of extreme Russian nationalism—the kind with anti-Semitism at its core. Now, both ardent patriot and unrepentant nostalgist for Soviet greatness, Prokhanov has waxed jubilant that yet another cycle has begun. The annexation of Crimea and bloody rise of pro-Russian separatists in Ukraine stand as irrefutable proof that Russia is on the right track once more—beginning another ascent while joyfully incurring the wrath of others. "America more and more is showing its profound hatred for Russia," he wrote early in 2014. "And that's a good sign: an Empire has been born." The fifth, by his count.[15]

One does not need to believe such metaphors literally or go down Prokhanov's extreme path in order to recognize their appeal. Christian or not, a cyclical view of history is inherently more optimistic and encouraging than a linear one which, by its very nature, presupposes a terminal point. It presents Russia as if protected by a special guardrail as it passes through time. It may come close to the edge, but never will it fall off into extinction. In the doomed year of 1918, the symbolist poet Alexander Blok famously pronounced that it is Russia's fate "to endure torment, humiliation and loss, yet she will emerge from such depths once again great, though in a new way."[16] He died that same year, not knowing how prophetic his words were, at least for those steeped in myth.

Viewing history this way also provides for a contiguity of space. During each cycle, Russia's political borders shift, yet in this mythic dimension its conceptual horizon remains constant. If an attack is the common experience of all on its land, then the sense of Russia or Russianness can swell to wherever the fighting occurs—even if it crosses into another country. This psychological reflex runs strongest in memories of World War II, when the distinction blurs between "Russian" and "Soviet."

President Putin put that slippage to good use, for example, in the May 9 platform of 2014 against the background of growing bloodshed in Ukraine. He declared, on the one hand, the holiday as Russia's, a celebration of "when the all-conquering strength of patriotism triumphs and when we feel in particularly sharp terms what it means to be faithful to the Motherland and how important it is to defend its interests." On the other, however, he made clear that the space which bore witness to duty and defense was larger than Russia's current territorial dimensions.

Playing with this notion, he delivered a roll call of the war's feats that first ran east to west, from the industrial plants of Siberia to partisans in the forests of Belarus. Then it turned north, to Leningrad, from there proceeding south through Moscow, Stalingrad, Sevastopol, and ending on the Dniepr River, where—unmentioned but obvious to all—Kiev, the capital of Ukraine, sits. The great expanse of *this* territory was where the "outcome of the war was determined," and where "the iron will of the Soviet people, their fearlessness and *stoikost,* saved Europe from slavery." Thus all who currently live on that "native land," no matter what citizenship they hold, owe a supreme debt to "our fathers, grandfathers and great-grandfathers who fought to their deaths."[17]

Russian weaponry in the Victory Day Parade, May 9, 2014, Red Square, Moscow. On the edifice of the building is a backdrop of the Order of the Patriotic War, awarded for exceptional conduct in battle during World War II. Pavel Golovkin / Associated Press.

Via the war, Putin swirls together the concepts of "us," "victory," and "motherland" that include Ukrainians and Belarussians as well. In the experiential melting pot he puts forth, national distinctions are, at first, meaningless: you were either on the good side, fighting for the motherland, or you were not. Yet at the same time, the motherland cannot be anything else but Russian. The implication is clear: those today in the Russian-Belarussian-Ukrainian triangle who oppose the motherland's interests only carry on the work of the former enemy which is why, once again, they deserve being called "Nazis" and "fascists."

Returning to the Roots

When considering the war myth's impact and endurance, a number of caveats arise that warrant attention. Most obvious is that not every work in Russian culture adheres to it. The Second World War has, besides Viktor Astafev, a host of other veterans-turned-writers, such as Vasil Bykov and Grigory Baklanov, whose novels and stories eviscerate any pretensions to it being a clash of absolutes; quite enough moral turpitude and villainy are shown to exist on all sides. Afghanistan brought prominence (and death threats) to Svetlana Alexievich in response to her *Zinky Boys* which, along with others, clarified what a catastrophic horror show that war was, again for all sides. Anna Politkovskaia's groundbreaking and fatally repercussive journalism on Chechnya is echoed in *One Soldier's War,* Arkady Babchenko's harrowing memoir of serving in both the first and the second Chechen conflicts. And in the case of Crimea, the text was written on the streets of Moscow when thousands demonstrated against annexation, though to no avail.

So too can the myth's core themes face challenges. All of the above have shown that blood, in quite liberal amounts, has been shed in vain; that defeat cannot always be recovered by the halo of "moral victory"; and that Russians can be as savage as the ones they fight. On this last note, Babchenko stands out, not the least for which because he was a both a survivor of and participant in the butchery in Chechnya. To what level it could descend we learn in a quiet aside about a unit that entered a village and found fellow Russians castrated and crucified in the main square. All the Chechen men were then rounded up and castrated alive, en masse. It took half a day.[18]

Core messages can also come under attack. Russia, like others in the nineteenth century, sold its territorial conquests as a civilizing mission. "Is it not obvious," wrote the historian Vasily Grigorev in 1840, "that Providence preserved the peoples of Asia from all foreign influences so that we could find them in an entirely undisturbed condition and therefore more inclined to accept the gifts we bring?"[19] No truer rebuttal came shortly thereafter from the brush of Russia's foremost painter on war, Vasily Vereshchagin.

On his canvases, far from bearing gifts, Russians brandish weapons as they march, fight, and die across central Asia. Noble cause finds no home in several of his more noted—and sometimes banned—

paintings. Instead the focus is on the price. In one, Russians wounded, bloodied, and bandaged lie in huddles at a field hospital; another opens onto bodies strewn across a field, naked and silent but here a mouth open, there a gaping hole visible—all inspired by Vereshchagin's encounter with Russians posthumously mutilated on a battlefield.

Most striking is when he trades realism for the purely symbolic, as in the 1871 *Apotheosis of War.* At its center, skulls are piled into a macabre pyramid; some are broken while others are frozen with jaws agape as if still screaming. Crows loom overhead, having removed the victims' eyes and the last bits of flesh; in the background a village lies shattered. Yet the effect does not end there. Though the pyramid invokes the legacy of Tamerlane, the scourge of central Asia in the fourteenth century, Vereshchagin added to the frame a caption that, as befitting a scene of destruction which shows no uniform or claims no side, reads simply: "To the memory of all great conquerors, past, present and future."

Interestingly, while this body of work brought criticism for being unpatriotic, it did not make Vereshchagin a pacifist. War was too much of an intoxicant in both aesthetic and psychological terms. Schooled as a naval cadet, he reenlisted in his thirties to fight in the Russo-Turkish War of 1877–1878. It took the life of his brother and almost claimed Vereshchagin himself, who suffered a grievous leg wound. After the war, he devoted his attention to a series of paintings inspired by the campaign of 1812 that followed the Tolstoyan message of the People's War while also offering famous profiles of Napoleon in defeat. (Vereshchagin was quite popular in America as well, where he scored success with, inter alia, a painting of Theodore Roosevelt charging up San Juan Hill during the Spanish-American War.) When war broke out between Russia and Japan in 1904, his fixation proved fatal. Though in his sixties, he sailed on the Pacific Fleet's flagship, *Petropavlosk,* as its official portraitist, and perished along with most of the crew when it struck a mine.

Another wounded veteran of the Russo-Turkish War also made a name by working contrary to expectation. While the war was popularized, quite successfully, as that of a paternal Russia marching to liberate other Slavs such as the Serbians and Bulgarians from their Muslim oppressors, the enduring piece of its literary legacy is a short story, "Four Days," by Vsevolod Garshin. Widely seen as the first example of stream-of-consciousness prose in Western literature, the entire story concerns the time a wounded Russian lies in the field, unable to move, next to the rotting body of the enemy he has killed. The corpse bloats under the fierce sun, maggots eat its flesh, and finally the face liquefies and slides off the skull. Only then does the protagonist see in it the human being who was once alive. A "murderer" is what he calls himself in Russia's most successful war between 1812 and 1945.

Even the demons of World War II can be humanized, as suggested by a few recent movies. To be sure, this would apply only to lower ranks wearing the uniform of the Wehrmacht, not the SS, but such a step was virtually unthinkable before. The boldest in that direction came in Georgii Vladimov's 1994 novel and recipient of the Booker Prize, *A General and His Army*, which gives a semi-sympathetic portrait of Russia's most notorious traitor, General Andrey Vlasov, who collaborated with the Germans after his capture in 1942. (He was hanged in Moscow in 1946, but his name has lived on as a catchword for all collaborators, or "vlasovites.")

And the doyen of them all, Tolstoy, completed his arc as war chronicler with a blistering pacifist manifesto following the outbreak of the Russo-Japanese War in 1904. Addressing the tsar as if he were a commoner, "Nikolai Romanov," he accused the monarch of consigning fifty thousand Russians to their death on "a foreign land" to which they had no just claim. While Tolstoy's estimate of casualties-to-be was low, his words rang true, which is why the government confiscated as many copies as it could—even after 1910, when the writer died and the war was long over.[20]

These exceptions show that the representation of war has never been a monochromatic phenomenon in Russia. Even at the height of Stalinism, there were stunning deviations from the norm, such as the veteran Viktor Nekrasov's 1946 novel *In the Trenches of Stalingrad,* which tempers its quasi-autobiographical tale of victory with details on Russians' cowardice, leaders' ineptitude, and the panicked flight east that brought the Germans to the city. Remarkably, it won the Stalin Prize but also had an equal impact on later revisionists, as a veteran-turned-writer concluded that "no other book had as much influence on the rest of our war literature and on each of us than did his novel."[21]

Yet it also holds true that these exceptions have not upset the war myth's dominance as it has passed through imperial, Soviet, and post-Soviet hands. That longevity is as much a measure of its adulatory power—Russia always held in a favorable light—as its go-anywhere, go-anytime quality. It can turn to almost any part of its history and take what it needs in order to weave vastly disparate events into a simple, self-reinforcing story based on an equally simple premise: Russia's experience of war is unique, and that has emphatically shaped the people and the nation.

Several paths issue from this premise. One even allows for self-parody without undermining the seriousness of the subject. The framework of Ilya Boiashov's 2008 novel *The Tankist or the White Tiger* reads as if a medieval chronicler had tried his hand at taking on World War II. Divine intercession, legendary resilience, unparalleled self-sacrifice, satanic invader—it's all there, but with a droll twist on nearly every page. The hero is a living incarnation of the Unknown Soldier. Found burned to a crisp inside a tank—with his eyelids fused and virtually no skin left on his body—he survives by a miracle. Unable to speak or communicate his identity, he is christened "Ivan the Foundling" and returns to service as a tank driver par excellence. God, the "Great Driver" in the Sky accompanied by nimbus-wreathed tank-angels, has granted him the special power to communicate with engine motors and a sixth sense to help hunt for German armor.

Ivan's crew members are equally legendary, though by way of sin. One is the champion of drink; the other of lust. Together their quarry is a phantomlike, indestructible Tiger tank that terrorizes the Russian lines. Despite several tanks being shot out from under them, so to speak, they pursue it all the way across Eastern Europe to Czechoslovakia until the final day of the war. By then Ivan is alone, but he sets out in a personally refitted, captured German light tank to slay "the dragon" that still lives on even after the war's end.

As much as Ivan's quest reads like a comic inversion of Captain Ahab's, the footnotes that undergird *The Tankist,* in Melville fashion, offer frank commentary on the inner workings of tanks, the scope of Soviet sacrifice, and Nazi genocide. In the same serious tone, Boiashov also highlights key revisionist points such as commanders' suicidal predilection for frontal attacks, the mass rape of German women by Red Army soldiers, non-accidental friendly fire, and the false claims made by Soviet histories. The mix of high and low make for an infectious, unpredictable novel, but it stays faithful to the overall script of Russia's distinctive experience of war. Its comic leavening, in other words, is not blasphemous, which explains why *The Tankist* was a finalist for the Great Book Award—akin to Russia's Pulitzer—the year it came out. And *The White Tiger,* the movie version made in 2012, was Russia's Oscar submission for Best Foreign Film. (It didn't win abroad but it did at home, earning Russia's own equivalent, the Golden Eagle.)

That, needless to say, is the path far less traveled. The one taken by the state dominates all others as it leads increasingly into a narrow, uncompromising corner. This is where documentaries such as *Death of an Empire: The Lesson of Byzantium* or novels the likes of *The Wall* reside, their field of vision rarely exceeding vociferous disdain for the West and nativistic genuflecting. At this extreme, they constitute national hagiographies that strike the same notes again and again with almost incantatory effect: tomorrow is always June 22; every action taken by outsiders reflects a plot with fatal designs on Russia; and a Judas is born each day.

At this level, alternative worldviews constitute blasphemy that also—as with virtually anything—can be whipped up as an existential threat. It comes not just with World War II and the passing of a law in 2014 making it illegal to publicly spread "falsehoods" about

Soviet actions during the conflict, but with Russia's entire military legacy and assumed mission in history. The very same law also criminalizes any public display of "disrespect" for "symbols of Russia's military glory." While now part of the legal code, this sentiment has long simmered.[22] The beginning of *The Military History of Our Country,* for example, instructs readers that nothing less than their survival as a people depends on getting that history right—and that was in 2003. As a case in point, warns *Death of an Empire,* the Byzantines' slide to extinction began when they let their sense of history become "ruinously self-disparaging." It "mocked their traditions" and undercut their "faith." Bereft of a sense of historical greatness, the army itself "fell into decay," and youth fell prey to foreign influences that lured them, along with the "best minds" of science, to the West.

Herein lie the main thrust and purpose behind the war myth's ascendancy. By embracing its historical record, Russians can avoid the fatal trap of diminished self-esteem. It erases downturns and defeats and flips demons like Stalin into palatable fare—all so as to ensure that Russians do not suffer any "guilt over the past," we learn from an official source. Instead, in their wake resounds the march of ten centuries of triumph and heroism. This banner runs "throughout the whole of Russian history" to the extent that it becomes nothing less than "the distinctive characteristic of Russians themselves." It also illuminates their mystical, unifying spirit that "no one has ever broken" and reinforces the idea that the people are "not only invincible" but also "capable of changing the fate of the world."[23]

There is no other story but war that in one narrative stroke answers these needs and also welds that sense of pride to a vital corollary: a cult of the state as an equal partner in delivering national greatness. For in this myth, its interests join lockstep in the same steady march. What else but war—or the threat thereof—warrants the concentration of power in its hands? What else projects Russia's much sought-after relevancy on a regional and global scale and turns voices of dissent into harbingers of treachery? Indeed, only this myth can champion isolation as a virtuous destiny, captured best by a favorite quip of Tsar

Alexander III, who came to the throne in 1881, that has made a come-back today on billboards and subway advertisements. "Russia has only two allies," he let be known. "Its army and its navy."

Of course, not all Russians, it must be noted, follow this path, and many cited above, such as Tolstoy and Alexander Pushkin, would never have traveled down it either. Even in his younger days, Tolstoy was cautionary about the ills of overblown patriotism, and Pushkin's "To the Slanderers of Russia" can seem mild compared with much of what one encounters today, especially from hot-mouthed commentators on television or the bevy of cranks and conspiracy theorists fronting as historians who champion a clash of civilizations between "the Russian World" and the rest. A fervent experimenter in the ways of transmitting history—by verse, fiction, drama, anecdote, or old-fashioned prose—Pushkin possessed the intellectual curiosity, creative brilliance, and sense of decency that would automatically disqualify him from their ranks. (Dostoevsky is another matter.)

Yet even if we stand on the side of a Tolstoy or a Pushkin, a reverse caveat rises before us. No matter how dogmatic this mythic narrative becomes, no matter how tight its scripting, or no matter how cartoonish its claims, it would be imprudent to dismiss it as a mere tool of the state, that is, propaganda to be ignored. A certain chicken-egg dynamic always obtains. Just as much as central authorities can manipulate the cultural and political climate for that narrative to blossom, its seeds, nevertheless, lie deep in the soil of Russian history. This fact arms the default premise of Russia's unique experience of war with fortitude, flexibility, and a degree of credibility that suggests that whatever flag might fly over the Kremlin—even perhaps a liberal-democratic one—some variant of this myth will live on as a defining mark of the nation and its people.[24]

To understand the grip this myth can have on the Russian collective imagination, it pays to return to the time when it was first coming into its own. In the spring of 1813, Vasily Norov was serving in Saxony as part of the campaign to push Napoleon out of German territories. He was a junior cavalry officer, twenty years old, and would soon be wounded. (His younger brother had already lost his foot at age seven-

Monument unveiled at Brest Fortress in 2011 to commemorate the seventieth anniversary of the German invasion. Its dedication reads, "To the heroes at the border and to the women and children who through their own courage passed into immortality." Author's personal collection.

teen manning a cannon at Borodino.) The elder Norov would survive the war, join the Decembrists, spend years in prison after their failed revolt, and eventually write an account of the war blending in his personal experiences. His letters home that spring repeat the usual grumblings about military service (low pay and so forth), but one from May includes a brief comment that speaks volumes.

> Everyone is promising buoyant success in carrying out our good intentions: to liberate from the French yoke all nations who took up arms against us in the previous campaign and to show that Russia was capable not only of destroying those who rose against it, but also that it is able to secure peace and order for all of Europe.[25]

Norov then abruptly excuses himself. There is no more time to write, since tomorrow they will attack the French. Nevertheless, his words foreshadow how expansive the myth would become, from the idea of a magnanimous Russia willing to give its life to save others, even allies such as Austria and Prussia, who just a year before had aided Napoleon's invasion, to that of the army's humanitarian purposes. They also bridge the oxymoron of a *pax Europa* guaranteed by its military supremacy. And with all of these assumptions wrapped in an allusion stretching back to the medieval past, then maybe, in the reality of the moment, someone like Norov could believe that Russia's destiny is not mythic at all, and that this truly is its neverending mission.

Epilogue

Even before the conflict in Ukraine, the twenty-first century has been witness to the drastic, seemingly irreversible hardening of Russia's war myth. For those who subscribe to it, the reason why inevitably points to the 1990s with the march of NATO toward the nation's borders. From this perspective, the coalition's move eastward constitutes a twofold betrayal when, in typical fashion, the West took advantage of a Russia reeling from its latest Time of Troubles. Not only were there false assurances that NATO would not expand, but the intent behind its embrace of former satellite states of the Soviet Union and three of its former republics has never been as benign as was offered by Zbigniew Brzezinski, once the National Security Advisor to President Jimmy Carter and a prominent supporter of the move. "NATO's expansion," he wrote in 1995, "should not be seen as directed against any particular state, but as part of a historically constructive process shaping a secure, stable and more truly European Europe."[1]

That NATO is now perched directly on Russia's border clearly demonstrates at whose expense this "constructive process" had to come. No matter if clothed in the robes of democracy, how can a growing military alliance not be another "Drang nach Osten," that is, the West's perpetual drive to the East? Even Mikhail Gorbachev, the last leader of the Soviet Union who became something of a star in the West in the 1990s, has called NATO's expansion its "worst blunder," one that has "irreparably damaged" relations between Russia and the West. Once more it pays to heed Boris Vasilev's observation when the process was in full swing. Russia's "genetic code" makes its people "eternal border guards" whose necessary qualities include "mistrust" and "suspicion" of those who are arrayed on the other side.[2]

If, following this line, the 2008 conflict with Georgia stopped NATO from nipping at Russia's southern heel, then the coalition's direct support for the protests that brought down Ukraine's pro-Kremlin government in 2014 constituted a full assault against Russia's front door. The annexation of Crimea in March that same year thus became Russia's first real victory against Western encirclement and gave birth to a "Russian spring," which, in the minds of the most fervent believers, could spark a "[re]gathering of the Russian lands," the peace-evoking euphemism describing how Moscow conquered, acquired, and came to control much of the Russian-speaking Orthodox world in the late Middle Ages.

Indeed, the conflict in eastern Ukraine, as presented by Russian political authorities and echoed in state-controlled media, folds precisely into the default mythic narrative, even as the government denies intervening militarily to support pro-Russian separatists: directly on its border Russia has again been called upon to protect others, but this time not just any "other." It is fellow Russians who have been attacked by Western-backed Ukrainian forces. Nevertheless, as per national character, Russia still plays the dove in this crisis, limiting itself, so runs the claim, to humanitarian aid.

In the West, the hardening of the narrative that Russia is not and cannot be "one of us" also seems irreversible, at least for the present time. Here the reason why starts with Vladimir Putin himself as the latest incarnation of its irrepressible belligerence. That he has revealed his true colors not just as an autocrat but even more so as an international bully necessitates turning history on its head in order to set the record straight. Thus in the 2008 clash with Georgia it is he, prime minister at the time, and not then–president of Georgia, Mikheil Saakashvili, who assumes the role of crazy, megalomaniac fanatic. The fact that his superior forces pummeled Georgia's and took control of the breakaway territories of Abkhazia and South Ossetia proved that "the bear is back on the prowl."[3] More ominously, the taking of Crimea and fomenting of unrest in eastern Ukraine smack of Hitler carving the Sudetenland away from Czechoslovakia in 1938, only to seize the rest of the country just months later.

Actions by the new Russia, in short, have given an extended lease to the assumption, as voiced typically by Western commentators long before the crisis in Ukraine, that Russia truly is a special kind of beast. Its "DNA," the popular French intellectual Alain Minc concluded in 2012, compels it "to expand and conquer," and the hardwiredness of its aggressive militarism has even operated as a fact in the hands of specialists like Brzezinski and another influential presidential advisor, Richard Pipes, who served on the National Security Council in the Reagan administration.[4] While commenting on Russia's Soviet empire (albeit shortly before it broke up), both were secure in their present-tense assertions that, in Russia's case, the nurturing effect of history has determined its very nature. Brzezinski located its "predatory character" on an ideational plane, a "Great Russian imperial consciousness" that began with Third Rome messianism in the fifteenth century and has continued in successive waves ever since. Pipes, in turn, as noted in Chapter 1, spelled out in precise historic, economic, geographic, and political terms why for Russia "expansion is not a phase but a constant."[5]

What has hardened on both sides is an essentialized view of Russia that runs as strong as ever, a full two centuries after it matured. Whichever "Russia" is invoked, its contents are accepted as innate and immutable—hence the ease with which a claimed trait is prefaced by an adverbial "again" or "once more." While with other subjects we might treat such an approach as problematic, with Russia it often seems the preferred one.

If the pitfalls inherent in employing such categories to describe a nation's behavior and interests are familiar, they resonate nonetheless when they impact policy or serve as a quick substitute for judicious and informed reasoning. Assuming that a nation or, for that matter, a people has something like a DNA, even if tendered as metaphor, can flatten conceptual horizons and drive meaningful discussion into the ground. For every assertion that "subduing neighboring peoples" is "part of Russia's genetic makeup," one can hear instead that its "genetic code" embraces "death for one's friends, for the people, for the fatherland"—the latter assertion being Putin's own. Either way, such bio-ethnic claims define and confine Russia's engagement with the world as one primarily of conflict. It is either manning its ramparts or seeking to expand. Causality becomes prescripted, since Russia can only be the unilateral aggressor or aggressee, which further suggests that the proper course of action, even if not intended, should be a military one.[6]

This is why, in part, World War II analogies enjoy currency in both camps. If Putin's aggressive designs invite comparison to Germany's prewar machinations—for Brzezinski he is "a partially comical imitation of Mussolini and a more menacing reminder of Hitler"—then anti-Russian protestors in Ukraine can be swept into the collective bin of "Nazis" or "fascists."[7] One can always question how sincere politicians or government officials are in using such language. However, its saturating effect provides adequate grounds for word and belief to feed off each other and, particularly on the street or on the Internet, lead to the factualization of historical analogies in the collective imagination of many. Either way, the one lesson Hitler holds for all is that in facing him or someone like him diplomacy is not an option.

The essentializing reflex and its "clash of civilizations" thrust are all the more injurious when applied to a place like Ukraine, where so many historical fault lines—political, national, religious—converge and where the historical memory of Hitler rings so tragically loud. This reflex ignores factors vital to the other's perspective which, in turn, help feed the very same stereotypes. The result can be a hyperextended sense of self-righteousness, as reflected in NATO's April 2014 fact sheet declaring that it "has treated" Russia "as a privileged partner" ever since the breakup of the Soviet Union. Or, as in Pipes's earlier

Cold War rendition, the same reflex can generate a sweeping dismissal of its invasion anxiety. The "record of history," he noted, "shows that far from being the victim of recurrent acts of aggression, Russia has been engaged for the past three hundred years with single-minded determination in aggressive wars, and that if anyone has reason for paranoia it would have to be its neighbors." From the perspective of Poland, the Baltic States, or now Ukraine, for example, one cannot disagree; but the aggregate historical record also suggests that if any country has earned the right to be paranoid about what goes on along and across its borders, then Russia is surely on the short list.[8]

Acknowledging this does not make one an apologist for Russia because it too carries blame for its Janus-faced reputation and not just—as many would assert—by its actions alone. The very nature of an exceptionalism claimed from the experience of war preordains such a fracture. When it is announced at the onset of *The Military History of Our Country* that what one can say about a nation's conflicts is the most important indicator of what one can say about that nation, then purveyors of the Russian myth become prisoners of their own making, unable to escape war as the baseline for discussion and thereby keeping the door permanently open on *all* of Russia's military actions, from the fall of Berlin in 1945 to that of Simferopol, the capital of Crimea, in 2014.

Moreover, one cannot ignore how Russia's war myth fans the fires of crude nativism and a xenophobic populism that does not want to be of a "West" if defined as a set of values and rights enshrined in liberal democracy. Deeper in that chain of thought stirs the conviction that Russia must break from the West because the latter truly is the root of Russia's troubles. NATO, so it goes, is the cause of turmoil and disorder in Ukraine; the United States, not Russia, covets hegemony. Indeed, if one goes back to the beginning, then cannot the case be made (and it has been) that the West, in fact, incited the Mongols to invade in the first place?[9]

Rehearsing, challenging, or even parodying the stories on which national reputations are built does not bind one to the assumption that all permutations are of equal validity or share moral equivalence. Russia, if a single conclusion might be drawn from its tumultuous history, is not for relativists. Yet in any serious attempt to understand its imaging, whether from inside or out, one imperative still stands: recognizing what kinds of stories can come into play, why they do, and what traction they can have with whom. Russia's case seems more intractable than that of others, since the war of words surrounding it is still locked, for the most part, in the same, centuries-long battle. In this there is a lesson for both Russophobe and Russophile alike: to live by the sword, rhetorically speaking, compels one to heed its double edge.

APPENDIX

NOTES

ACKNOWLEDGMENTS

INDEX

Appendix: Filmology

Following are those Russian movies, miniseries, and television shows referenced in the text, by English translation, Russian title, director, and year of release.

Admiral [Admiral] (Andrei Kravchuk, 2008).

Afghan Fracture [Afganskii izlom] (Vladimir Bortko, 1991).

Alexander Nevsky [Aleksandr Nevskii] (Sergei Eisenstein, 1938).

And Quiet Flows the Don [Tikhii Don] (Sergei Urusliak, 2015).

And the Dawns Here Are Quiet [A zori zdes' tikhie] (Stanislav Rostotskii, 1972).

Ballad of a Soldier [Ballada o soldate] (Grigorii Chukhrai, 1959).

Breakthrough [Proryv] (Vitalii Lukin, 2006).

Brest Fortress [Brestskaia krepost'] (Aleksandr Kott, 2010).

Burnt by the Sun [Utomlennye solntsem] (Nikita Mikhalkov, 1994).

Burnt by the Sun—2 [Utomlennye solntsem-2] (Nikita Mikhalkov, 2010, 2011).

Checkpoint [Blokpost] (Aleksandr Rogozhkin, 1998).

Come and See [Idi i smotri] (Elem Klimov, 1985).

The Cranes Are Flying [Letiat zhuravli] (Mikhail Kalatozov, 1957).

Death of an Empire: The Lesson of Byzantium [Gibel' imperii: Vizantiiskii urok] (Olga Savostianova, 2008).

Defense of Sevastopol [Oborona Sevastopolia] (Vasilii Goncharov and Aleksandr Khanzhonkov, 1911).

Destiny of a Man [Sud'ba cheloveka] (Sergei Bondarchuk, 1959).

Dr. Zhivago [Doktor Zhivago] (Aleksandr Proshkin, 2006).

Fall of the Empire [Gibel' imperii] (Vladimir Khotinenko, 2004).

The Honor Is Mine [Chest' imeiu] (Viktor Buturlin, 2004).

Life and Fate [Zhizn' i sud'ba] (Sergei Ursuliak, 2012).

Minin and Pozharsky [Minin i Pozharskii] (Vsevolod Pudovkin and Mikhail Doller, 1939).

My Name Is Ivan [Ivanovo detstvo] (Andrei Tarkovskii, 1962).

Ninth Company [9 rota] (Fyodor Bondarchuk, 2005).

Olympius Inferno [Olympius Inferno] (Igor Voloshin, 2009).

One-Two, Soldiers Were Going [Aty-baty, shli soldaty] (Leonid Bykov, 1977).

Penal Battalion [Shtrafbat] (Nikolai Dostal, 2004).

Prisoner of the Mountain [Kavkazskii plennik] (Sergei Bodrov, 1996).

Purgatory [Chistilishche] (Aleksandr Nevzorov, 1997).

72 Meters [72 metra] (Vladimir Khotinenko, 2004).

1612: A Chronicle of the Time of Troubles [1612: Khroniki smutnogo vremeni] (Vladimir Khotinenko, 2007).

SMERSH [SMERSH] (Zinovii Roizman, 2007).

Stalingrad [Stalingrad] (Fyodor Bondarchuk, 2013).

Star [Zvezda] (Nikolai Lebedev, 2002).

They Fought for the Motherland [Oni srazhalis' za Rodinu] (Sergei Bondarchuk, 1975).

The Third Reich versus the Third Rome [Tretii Reikh protiv Tret'ego Rima] (Vladimir Novikov, 2008).

Thunder at the Gates [Grozovye vorota] (Andrei Maliukov, 2006).

Variag [Kreiser "Variag"] (Viktor Eisymont, 1946).

War and Peace [Voina i mir] (Sergei Bondarchuk, 1966–1967).

The White Tiger [Belyi tigr] (Karen Shakhnazarov, 2012).

Notes

Prologue

1. Frantisek Palacky, from Hans Kohn, "Introduction," in *Russian Imperialism from Ivan the Great to the Revolution,* ed. Taras Hunczak (New Brunswick, NJ: Rutgers University Press, 1974), 9.

2. Nikolay Berdyaev, *The Russian Idea,* trans. R. M. French (1947; reprint, Hudson, NY: Lindisfarne, 1992), 23.

3. Antonio Possevini, *Istoricheskie sochineniia o Rossii XVI veka* (Moscow: Izdatel'stvo Moskovskogo universiteta, 1983), 46.

1. Pedigree

1. "Slova Serapiona Vladimirskogo," in *Pamiatniki literatury drevnei Rusi: XIII vek,* ed. L. A. Dmitrieva and D. S. Likhachev (Moscow: Khudozhestvennaia literatura, 1981), 447, 449.

2. If, as Daniel Rowland has argued, in contemporary usage the concept of New Israel was more important than that of the Third Rome, in the mythic view of Russian history the latter reigns supreme, especially today, as the marker of Russian exceptionalism as a divine gift. See his "Moscow—The Third Rome or the New Israel," *Russian Review* 55, no. 4 (1966): 591–614.

3. Jaroslav Pelenskii, *Russia and Kazan: Conquest and Imperial Ideology (1438–1560s)* (The Hague: Mouton, 1974), 541.

4. *The History of Kazan,* from *Pamiatniki literatury drevnei Rusi: Seredina XVI veka,* ed. L. A. Dmitrieva and D. S. Likhachev (Moscow: Khudozhestvennaia literatura, 1985), 300–565.

5. N. F. Droblenkova, *Novaia povest' o preslavnom Rossiiskom tsarstve i sovremennaia ei agitatsionnaia patrioticheskaia pis'mennost'* (Moscow: Izdatel'stvo Akademii nauk, 1960), 189–209. The anonymous seventeenth-century pamphlet, inspired by Hermogen and from which these words are quoted, also praises him as "Christ's warrior" armed with "God's word" who stands astride their land as its "steadfast pillar" that will never fall. For a road map to the sheer complexity of this unprecedented chapter of Russian history, see Chester Dunning, *Russia's First Civil War: The Time of Troubles and the Founding of the Romanov Dynasty* (University Park: Pennsylvania State University Press, 2001).

6. On the true nature of Russian-Mongol political and military affairs and for the argument that the latter's impact was not solely negative on Russia, see the third volume of George Vernadsky's series *A History of Russia,* entitled *The Mongols and Russia* (New Haven, CT: Yale University Press, 1953); Henryk Paszkiewicz, *The Rise of Moscow's Power,* trans. P. S. Falla (New York: Columbia University Press, 1983); and Charles Halperin, *Russia and the Golden Horde: The Mongol Impact on Medieval Russian History* (Bloomington: Indiana University Press, 1985). The chronicles themselves are highly subjective accounts of events in Rus, generally omitting, for example, collaboration with heathen or heretical neighbors and treating political conflicts in almost exclusively religious tones. However, the very fact of this bias makes them central to Russia's grand narrative of war, since they are precursors of the simplified, black-and-white version of its conflicts that is favored by mythic history.

7. See John Fennell, *The Crisis of Medieval Russia, 1200–1304* (London: Longman, 1983), 103–106; and Mari Isoaho, *The Image of Alexander Nevsky in Medieval Russia* (Leiden: Brill, 2006), 183–190.

8. "Metropolit Kirill prizyvaet rossian otdat' svoi golosa Aleksandru Nevskomu v reitinge 'Imia Rossii,'" October 6, 2008, http://www.pravoslavie.ru/jurnal/27826.htm.

9. For a history of Russia's wars from the premodern period to the beginning of the twenty-first century, see David Stone, *A Military History of Russia from Ivan the Terrible to the War in Chechnya* (Westport, CT: Praeger Security International, 2006).

10. Vasily Trediakovsky, "Panegyric Verses to Russia," in *The Literature of Eighteenth-Century Russia*, vol. 1, ed. and trans. Harold B. Segel (New York: Dutton, 1967), 166. I have substituted "the radiant" for "a radiant"; Iurii Golotiuk, "Rossiiskie pogranvoiska otnyne sluzhat Bogu i Otechestvu," *Segodnia*, March 17, 1995, 2.

11. George Fedotov, *The Russian Religious Mind* (Cambridge, MA: Harvard University Press, 1946), 361.

12. "Letopisnaia povest' o Kulikovskoi bitve," in *Pamiatniki literatury drevnei Rusi: XIV-seredina XV veka*, ed. L. A. Dmitrieva and D. S. Likhachev (Moscow: Khudozhestvennaia literatura, 1981), 117–123.

13. "Obrashchenie mitropolita Moskovskogo i Kolomenskogo Sergiia (Stragorodskogo) pastyryam i pasomym Khristovoi Pravoslavnoi Tserkvi," in *Russkaia pravoslavnaia tserkov' v gody otechestvennoi voiny, 1941–1945 gg* (Moscow: Izdatel'stvo Krutitskogo podvor'ia, 2009), 38–40.

14. Ushakov's elevation to become patron saint of the strategic air wing was made in 2005. See "Slovo Sviateishego Patriarkha Aleksiia v Shtabe Dal'nei aviatsii VVS Rossii," September 27, 2005, http://www.patriarchia.ru/db/text/50591.html.

15. V. A. Zolotarev et al., *"Skazhite vsem, chto Rus' vsegda zhiva." Ratnye dela otechestva: Rus' i iunaia Rossiia VI–XVIvv* (Moscow: Animi Fortitudo, 2004), 32; A. E. Savinkin et al., *Khristoliubivoe voinstvo: Pravoslavnaia traditsiia Russkoi Armii* (Moscow: Russkii put', 2006), 481.

16. V. V. Abaturov et al., *Otechestvennaia voennaia istoriia*, vol. 1 (Moscow: Zvonnitsa-MG, 2003), 97.

17. "Poslanie Sviateishego Patriarkha Moskovskogo i vseia Rusi Aleksiia II po sluchaiu prazdnovaniia 625-letiia pobedy na Kulikovom pole," September 21, 2005, http://www.pleskovo.ru/index.php?name=kulikov2.

18. Richard Pipes, *Russia under the Old Regime* (New York: Charles Scribner's Sons, 1974), 83 (emphasis in the original), 80; Richard Pipes, *Survival Is Not Enough: Soviet Realities and America's Future* (New York: Simon and Schuster, 1984), 39.

19. Abaturov et al., *Otechestvennaia voennaia istoriia*, 1:192; S. Z. Kodzova, ed., *Istoriia Kryma* (Moscow: OLMA Media Grupp, 2015), 113.

20. George Vernadsky, ed., *A Source Book for Russian History from Early Times to 1917*, vol. 3 (New Haven, CT: Yale University Press, 1972), 610.

21. Boris Vasilev, *Liubi Rossiiu v nepogodu* (Moscow: Vagrius, 2008), 8.

22. Michael Cherniavksy, "Russia," in *National Consciousness, History and Political Culture in Early-Modern Europe,* ed. Orest Ranum (Baltimore, MD: Johns Hopkins University Press, 1975), 121 (emphasis in the original). On Russia's military history at this time, see Carol B. Stevens, *Russia's Wars of Emergence: 1460–1730* (New York: Pearson Longman, 2007).

23. Fyodor Dostoevsky, *Polnoe sobranie sochinenii v tridtsati tomakh,* vol. 25 (Leningrad: Nauka, 1983), 49, 22.

24. Heinrich von Staden's plans are in *The Land and Government of Muscovy,* ed. and trans. Thomas Esper (Stanford, CA: Stanford University Press, 1967); Andrew Wilson, *Ukraine Crisis: What It Means for the West* (New Haven, CT: Yale University Press, 2014), vii.

25. *Velikaia Otechestvennaia voina v dvenadtsati tomakh,* vol. 12, ed. S. K. Shoigu et al. (Moscow: Kuchkovo pole, 2015), 677–678; *Istoriia Velikoi Pobedy,* ed. V. A. Zolotarev, in the series *Voennaia istoriia Gosudarstva Rossiiskogo,* (Moscow: Animi Fortitudo, 2005), 623.

26. Yevgeny Yevtushenko, "Nepriavda," in *Ves' Evtushenko: Stikhi i poemy, 1937–2007* (Moscow: Slovo, 2007), 679–690.

27. Alexander Pushkin, letter of October 19, 1836, in *Polnoe sobranie sochinenii,* vol. 16 (Moscow: Voskresenie, 1997), 171.

2. A Myth Comes of Age

1. Karl Marx, "Poland's European Mission," in *The Russian Menace to Europe,* ed. Paul W. Blackstock and Bert F. Hoselitz (Glencoe, IL: Free Press, 1952), 106.

2. Fyodor Glinka, "O neobkhodimosti imet' istoriiu Otechestvennoi voiny 1812 goda," in "Biblioteka internet-proekta '1812 goda,'" www.museum .ru/museum/1812/library/Glinka3/index.html.

3. Fyodor Glinka, "Ocherki Borodinskogo srazheniia," in *1812: Borodinskaia bitva* (Moscow: Iauza-Eksmo, 2009), 7–113; Sergei Glinka, "Iz zapisok o 1812 gode," in *1812 god v russkoi poezii i vospominaniiakh sovremennikov* (Moscow: Pravda, 1987), 394–491.

4. *A Source Book for Russian History from Early Times to 1917,* vol. 2, ed. George Vernadsky (New Haven, CT: Yale University Press, 1972), 499. I have replaced "fatherland" with "country."

5. On this event, see Richard S. Wortman, *Scenarios of Power: Myth and Ceremony in Russian Monarchy*, vol. 1 (Princeton, NJ: Princeton University Press, 1995), 113.

6. Denis Davydov, *Voennye zapiski* (Moscow: Voennoe izdatel'stvo, 1982), 127.

7. Ibid., 91.

8. Ibid., 249.

9. Karolina Pavlova, "Moskva," in *Sbornik stikhov i pesen ob Otechestvennoi voine*, www.museum.ru/museum/1812/Library/poetry/content.html; "Kak na gorochke stoiala Moskva," in *Sbornik stikhov i pesen ob Otechestvennoi voine*, www.museum.ru/museum/1812/Library/content.html.

10. Sergei Glinka, "Iz zapisok o 1812 gode," 399.

11. Pamfil Nazarov, "Zapiski soldata Pamfila Nazarova," *Russkaia starina* 12 (1878): 529–556.

12. Vissarion Belinsky, *Polnoe sobranie sochinenii*, vol. 4 (Moscow: Izdatel'stvo Akademii nauk SSSR, 1954), 7–9.

13. Mikhail Lermontov, *Strannyi chelovek*, in *Sobranie sochinenii*, vol. 3 (Moscow: Khudozhestvennaia literatura, 1965), 321. For a discussion of how Russian-ness in 1812 and wars following manifested itself visually for over the next century, see Stephen M. Norris, *A War of Images: Russian Popular Prints, Wartime Culture and National Identity, 1812–1945* (DeKalb: Northern Illinois Press, 2006).

14. Lev Tolstoy, *Sobranie sochinenii v dvadtsati dvukh tomakh*, vol. 7 (Moscow: Khudozhestvennaia literatura, 1981), 130, 142–143, 181.

15. Ivan Turgenev in *L. N. Tolstoi v russkoi kritike*, ed. S. P. Bychkov (Moscow: Khudozhestvennaia literatura, 1952), 297–298; Lev Korneshov, "Bol'she, chem liubov'," *Otchizna* 9 (1978): 3.

16. Nikolai Karamzin, "O liubvi k otechestvu i narodnoi gordosti," in *Izbrannye stat'i i pis'ma* (Moscow: Sovremennik, 1982), 94.

17. Dostoevsky, *Complete Letters*, vol. 3, ed. and trans. David Lowe (Ann Arbor, MI: Ardis, 1990), 288; J. L. Black, *Nicholas Karamzin and Russian Society in the Nineteenth Century: A Study in Russian Political and Historical Thought* (Toronto: University of Toronto Press, 1975), 149.

18. Nikolai Karamzin, *Istoriia Gosudarstva Rossiiskogo: Polnoe izdanie v odnom tome* (Moscow: Alfa-Kniga, 2009), 409, 518.

19. Nikolai Karamzin, "Osvobozhdenie Evropy i slava Aleksandra I," in *Polnoe sobranie stikhotvorenii*, ed. Iu. Lotman (Moscow-Leningrad: Sovetskii pisatel', 1966), 300–311.

20. Gavrila Derzhavin, "Gimn liro-epicheskii na prognanie frantsuzov iz otechestva," *Sbornik stikhov i pesen ob Otechestvennoi voine,* www.museum .ru/museum/1812/Library/content.html.

21. L. G. Beskrovnyi, *Otechestvennaia voina 1812 goda* (Moscow: Izdatel'stvo sotsial'noi-ekonomicheskoi literatury, 1962), 28.

22. Nadezhda Durova, "Kavalerist-devitsa: Proisshestvie v Rossii," in *Kavalerist-devitsa: N. A. Durova v Elabuge,* ed. A. I. Begunova (Moscow: Reittar, 2003), 157. Her memoirs have been translated as *The Cavalry Maiden: The Journals of a Russian Officer in the Napoleonic Wars,* ed. and trans. Mary Fleming Zirin (Bloomington: Indiana University Press, 1988).

23. Andrei Naumov, ed., *Kulikovo pole. Antologiia publikatsii XIX–XX vekov* (Tula: Kulikovo pole, 2014), 205–238.

24. George Vernadsky, *The Mongols and Russia* (New Haven, CT: Yale University Press, 1953), 379.

25. Avraamy Palitsyn's account of the siege of the Holy Trinity–St. Sergius Monastery is from *Skazanie Avraamiia Palitsyna ob osade Troitse-Sergieva monastyria,* in *Biblioteka literatury drevnei Rusi,* vol. 14, ed. D. S. Likachev et al. (St. Petersburg: Nauka, 1997), 238–355.

26. Karamzin, *Istoriia Gosudarstva Rossiiskogo,* 1186; Sergei Kedrov, "Avraamii Palitsyn, kak pisatel': Novoe issledovanie," *Russkii arkhiv* 8 (1886): 519.

27. Apollon Maikov, "Uprazdnennyi monastyr'," in *Izbrannye proizvedeniia* (Leningrad: Sovetskii pisatel', 1977), 371.

28. Sergei Glinka, "Iz zapisok o 1812 gode," 450.

29. Fyodor Dostoevsky's comments on Russian exceptionalism are from *Dnevnik pisatelia,* in *Polnoe sobranie sochinenii v tridtsati tomakh* (Leningrad: Nauka, 1972) as follows, indicating the volume, the diary entry by month, as he did, and then page: "predestined and created," vol. 25 (April 1877), 100; "blessed and genuine union of all humanity," vol. 25 (July–August 1877), 195; "taking up arms," vol. 25 (April 1877), 99; "money and the scientific organization," vol. 25 (April 1877), 98; "true exaltation of Christ's truth," vol. 23 (June 1876), 50.

30. For a broader discussion of how Russia marshaled its distant past for nationalist purposes in the nineteenth century, see Olga Maiorova, *From the Shadow of Empire: Defining the Russian Nation through Cultural Mythology, 1855–1870* (Madison: University of Wisconsin Press, 2010).

31. Nikolai Sukhotin, *Voina v istorii russkogo mira* (St. Petersburg: Sklad u V. A. Berezovskago, 1898), v, 38.

32. Nikolai Sukhotin, *Voina v istorii russkogo mira* (1898; reprint, Moscow: Antologiia otechestvennoi voennoi mysli, 1998), 4.

33. Friedrich Engels, "The Foreign Policy of Russian Czarism," in Blackstock and Hoselitz, *The Russian Menace to Europe,* 28, 39.

34. Firuz Kazemzadeh, "Russian Penetration of the Caucasus," in *Russian Imperialism from Ivan the Great to the Revolution,* ed. Taras Hunczak (New Brunswick, NJ: Rutgers University Press, 1974), 261.

35. Astolphe Marquis de Custine, *Journey for Our Time,* trans. Phyllis Penn Kohler (New York: Pellegrini & Cudahy, 1951), 98; on the dismissal by Polish intellectuals of Russian Slavicness, see Serhiy Bilenky, *Romantic Nationalism in Eastern Europe* (Stanford, CA: Stanford University Press, 2012), 64.

36. Custine, *Journey for Our Time,* 169.

37. George Curzon, *Russia in Central Asia in 1889 and the Anglo-Russian Question* (London: Longmans, Green, 1889), 319; Robert Kagan, "The New Russophobes Are Here," *Weekly Standard,* July 1, 1996, 25.

38. James Doolittle et al., "Report on the Covert Activities of the Central Intelligence Agency," 1954, 2, https://cryptome.org/cia-doolittle/cia-doolittle .htm. On the invoking of Peter I's testament in the twentieth century, see Albert Resis, "Russophobia and the 'Testament' of Peter the Great, 1812–1980," *Slavic Review* 44, no. 4 (1985): 681–693; George Will, "NATO's Role in a Peaceful Europe," *Baltimore Sun,* June 13, 1996, http://articles.baltimoresun .com/1996-06-13/news/1996165054_1_nato-russia-rulers; Edward Lucas, *The New Cold War: Putin's Russia and the Threat to the West* (New York: Palgrave Macmillan, 2008), 12.

3. The Burden of Victory

1. Stephen G. Fritz, *Ostkrieg: Hitler's War of Extermination in the East* (Lexington: University Press of Kentucky, 2011), 299.

2. Elena Kochina, *Blockade Diary,* trans. Samuel C. Ramor (Ann Arbor, MI: Ardis, 1990), 65.

3. Max Hastings, *Inferno: The World at War, 1939–1945* (New York: Alfred A. Knopf, 2011), 140. I have changed the original, substituting "engagement" for "clash" in order to make the statement logically consistent with the phrase "from conception to execution."

4. Chris Bellamy, *Absolute War: Soviet Russia in the Second World War* (New York: Alfred A. Knopf, 2007), 5; Hastings, *Inferno,* 596.

5. Lidia Ginzburg, *Blockade Diary,* trans. Alan Myers (London: Harvill Press, 1995), 3.

6. Alexander Tvardovsky, *Vasilii Tyorkin* (Moscow: Raritet, 2000), 34–35. I have substituted "Alyosha" for "Fom" (Thomas) on the assumption that to the nonnative speaker it would sound more characteristically Russian (which is Tvardovsky's intent) and because of its close rhyme with "Russia."

7. On the state-enforced memory of the war in the Soviet Union, see Nina Tumarkin, *The Living and the Dead: The Rise and Fall of the Cult of World War II in Russia* (New York: Basic Books, 1994).

8. Viktor Astafev, *Proklyaty i ubity* (Moscow: Eksmo, 2005). It was published in two parts in the journal *Novyi Mir* in 1992 (issues 10–12) and 1994 (issues 10–12); it has not been translated into English. His comments that follow on the political officer's abuse of women are from "Snachala snariady, potom liudi," *Rodina* 6–7 (1991): 52–56; on the falseness of official Soviet history and on the impression of defeat in the war, see his "Polupravda nas muchila . . . ," *Voprosy istorii* 6 (1988): 34. For an example of the Dniepr as the "River of Heroes," see N. I. Lutsev et al., *Dnepr—reka geroev* (Kiev: Izdatel'stvo politicheskoi literatury Ukrainy, 1988), the preface for which was written by General Moskalenko, commander of the 38th and then 40th Armies there and who is quoted here.

9. Vladimir Tsvetkov, *Zvezdy mertsaiut* (Orel: Veshnie vodi, 2002). He is one of the few memoirists to describe at length the rapes and looting carried out in Germany and Eastern Europe. For an in-depth account of the experiences of the common Soviet soldier in World War II, see Catherine Merridale, *Ivan's War: Life and Death in the Red Army, 1939–1945* (New York: Metropolitan Books, 2006).

10. Sergei Poliakov, "Zapiski malen'kogo soldata o bol'shoi voine," *Sever* 9 (1995): 117.

11. Viacheslav Kondratev, "Paradoks frontovoi nostalgii," *Literaturnaia gazeta,* May 9, 1990, 9. His World War I–esque comments are from "Ne tol'ko o svoem pokolenii," *Kommunist* 7 (1990): 113–117. The "harvest of corpses" comes from Vladimir But's quasi-autobiographical novel *Trava sorok tret'ego goda* (Moscow: Vagrius, 1996).

12. The first six volumes of *Velikaia Pobeda* [The Great Victory] bear the title *65 let Velikoi Pobedy* [65 years of the Great Victory] (Moscow: Izdatel'stvo "MGIMO-Universitet," 2010); the final nine appeared under the second, shortened title. Subsequent citations are identified here by volume and page:

"defended the planet from the forces of evil" (1:29); "many innocent people" (1:30); "butchers" (8:146), "Asian barbarism" (1:51); on the Korolev brothers (7:352); "paid for by the blood" (1:38); "an attempt to form a new pan-European identity" (8:301).

13. *Velikaia Otechestvennaia voina v dvenadtsati tomakh*, vol. 7, ed. S. K. Shoigu et al. (Moscow: Kuchkovo pole, 2013); Vladimir Bushin, *Za rodinu, za Stalina!* (Moscow: Eksmo, 2003); Nikolai Chervov, *Provokatsii protiv Rossii* (Moscow: Olma Press, 2003); Vladimir Karpov, *Generalissimus* (Kaliningrad: Iantarnyi skaz, 2002); and Aleksandr Ognev, *Traditsii, voina i sud'ba Rossii* (Tver: Zolotaia bukva, 2004). All are veterans of the war.

14. *Velikaia Otechestvennaia voina*, 12:13.

15. Stephen Ambrose, *D-Day, June 6, 1944: The Climactic Battle of World War II* (New York: Simon & Schuster, 1994), 107.

16. Just as with overall Soviet losses in World War II, the precise number of people who perished during the siege of Leningrad is also unknowable. Some calculations focus on civilian deaths in the city itself while not counting the environs; others just on civilians, but leaving out soldiers who died defending it. Following Harrison Salisbury's estimate that combines all three, more than a million would be the likely number of victims in Leningrad and the surrounding region. See *The 900 Days: The Siege of Leningrad* (New York: Harper & Row, 1969), 516.

17. David McCullough, *Truman* (New York: Simon & Schuster, 1992), 262.

18. Alexander Pushkin, "Klevetnikam Rossii," in *Polnoe sobranie sochinenii v desiati tomakh*, vol. 3 (Moscow: Izdatel'stvo Akademii Nauk SSSR, 1963), 222–223.

19. Vladimir Medinsky, *Voina: Mify SSSR, 1939–1945* (Moscow: Olma Media Grupp, 2011), 615.

20. *Velikaia Otechestvennaia voina*, 12:693.

21. Boris Sokolov, *Okkupatsiia: Pravda i mify* (Moscow: Ast-Press, 2002).

22. Chervov, *Provokatsii protiv Rossii*, 378; D. A. Petukhov and M. N. Murashova, *Pobediteli* (Moscow: Metagalatika, 2005), 31; Vladimir Rostkovskii, *Verkhovnyi Glavnokomanduiushchii* (Moscow: Kraft, 2005), 3.

23. Vasily Grossman, *Life and Fate: A Novel*, trans. Robert Chandler (New York: Harper & Row, 1986).

24. Viktoria Pimenova, ed., *Boklada Leningrada: Narodnaia kniga pamiati* (Moscow: AST, 2014), 133, 69, 64.

4. Halo of Blood

1. Donald S. Detweiler, ed., *World War II German Studies,* vols. 18 and 19 (New York: Garland, 1979), 18:2, 4; 19:14, 15, 19.

2. General Max Simon, commander of the SS-Totenkopf Division and later of the XIII SS Corps, writing in 1949, in ibid., 19:3–4.

3. Frederick the Great's alleged statements and other opinions of the Russian military during the Seven Years' War are from Christopher Duffy, *Russia's Military Way to the West: Origins and Nature of Russian Military Power, 1700–1800* (London: Routledge & Kegan Paul, 1981), 74, 80, 177.

4. On the development of the Russian Army from the premodern period through the imperial age, see John Keep, *Soldiers of the Tsar: Army and Society in Russia, 1462–1874* (Oxford: Clarendon Press, 1985).

5. The size of each army at Borodino is still debated, as are the numbers of casualties, understood as the combined number of dead and wounded to the degree of being out of action. See Alexander Mikaberidze, *The Battle of Borodino: Napoleon against Kutuzov* (Barnsley: Pen & Sword Military, 2007), 50–51.

6. The commander with three hundred men at evening roll call was General Mikhail Voronstov of the Second Combined Grenadier Division, quoted from Mikaberidze, *The Battle of Borodino,* 109. Bagration's statement is quoted from the same source, 108. The belief in 50 percent losses by Russians has become canonical. See, for example, one of the earliest histories of the 1812 campaign, D. Buturlin, *Istoriia nashestviia Imperatora Napoleona na Rossiiu v 1812-m godu* (St. Petersburg: Izdanie knigoprodavtsa Aleksandra Smirdina, 1837), 261; or the jubilee history of 1912, A. K. Dzhivelegov et al., *Otechestvennaia voina i russkoe obshchestvo, 1812–1912: Iubileinoe izdanie,* vol. 4 (Moscow: Sytin, 1912), 28: "In all of modern history, there has never been a more bloody battle than Borodino. Nor has there ever occurred the event where an army, having withstood losses of 50 percent, was still capable the next day of continuing action."

7. Count Philippe-Paul de Ségur, *Napoleon's Russian Campaign,* trans. J. David Townsend (Alexandria, VA: Time-Life Books, 1980), 80; *With Napoleon in Russia: The Memoirs of General de Caulaincourt, Duke of Vicenza,* ed. Jean Hanoteau (New York: W. Morrow and Company, 1935), 103.

8. Fyodor Glinka, "Ocherki Borodinskogo srazheniia," in *1812: Borodinskaia bitva* (Moscow: Iauza-Eksmo, 2009), 62.

9. Mikhail Lermontov's "Borodino" was written in 1837; Karolina Pavlova's "Moscow," in 1844. Both in *Sbornik stikhov i pesen ob Otechestvennoi voine,* www.museum.ru/museum/1812/Library/content.html.

10. Mikhail Dragomirov's review of *War and Peace* ("Razbor 'Voiny i mira' ") and "A Note on the Russian Soldier" are from his *Ocherki* (Kiev: Izdanie knigoprodavtsa N. Ia. Ogloblina, 1898), 4–137, 138–149.

11. V. F. Greene, *Sketches of Army Life in Russia* (New York: Charles Scribner's Sons, 1881), 48–50.

12. On Russian casualties as a point of pride, see N. P. Mikhnevich, *Osnovy russkogo voennogo iskusstva* (Moscow: Tipografiia Shtaba Otdel'nogo korpusa Pogranichnoi strazhi, 1898), 171–175. On the Russian military in this period, see Bruce W. Menning, *Bayonets before Bullets: The Russian Imperial Army, 1861–1914* (Bloomington: Indiana University Press, 1992).

13. Sergei Smirnov, *Brestskaia krepost'* (Moscow: Raritet, 2000), 225.

14. Konstantin Siminov's words on the Brest-Berlin connection are cited in Vladimir Beshanov, *Brestskaia krepost'* (Moscow: Iauza-Eksmo, 2009), 291. As a sign of the strength of the myth of Brest as the first step to victory, even Beshanov, one of the most prolific revisionist historians, comes to the same conclusion.

15. Boris Vasilev, *His Name Was Not Listed,* trans. Robert Daglish (Moscow: Progress Publishers, 1978), 187. (The Russian version first appeared in 1974.) On Vladimir Putin's recommendations, see "The Reading List," *World War II* 25, no. 6 (March–April 2011): 16.

16. Randy Roberts and James S. Olson, *A Line in the Sand: The Alamo in Blood and Memory* (New York: Free Press, 2001), 223.

17. Lev Tolstoy, "Proekt o pereformirovanii armii," in *Sobranie sochinenii v 22-ukh tomakh,* vol. 16 (Moscow: Khudozhestvennaia literatura, 1983), 399.

18. Vladimir But, *Trava sorok tret'ego* (Moscow: Vagrius, 1996), 240.

19. Evgeny Martynov, *Iz pechal'nogo opyta Russko-Iaponskoi voiny* (St. Petersburg: Voennaia tipografiia, 1906), 83, 88.

20. Franz Halder, *The Halder Diaries: The Private War Journals of Colonel General Franz Halder,* vol. 6, *The Campaign in the Balkans and Russia: 21 February–31 July 1941* (Boulder, CO: Westview Press, 1976), 183.

21. F. W. von Mellenthin, *Panzer Battles: A Study of the Employment of Armor in the Second World War* (Norman: University of Oklahoma Press, 1956), 293; Ronald Smelser and Edward J. Davies II, *The Myth of the Eastern*

Front: The Nazi-Soviet War in American Popular Culture (New York: Cambridge University Press, 2008), 69.

22. Maurice Baring, *With the Russians in Manchuria* (London: Methuen, 1906), 183.

23. Greene, *Sketches of Army Life in Russia,* 25–26.

24. On Boris and Gleb and the significance of death as an accepted role or outcome of a leader's duty in medieval Russia, see Michael Cherniavsky, *Tsar and People: Studies in Russian Myths* (New Haven, CT: Yale University Press, 1961), 8–22. For a broader discussion of their legacy, see Gail Lenhoff, *The Martyred Princes Boris and Gleb: A Socio-Cultural Study of the Cult and the Texts* (Columbus, OH: Slavica Publishers, 1989).

25. E. M. Saenkova and N. V. Gersimenko, *Ikony sviatykh voinov* (Moscow: Interbuk-biznes, 2008), 3 (emphasis added).

5. Defeat Undone

1. Svetlana Alexievich, *Zinky Boys: Soviet Voices from the Afghanistan War,* trans. Julia and Robin Whitby (New York: W. W. Norton, 1992), 111.

2. Artyom Borovik, *The Hidden War: A Russian Journalist's Account of the Soviet War in Afghanistan* (New York: Grove Press, 1990), 176.

3. The secret documents from the Kremlin were published in "Sekretnye dokumenty iz osobykh papok: Afganistan," *Voprosy istorii* 3 (1993): 3–33.

4. Alexievich, *Zinky Boys,* 6, 17.

5. Ibid., 124.

6. Valery Kichin, writing for *Rossiiskaia gazeta,* October 1, 2005, https://rg.ru/2005/10/01/9rota.html.

7. Edward Porter, "9th Company," *Sunday Times* (London), February 18, 2007, 14; Denise J. Youngblood, *Russian War Films: On the Cinema Front, 1914–2005* (Lawrence: University Press of Kansas, 2007), 208.

8. Boris Gromov, *Ogranichennyi kontingent* (Moscow: Progress, 1994), 331.

9. "Putin Praise for Russian War Film," BBC News, November 8, 2005, http://news.bbc.co.uk/go/pr/fr/-/2/hi/entertainment/4416674.stm.

10. Walter Lord, *Day of Infamy* (New York: Holt, 1957), 106, 113, 153.

11. Frederick Grossmith, *Dunkirk—A Miracle of Deliverance* (London: Bachman and Turner, 1979), 8.

12. Lev Tolstoy, "O tsarstvovanii imperatora Aleksandra II-go," in *Polnoe sobranie sochinenii,* vol. 17 (Moscow: Gosudarstvennoe izdatel'stvo khudozhest-

vennoi literatury, 1936), 360–362 (the article was written in 1877 but was not published); Friedrich Engels, "The Foreign Policy of Russian Czarism," in *The Russian Menace to Europe*, ed. Paul W. Blackstock and Bert F. Hoselitz (Glencoe, IL: Free Press, 1952), 45.

13. Orlando Figes, *The Crimean War: A History* (New York: Metropolitan Books, 2010), 163.

14. On the Russian military during this period, see John Shelton Curtiss, *The Russian Army under Nicholas I, 1825–1855* (Durham, NC: Duke University Press, 1965).

15. Fyodor Tiutchev, "Iz pisem F. N. Tiutcheva," *Russkii arkhiv* 2 (1899): 277, 273; Vera Golovina from *Otechestvennaia voina 1812 goda v kul'turnoi pamiati Rossii*, ed. L. V. Mel'nikova (Moscow: Kulikovo pole, 2012), 244; Fyodor Glinka, "Ura," 1854, http://lib.russportal.ru/index.php?id=authors.glinka_th.glinka_th1854_00_0001.

16. Tolstoy, letter of November 29, 1854, in *Polnoe sobranie sochinenii*, vol. 59 (Moscow: Khudozhestvennaia literatura, 1935), 281.

17. Tolstoy, *Polnoe sobranie sochinenii*, vol. 47 (Moscow: Gosudarstvennoe izdatel'stvo khudozhestvennoi literatury, 1937), 42, 41, 60.

18. Ilya Ehrenburg, in *The Heroic Defence of Sevastopol* (Moscow: Foreign Languages Publishing House, 1942), 15; Erich von Manstein, *Lost Victories* (Chicago: H. Regnery, 1958), 188.

19. The 1904 commemorative history is "Oborona Sevastopolia. Istoricheskii ocherk," by A. Zaionchkovskii, reprinted in *Sevastopol: Istoricheskaia povest'*, vol. 1, ed. V. S. Frolova (Sevastopol: Ekosi-Gidrofizika, 2002), 141–206. For another such reprint, see also K. V. Lukashevich, *Oborona Sevastopolia i ego slavnye zashchitniki* (Moscow: STSL, 2014).

20. "Der 'Varjag'" was written by Rudolf Greinz. Suspicions as to its mock-heroic status have been raised at http://svidetel-fryaz.livejournal.com/17423.html#cutid2. The poem was actually beaten to the press by a Russian one, "Cold Waves Lapping," and it too was turned into a song, but "Variag," of course in Russian translation, endures as *the* one.

21. E. V. Lozovskii and M. V. Muzalevskii, *Vo slavu russkogo flaga* (Moscow: Kavaler 2014), 12. Memorabilia of the sailors' various receptions, including fliers and postcards, have been reproduced in *Variag: Stoletie podviga, 1904–2004*, ed. V. I. Kataev and V. V. Lobytsin (Moscow: Soglasie, 2004).

22. Rafail Melnikov, *Kreiser "Variag"* (Leningrad: Sudostroenie, 1975), 6.

23. The return of the bow flag and related events are given in A. L. Khazin, *Obretenie Rossiei relikvii kreisera "Variag" i kanonerskoi lodki "Koreets"* (Moscow: Fond sodeistviia razvitiiu druzheskikh otnoshenii s Respublikoi Koreia, 2010).

24. M. V. Oskin, *Neizvestnye tragedii pervoi mirovoi* (Moscow: Veche, 2011), 419. For similar interpretations of Russia's role in World War I, see also Viacheslav Shatsillo, *Pervaia mirovaia voina 1914–1918* (Moscow: Olma, 2003); Viacheslav Bondarenko, *Uteriannye pobedy Rossiiskoi imperii* (Minsk: Kharvest, 2010); Natalia Narochnitskaia, *Zabytaia voina i predannye geroi* (Moscow: Veche, 2011). Aleksei Oleinikov has claimed that Russia's role was "the *decisive* one" in the Allied victory. See *Rossia—Shchit Antanty* (St. Petersburg: Piter, 2016), 13 (emphasis in the original). In *The Great War in Russian Memory* (Bloomington: Indiana University Press, 2011), Karen Petrone has argued that its memory was preserved in several venues like statuary. None of them, however, were of mythic status, which is why in Russia today it is sometimes referenced as "forgotten." For an introduction to Russia's experience of World War I, see W. Bruce Lincoln, *Passage through Armageddon: The Russians in War and Revolution, 1914–1918* (New York: Simon and Schuster, 1986).

25. Vladimir Putin, "Otkrytie pamiatnika geroiam Pervoi mirovoi voiny," August 1, 2014, http://news.kremlin.ru/news/46385.

6. Deadliest Sin

1. Iurii Gotye, *Smutnoe vremia: Ocherk istorii revoliutsionnykh dvizhenii nachala XVII stoletiia* (Moscow: Gosizdat, 1921), 3. The text was written in 1919. His French ancestors, with the surname of "Gautier," came to Russia in the eighteenth century. The spelling of his name as "Gotye" reflects the transliteration from the Russian "Got'e."

2. Iurii Gotye, *Time of Troubles: The Diary of Iurii Vladimirovich Got'e. July 8, 1917 to July 23, 1922,* trans. Terence Emmons (Princeton, NJ: Princeton University Press, 1988), 28, 42.

3. Isaak Babel, "Sol'," in *Sochineniia v dvukh tomakh*, vol. 2 (Moscow: Khudozhestvennaia literatura, 1990), 76.

4. *The Nikonian Chronicle: From the Beginning to the Year 1132*, vol. 1, trans. Serge A. and Betty Jean Zenkovsky (Princeton, NJ: Kingston Press, 1984), 151.

5. Metropolitan Ioann, *Odolenie smuty,* n.d., http://social-orthodox.info /pages/1_3_snychev.htm.

6. Vladimir Putin, "Poslanie Federal'nomu Sobraniiu Rossiiskoi Feder-atsii," April 25, 2005, http://kremlin.ru/events/president/transcripts/22931; "O strategii razvitiia Rossii do 2020 goda," February 2, 2008, http://president .kremlin.ru/text/appears/2008/02/159528.shtml.

7. Marina Tsvetaeva, "Okh, gribok ty moi . . . ," in *Stikhotvoreniia i poemy* (Leningrad: Sovetskii pisatel', 1990), 185; Tikhon, "Poslanie Sviateishego Patriarkha Tikhona ot 5(18) marta 1918," http://azbyka.ru/otechnik/Tihon _Belavin/poslanie-patriarha-tihona-po-sluchaju-zakljuchenija-brestskogo -mira/.

8. Patriarch Kirill, "Slovo Sviateishego Patriarkha Kirilla posle bogoslu-zheniia v vosstanovlennom Fedorovskom sobore Sankt-Peterburga," September 14, 2013, http://www.patriarchia.ru/db/print/3233663.html.

9. Chris Baldwin, "Action Movie an Allegory for Putin's Russia," Reuters, www.reuters.com/articlePrint?rticleID=USIndia-30309520071103. For a broader discussion of how Russian cinema, with state support, has mobilized the past for present-day purposes, see Stephen M. Norris, *Blockbuster History in the New Russia: Movies, Memory and Patriotism* (Bloomington: Indiana University Press, 2012).

10. Nikolai Karamzin, *Istoriia Gosudarstva Rossiiskogo: Polnoe izdanie v odnom tome* (Moscow: Alfa-Kniga, 2009), 1251; Vladimir Medinsky, *Stena* (Moscow: Olma Media Grupp, 2012), 606.

11. M. A. Pis'mennyi, *Zhitie Aleksandra Nevskogo* (Moscow: Ripol Klassik, 2003), 65.

12. Aleksei Shishov, *Aleksandr Nevskii: Sviatoi kniaz'-ratoborets* (Moscow: Veche, 2006), 8; Boris Vasilev, "Patriot skvoz' pritsel istorii," in *Liubi Rossiiu v nepogodu* (Moscow: Vagrius, 2006), 215.

13. Pis'mennyi, *Zhitie Aleksandra Nevskogo,* 14.

14. "Metropolit Kirill prizyvaet rossian otdat' svoi golosa Aleksandru Nevskomu v reitinge 'Imia Rossii,'" October 6, 2008, www.pravoslavie.ru /news/print27826.htm.

15. Dmitry Medvedev, "Obrashchenie k chitateliam," in *Aleksandr Nevskii: Gosudar', diplomat, voin,* ed. P. G. Gaidukov and P. P. Shkarenkov (Moscow: MGIMO, 2010), 8–9.

16. Pis'mennyi, *Zhitie Aleksandra Nevskogo,* 130, 7.

17. A. Bondarenko and N. Efimov, eds., *Zagadochnye stranitsy russkoi istorii* (Moscow: Reitar, 2008), 14; Viacheslav Kozliakov, *Smuta v Rossii: XVII vek* (Moscow: Omega, 2007), 443.

18. Vladimir Putin, "Vystuplenie na tseremonii vstupleniia v dolzhnost' Prezidenta Rossii," May 7, 2000, http://news.kremlin.ru/transcripts/21399/print.

7. War Neverending

1. Petr Tiukhov, "Dnevnik Generala P. G. Tiukhova," *Istoricheskii arkhiv* 2 (2000): 90. (He was a colonel at the time of writing this entry.) The novel's title refers to the leader of the Mongol invasion, also known as Batu, who was a grandson of Genghis Khan.

2. Anna Politkovskaya, *A Small Corner of Hell: Dispatches from Chechnya* (Chicago: University of Chicago Press, 2003).

3. "Putin, Ivanov and Kadyrov Claim Peace Is at Hand," *Chechnya Weekly* 8, no. 7 (February 15, 2007), https://jamestown.org/program/putin-ivanov-and-kadyrov-claim-peace-is-at-hand-2/.

4. S. Iu. Semeniuta et al., eds., *Shag v bessmertie* (Pskov: 76-aia gvardeiskaia desantnaia diviziia, 2000), 27.

5. Vladimir Putin, "Vystuplenie na prazdnike, priurochennom k 70-letiiu Vozdushno-desantnykh voisk," August 2, 2000, http://president.kremlin.ru/text/appears/2000/08/28818.shtml.

6. Semeniuta et al., *Shag v bessmertie,* 19.

7. In 2000, the same year of the *Kursk* disaster, a novella, *72 Meters,* by Alexander Pokrovsky was published that describes a similar fate befalling a submarine. However, since the film came out in 2004, it would have been quite difficult for Khotinenko to make it—and a Russian audience to view it—without the fate of *Kursk* in mind first and foremost.

8. Vladimir Putin, "Obrashchenie Prezidenta Rossiiskoi Federatsii," March 18, 2014, http://news.kremlin.ru/news/20602/print.

9. *Velikaia Otechestvennaia voina v dvenadtsati tomakh,* vol. 12, ed. S. K. Shoigu et al. (Moscow: Kuchkovo pole, 2015), 698, 715.

10. Vladimir Putin, "Vystuplenie na voennom parade v chest' 62-i godovshchiny Pobedy v Velikoi Otechestvennoi voine," May 9, 2007, http://president.kremlin.ru/text/appears/2007/05/127757.shtml.

11. Lawrence James, *The Rise and Fall of the British Empire* (New York: St. Martin's Press, 1994), 30 (emphasis in the original).

12. Anon., *The History of Kazan,* in *Pamiatniki literatury drevnei Rusi: Seredina XVI veka,* ed. L. A. Dmitrieva and D. S. Likhachev (Moscow: Khudozhestvennaia literatura, 1985), 305, 311.

13. Mikhail Menshikov's comparison of Russia to Christ's passions is from his 1908 "Molitva za Rossiiu," reprinted in A. E. Savinkin et al., *Khristoliubivoe voinstvo* (Moscow: Russkii put', 2006), 14–18.

14. Nikolai Triapkin, "Mat'," in *Goriashchii Vodolei* (Moscow: Molodaia gvardiia, 2003), 409–410.

15. Alexander Prokhanov, "Simfoniia 'Piatoi Imperii,'" http://litmir.net/br/ ?b=109229&p=1.

16. Alexander Blok, "Intelligentsiia i revoliutsiia," in *Sobranie sochinenii v shesti tomakh,* vol. 5 (Moscow: Pravda, 1971), 396.

17. Vladimir Putin, "Parad Pobedy na Krasnoi ploshchadi," May 9, 2014, http://news.kremlin.ru/news/20989/print.

18. Arkady Babchenko, *One Soldier's War,* trans. Nick Allen (New York: Grove Press, 2007), 145–146.

19. Mark Bassin, *Imperial Visions: Nationalist Imagination and Geographical Expansion in the Russian Far East, 1840–1865* (New York: Cambridge University Press, 1999), 54.

20. Lev Tolstoy, "Odumaites'," in *Polnoe sobranie sochinenii,* vol. 36 (Moscow-Leningrad: Khudozhestvennaia literatura, 1936), 137.

21. Grigory Baklanov, *Dorogi prishedshikh s voiny* (Moscow: Pushkinskaia biblioteka, 2005), 378.

22. *Ugolovnyi kodeks Rossiiskoi Federatsii,* Glava 34, Stat'ia 354.1 "Reabilitatsiia natsizma" [Criminal Code of the Russian Federation, Chapter 34, Article 354.1, "The Rehabilitation of Nazism"], http://www.uk-rf.com/glava34.html.

23. *Velikaia Otechestvennaia voina,* 12:699; *Velikaia Otechestvennaia voina v dvenadtsati tomakh,* vol. 1, ed. S. K. Shoigu et al. (Moscow: Kuchkovo pole, 2011), 920; *Velikaia Otechestvennaia voina,* 12:679, 1:903.

24. According to the data of a noted sociologist, even before the ascendancy of President Putin, a majority of Russians saw their country in the twentieth century as "never the aggressor" but rather "the victim of war in the majority of cases." Lev Gudkov, *Negativnaia identichnost'. Stat'i 1997–2002 godov* (Moscow: Novoe literaturnoe obozrenie, VTsIOM-A, 2004), 139.

25. Vasilii Avram Norov, "Original'nye pis'ma iz Armii 1812–1813 godov," in *Reka vremeni: Kniga piataia* (Moscow: Ellis Lak, 1996), 68.

Epilogue

1. Zbigniew Brzezinski, "A Plan for Europe: How to Expand NATO," *Foreign Affairs* 74, no. 1 (January / February 1995): 34.

2. Natalia Narochnitskaia, *Za chto i s kem my voiuem* (Moscow: Minuvshee 2005), 67; Mikhail Gorbachev, *The New Russia*, trans. Arch Tait (Malden, MA: Polity Press, 2016), 306–307; Boris Vasilev, *Liubi Rossiiu v nepogodu* (Moscow: Vagrius, 2006), 8.

3. "The Bear Is Back on the Prowl" is the title of Vivienne Walt's article in *Time,* August 25, 2008, 28–29.

4. Alain Minc, *L'âme des Nations* (Paris: Grasset, 2012), 137.

5. Zbigniew Brzezinski, *Game Plan* (Boston: Atlantic Monthly Press, 1986), 21; Richard Pipes, *Survival Is Not Enough: Soviet Realities and America's Future* (New York: Simon and Schuster, 1984), 37.

6. Marcel H. Van Herpen, *Putin's Wars: The Rise of Russia's New Imperialism* (New York: Rowman & Littlefield, 2014), 2; Vladimir Putin, "Priamaia liniia s Vladimirom Putinym," April 17, 2014, http://kremlin.ru/events/president/news/20796.

7. Zbigniew Brzezinski, "What Is to Be Done? Putin's Aggression in Ukraine Demands a Response," *Washington Post,* March 3, 2014, https://www.washingtonpost.com/opinions/zbigniew-brzezinski-after-putins-aggression-in-ukraine-the-west-must-be-ready-to-respond/2014/03/03/25b3f928-a2f5-11e3-84d4-e59b1709222c_story.html.

8. NATO Fact Sheet, "Russia's Accusations—Setting the Record Straight," April 2014, http://www.nato.int/cps/en/natolive/topics_109141.htm; Pipes, *Survival Is Not Enough,* 38.

9. On the West's ostensible collusion with the Mongols, see, for example, Iurii Denisov, *Kto zakazal tataro-mongol'skoe nashestvie?* (Moscow: Flinta, 2008).

Acknowledgments

Parts of this book revisit themes first explored in a number of venues, including the journals *Slavic Review, History and Memory,* and *History Today,* as well as two critical anthologies, *The Long Aftermath: Cultural Legacies of Europe at War, 1936–2016* and *The Roots of Nationalism: National Identity in Early Modern Europe, 1600–1815,* published in 2016 by Berghahn and Amsterdam University Press, respectively. It has been my aim in *Russia: The Story of War* not only to expand upon that material in a more accessible format but also to develop its importance by showing how its signature points are all interconnected. The war myth, as I hope to have demonstrated, permeates so much of Russian culture and, as a consequence, offers a rich and poignant vein from which to construct national identity. However, it is often difficult for outsiders to recognize the broader canvas on which it can operate—one that many Russians have internalized for generations. Whether the result as given here is a successful one, I leave for others to decide.

In thinking about and writing this book, I have incurred a number of debts that the following words cannot begin to cover. Daniel Mulholland and Stephen Norris read earlier versions of this manuscript, and their collective insight as historians of Russia has proven invaluable and has helped make the finished product much stronger.

The two anonymous reviewers for Harvard University Press also offered salubrious commentary and challenges that have helped me avoid potential pitfalls. The sound input of Nina Tumarkin, Jonathan Brunstedt, Hugh Olmsted, and Adrianne Harris, whether given at conference panels or in other discussions, has also enriched these pages. To all I am grateful. Any mistakes or errors, however, remain in my sole possession.

I would also like to express my deep gratitude to Lisa Adams of the Garamond Agency not only for her unstinting support and advice, always on target, but also for her enviable patience in handling my too-many-to-count questions. This book would not have appeared without her efforts. The same must be said as well of Kathleen Mc-Dermott, Executive Editor for History at Harvard University Press, who is a model of professionalism blessed with an intuitive knack to know just how things should be. I would also like to thank her helpful, ever-courteous staff and Isabelle Lewis, who produced the supporting maps. My gratitude extends as well to Tufts University for providing a semester's leave when it came time to set pencil to paper.

My students have been unwitting guinea pigs in the writing of this book, and I have learned a lot from them. I thank them for their input (even though they probably didn't know I was writing one) and tolerance for my classroom tics and other idiosyncrasies, especially my penchant for mixing metaphors. (No doubt one already lurks nearby.) Since I have been department chair while doing the final writing and edits, I must single out its staff members, Vicky Cirrone and Caroline Harrison, for their incredible work in the department (because they're the ones who really run it) and their indefatigable good cheer no matter the tally of my personal gaffes on any given day. And a glass must be raised to Lyonya and Ira for their exceptional hospitality during my many stays in Moscow.

Finally—and here the words truly are inadequate—I must thank my wife, Gina, and our son, Alessandro, to whom this book is dedicated. They are my pillars of strength, particularly when I have been on long sojourns in Russia or, for that matter, in the library here. Now that the book is complete, I hope that in some small way it will atone for those absences and all the other myriad ways my time has been claimed by what has been one of the most challenging things I've ever written—but also one of the most rewarding.

Index